Sunshine follows the Rain

Polly Holden

authorHOUSE®

AuthorHouse™
1663 Liberty Drive
Bloomington, IN 47403
www.authorhouse.com
Phone: 1-800-839-8640

Published by AuthorHouse   06/13/2012

ISBN: 978-1-4685-7910-9 (sc)
ISBN: 978-1-4685-7911-6 (e)

When faced with adversity
There is always a way out.
If you can't see it.
Search until you find it.

PROLOGUE

At the end of the Second World War most of Europe was in a terrible mess devastated by the most destructive war ever to hit mankind and Britain although on the winning side was no exception.

Whereas in the First World War most of the damage was confined to certain areas where the fighting had been most severe, this world war had seen the terrible ruin of whole cities and with it people's homes and their way of life.

In normal circumstances after a war, prisoners are repatriated back to their country of origin as soon as can be arranged as the Geneva agreement requires; at the end of this war with no formal peace treaty signed the Geneva treaty didn't have the force of law behind it.

Clement Atlee the newly elected British Prime Minister declared he wouldn't send home the well over a quarter of a million German prisoners of war captured by the British and Americans, and now housed in Britain.

The House of Commons agreed with the Prime Minister; with half of London and most major cities nationwide in a state of severe destruction and with more than four million homes completely destroyed they deemed it only right that these men help put right the damage wrought by their nation.

Although the British Prime Minister knew it was Adolf Hitler who gave the orders to the German army and everyone else had to obey he was concerned because most of the young men who now reposed in the prisoner of war camps had the Nazi way indoctrinated into them from their impressionable young teenage years.

So Atlee decreed it was necessary for these men to be told and shown exactly what Hitler had been responsible for; the concentration camps for example and the killing of so many innocent people especially the Jewish race.

Possibly at the back of Atlee's mind was he didn't want a repeat of the type of socialism of Hitler's type to surface again, especially as Germany had been responsible for the last two most violent wars in history.

At first the men were mostly housed in the compounds left by the American, Canadian, Polish, Italians and Free French as they waited for the invasion of France in 1944, due to the considerable numbers of PoW's involved, other accommodation like large country houses were also requisitioned for use.

During this time the men were kept under armed guard, then there began a pattern of forced education for the PoW's, with many lectures and films about Hitler's' terrible regime given for many weeks to indoctrinate them into the truth of the Nazi rule and how evil it was,

Because so many of the British Servicemen were still overseas supervising the clear up there before the general demobilization, man power in the U.K. was in short supply, it was then agreed by the government that some working parties of PoW's were to be sent out from their enclosures to work on the land, help with road building and serve as general laborers clearing up the rubble caused by extensive bombing in the cities.

The food situation was bleak, rationing being very severe, so 90% of these men were used to work on the land, with men moved around the country to where labor was most required.

As time went by the prisoners became very restless, they were anxious to go home especially when they heard their families and cities were in with many ways worse off than the situation here in Britain.

Very soon these men began to protest; fed up with moving from camp to camp and being behind barbed wire fences under armed guard after their hard working day, the men argued they were needed in their homeland.

They began to insist they were not prisoners of war and that they were being treated as forced labor, this they said was against their human rights. They also pointed out to the British Authorities that if they not become soldiers under Adolf Hitler they would have been shot. Prime Minister Atlee turned a deaf ear and stuck his heels in; he would not be moved to submission on this issue for some considerable time

The men had been used to army discipline so their quarters were kept in good order, they often painting scenes from home on the bare wars of the huts in which they were held, during the time they were confined they whittled away at wood, making children's toys together with other things, and outside within the bounds of the compound, vegetables and flowers filled any available space grown by the inmates.

Eventually Atlee found he had to bow to public pressure and it was decided by the government to gradually allow the men more freedom in the local communities.

With this in mind a pamphlet was issued by the council of churches to help the situation.

It said in part that the prisoners had special difficulties and were in a difficult physiological position being in the side of a nation who had lost a calamitous war; it went on to point out these men were human beings and should be treated by the church fittingly

It also stated that the majority of these men were either of the Protestant or Catholic religion as were their captors and they were therefore brothers, so it was proper to treat these people in a Christian way; it explained that a handshake in German was the same as a handshake in English.

Many of the ministers' local to the camps took up the challenge outlined in the pamphlet getting permits to visit the men where they were held.

To begin with the clergymen held services for the men where they were confined; but as time passed by the men were encouraged to go to the morning services at the local church accompanied by their warders.

Although fraternization with the local population at this time wasn't allowed, the men did mix with other workers where work parties were sent out to local farms or whenever else their labor was required and in the most part got on well with the local inhabitants.

Gradually things began to change, around the time of Christmas 1946, it was suggested the men be allowed to spend the festive season with local families and this was deemed a success, although there were objections by some people particularly those in close knit communities.

Mr. Atlee again faced with pressure from the public to allow these men to return to their country of origin, so at the beginning of 1947 it was declared that repatriation could begin.

It began very slowly at first with just 3,000 a month out of a quarter of a million men allowed to go home, the authorities making sure those who did go had it firmly fixed in their minds what a catastrophe Adolf Hitler had caused, so that the same thing wouldn't be allowed to happen again.

As 1947 progressed, repatriation continued apace with more than 15.000 a month allowed to return to their homeland, each kitted out with suits and shoes.

The men remaining here were no longer confined to the camps and during their spare time, they were allowed to mix with the general public.

With Germany now divided and the Russians now in control of a swath of their country, a lot of the PoW's from this area didn't want to go back, especially when they heard from other men who had returned how bad things were there.

Then there were the men who met British girls, fell in love, and had another reason not to go home!

RATIONING

Rationing came in at the start of the war and remained for quite a few years afterwards but it was the early 1950's before certain things like sweets became generally available again.

Each family was issued with a ration book which detailed their food entitlement and clothing coupons

To start with each person was allowed 16 points per month to use on whatever items they wished from the stocks available.

Most householders registered at their local shop and then used their points exclusively at this shop, this was necessary so that that shop could be provided with enough goods to meet the demand of their registered customers.

The number of points was later raised to twenty per month although some items like fish and potatoes were never rationed; fish was often in short supply owing to the blockade of the beaches and ports.

Some imported goods were not available at all, bananas being one such item,

In addition each family was allowed a pint of milk extra. For the young cod liver oil, and orange juice with a double allowance of eggs, although powdered egg was available.

Children under the age of five were allowed a half ration of meat, and children between the ages of five and sixteen held a separate blue ration book which entitled them to fruit and other health foods (virol for example)

All other ration books were a buff colour.

Additional rations were given to expectant mothers, and people with special diet needs.

Typical weekly rations were

- 2oz Bacon
- 4oz Margarine
- 4oz Sugar
- 8 oz. of meat to the value of 1/6
- 1 egg per week
- Three pints of milk occasionally dropping to two pints
- 2 oz. of cheese (farm workers got more as their job was deemed necessary to help the rationing at home)
- 2oz of tea
- 1 lb. of jam every two months
- Dried egg one packet every four weeks
- Sweets 12 oz. every four weeks

CHAPTER ONE

October 1945

A slight bump shook the American troopship as it slid alongside the dock, the gale force winds that had thrashed the vessel in mid Atlantic for the past week still hadn't abated which meant tying up at the dockside had still been precarious even in these somewhat calmer waters.

Karl went up the narrow ladder that led to the restricted deck reserved for the prisoners of war to see his first glimpse of his former enemy's country.

Leaning against the ships rail and taking a deep inward breath he surveyed the scene before him. With the wind blowing cold from the land against his face he could still detect the smell of the salty sea, yet this was now mixed with the odour from the docks and the earth, faintly in the background he could detect the scent of brick dust with the smell that hangs about following bad fires.

He knew Goering's Luftwaffe had done immense damage to London and the cities in the south, what he hadn't realized was how much this part of the north west of the country had suffered judging by the piles of rubble still waiting clearance in the foreground and the huge gaps in the warehouses alongside the waterfront the bombing here had been very severe.

Looking just beyond the dockside he saw there were bombsites in the near vicinity also.

'Yes Liverpool was badly hit by Incendiary bombs.' One of the warders who were in charge of the PoW's and who had followed him up the ladder now spoke as he followed Karl's gaze.

Concern showed in the warder's face as he now continued the conversation.

'It's even worse in the interior! When I came here a few weeks ago I was able to look round and I can tell you I was really shocked.' The warden lowered his voice.

'We in the USA have suffered nothing like these people on this side of the pond, Pearl Harbour was nothing compared with the devastation here, and it's even worse over on the mainland of Europe I am told!'

A shiver went down Karl's spine when he heard those words and he hung his head suddenly ashamed that Germany had been part of such destruction and that he was a member of that race.

'Here look through this, and then you can see more.' The warder held out a telescope he'd been holding in his hand to Karl, pointing to the direction just ahead adding sadly.

'Now you can really see what a real mess was made of the city!'

Reluctantly lifting it to his eye, Karl looked out over the metropolis; he did't really want to observe the harm done by the nation he had been a part of; yet to reject the warders offer it would have seemed impolite.

The scene that greeted him shocked him to the core; he wasn't prepared for such damage; after nearly a year in an American detention centre he'd almost forgotten how bad the war had been.

Whole streets before him had been razed to the ground and looking of the blackened walls that were still standing fires caused by the bombing had been horrendous.

Through the powerful telescope he saw a few children playing amongst rubble, he could see clearly their pale faces and worn clothing, several older people their faces sad were stooped over as they carried what appeared to be shopping bags along the narrow streets

Aware the situation on the continent was still terrible, it was no surprise to him that there was an absence of young men and women, obviously the majority of the younger generations were still on active duty elsewhere.

He quickly removed the telescope from his eyes; he'd seen enough, this had really shaken him!

What had his race had done to this city, and if it was like this here what was the damage like to the rest of the country? Rumour was rife amongst his fellow prisoners that they wouldn't be going home for some considerable time; because the British Prime Minister had said the men had to help put right the damage done.

Sudden fear gripped him; he and his fellow prisoners were now at the mercy of this people so how were they going to face them?

'Can I have a look?' Karl turned round to see the warder had been replaced by a fellow prisoner speaking to him in their native tongue; Karl's spirits fell as he recognized the voice at his elbow turning round he looked straight into the beady eyes a fellow detainee whose face still had whey colour about the gills after the rough crossing.

It was Heinz.

Karl quietly passed the telescope to the other man who raised it to his eye, a scornful smile played round his mouth as he took in the scene that unfolded before him; there was no mistaking the pride in his next words.

'Well we certainly did some damage to this place!' His speech made Karl feel very uneasy, he had never really connected with Heinz, there was something cruel about him which was the reason he'd been such a good Nazi commanding officer before their capture. A Nazi through and through with a rigid attitude; he rarely smiled except at someone's misfortune.

Heinz had seen much active service during the war before being taken captive, and he still thought his authority counted for something when he was amongst fellow prisoners, most of the men now poked fun at him behind his back and ignored any commands he gave, Karl thought perhaps it was because Heinz had seen so many dreadful things during the war he'd got hardened to the awfulness of it all, and accepted these things as normal.

From the conversations Karl personally had recently with the older man he had gleaned that Heinz still believed that Adolph Hitler wasn't a bad man and the 3rd Reich would raise again despite their defeat.

Heinz even questioned the fact that Adolph Hitler was dead!

A spiteful look came over Heinz's face and his German became excitable as he pointed out something on the waterfront and to what was obviously a red brick church building behind it.

'Anyway it's not as badly damaged as some of our cities look over there some of the buildings are still standing.' His voice boomed out.

'My sister in a letter told me that Dresden was almost razed to the ground, and so is much of Berlin!'

Karl chose not to reply as Heinz silently passed the telescope back to him, he knew Dresden had been badly bombed, he himself had lived in the countryside quite close to this city before the war; but then many places had been bombed back in Germany, dwelling on that wasn't going to help the present situation.

3

Seeing that Karl wasn't going to be drawn into his conversation Heinz turned on his heels and marched away down to the bowels of the ship, without a glance behind.

Karl watched him go looking at his tall straight back and clipped heels.

Although of the same nationality the two men couldn't be more different, dark haired Heinz was sharp faced and very thin, handsome blonde headed Karl was more the Arian type favored by Hitler, his broad muscular shoulders and well-built physique stood out making him look wider than he actually was. Yet in nature they were complete opposites, Heinz was the Nazi and Karl ashamed over the havoc his nation had created.

Karl looked again over the ships rail, the sun chose that moment to peep through the clouds making everything seem a little brighter, yet it didn't reach down to Karl's stone like heart beating in his chest.

Here he was a young man, who should be filled with optimism for the future, but he had seen so much suffering during his youthful life thanks to the war, it almost seemed he'd lived a lifetime already although in fact he wasn't quite twenty years old.

As it often did at these times of melancholy his thoughts turned once more to Wilhelm.

If only he was here with him now things would be more bearable.

It had been a terrible shock when he'd been killed during the battle which resulted in their capture by the Americans.

They had been companions since childhood, their parents also being great friends through the hard years of the 1930's when food and jobs were scarce, joining the Hitler youth together they had been drawn along by the general excitement exuded by a Fuehrer who believed the 3rd Reich would last a thousand years.

Jointly they had been pleased to participate in the euphoria that existed then; especially as they were in their impressionable early teens.

His father's words spoken then often came back to haunt Karl now.

'The elation and adoration that was going on then with Hitler will eventually end in disaster.' On reflection how right his father had been!

Now Karl wasn't even sure his father or any of his family were still alive he'd heard nothing from them since he'd been taken captive. He knew that the axis powers had taken over their homeland and they were going to be in the Russian sector of a divided fatherland, which meant things would not bode well for them, even if they had escaped the ravages of the war.

The war had already raged for three and a half years old when he and Wilhelm got their first posting together in France at the age of 17, joining the grenadiers of the 916th infantry regiment 352nd infantry division; under the care of their commanding officer Heinz, in the Normandy area of France.

Until the invasion came life had been good, it had been an easy task to supervise the French people even though they both often felt uncomfortable about the hatred in people's eyes as they went about their tasks.

They learnt to ignore this because the Germans had the upper hand.

Heinz had made it clear he took pleasure in being the aggressor, for Karl and Wilhelm it was just a job to do, when speaking together privately they both agreed it wasn't something they really enjoyed.

The German army had been totally unprepared for the offensive when it came; those in authority had been convinced it would come from a different direction, possibly the Calais area so it was a shock when their division found themselves invaded by the enemy led by the Americans.

It was a long drawn out battle lasting several weeks, as the Americans and British began to gain the upper hand some German units got ready to surrender knowing that the backup from the air on the enemy side was superior.

Heinz decided the men under his control were not going to give up without a struggle, they were told to march.

Even when they passed armed vehicles with white flags in strategic spots as a signal to the advancing enemy, Heinz contended he wasn't going to give up without a fight. Armed with sub machine guns, they smothered their faces with dust; chicken wire on their helmets covered with foliage for extra camouflage meant they made the most of the terrain which remarkably lent itself to defensive warfare their grey-green uniforms blending well into the surrounding countryside.

They dug in at the edge of a forest that lined a Normandy road, firmly entrenched their unit held the area to the south west of the Cerisy forest for some considerable time. A small back up group of Germans checked every move the Americans made to break through their lines and advance towards the south; on the face of it, it seemed for the present they were safe.

Deep inside fear gripped Karl, knowing the allied forces had great power behind them and that the German Army's main back up was days away.

As time moved on the allied bombers dropped many shells, it was terrifying, yet somehow their unit still held out.

It came to an end on a damp misty night when the Americans closed in on their stronghold where they had bedded down for the night after a day of defensive fighting by the front line troops

Karl felt in the small pocket on one side of his belt for a magazine loading tool he knew was there, he was fearful of using the gun to kill yet aware he would have to do it, it was kill or be killed.

Fortunately he was spared this when a sharp report came whizzing through the air and a grenade landed by their side scattered them in all directions out of their stronghold into the turnip fields surrounding them, there they were rounded up by the enemy.

Hands on heads they sat together surrounded by their captors.

Karl thought Wilhelm was with them, it wasn't until the Americans removed some bodies from the hideout he realized some of his comrades hadn't made it.

Looking round for his friend, he saw the broken down body of a panzer soldier being carried by two US marines from their stronghold, a blonde forelock fell over a bloodstained face, sightless eyes were staring straight ahead, hands were hanging limply down over the stretcher.

Shocked to the core Karl knew immediately that his friend Wilhelm was dead.

Things happened speedily after that; their units together with several others were shipped out to the USA where they spent the best part of a year in a detention centre; they were not badly treated, but freedom was curtailed.

When news came through that the war was over the prisoners looked forward to being repatriated back to their home country.

It was some considerable time before the call came for them to be moved and when it did the excitement that went through the men quickly turned to despair when they were informed that instead of going back to Germany to help clear up the mess left by the war in their native land; they were heading to England on the orders of the British Prime Minister to help clear up the chaos left by the 3rd Reich.

In many cases the these men didn't know whether their dear ones were dead or alive, and for all of them there was a certain fearful dread for what the future held, how would their former enemy treat them?

After what Karl had just witnessed through the telescope he could understand a little of what the British government were about, if it was this bad here it must be just as bad or even worse elsewhere?

'Finished with the telescope then?' The warder was back at Karl's elbow; Karl smiled as he passed the borrowed item back to its owner.

'Not a nice scene was it!' Karl unable to trust his voiced nodded in agreement.

'At least those three buildings on the water front have survived; see that one there.' Karl's eyes followed to where the warder pointed, this building had a huge clock face was decorated with statues and what seemed like at this distance birds.

'That is the liver building. 'The warder explained pointing it out.

'I'm told these three buildings are known locally as the three graces.' The warder paused.

'The birds on the top are known as the 'liver birds' did you know they were designed by a fellow country man of yours?'

'Really.' Karl looked impressed.

'Yes he had the same first name as you, but I can't remember his surname, he designed some things in the U.S. also, that is why I know something about him, I gather he left Britain just before the outbreak of the last war because your nationality had become rather unpopular.' The warder looked sheepish and quickly changed the subject when he saw Karl's cheeks redden.

See the reddish building over there.' Karl followed his gaze.

'That is the Anglican cathedral, nice to think that survived the bombing!'

The warder turned the other away pointing to a group of men on the dockside below beneath a brick wall so they could shelter from the wind.

Some were sitting some standing but they all appeared to be taking something from what seemed like newspaper and putting it in their mouths.

The warder had a cheeky grin on his face as he said.

'That's a better scene; those blokes seem to be cheerful don't they?'

'What are they doing?' Karl asked his curiosity aroused.

'You've got to hand it to those limey's.' The warder was now grinning from ear to ear.

'They do like their fish and chips and that is the way they eat them! I understand it is one of the few things not on ration so I suppose you can't blame them. It has been very tough the rationing here. You fellows have done well being with us in the U.S.'

'I must admit we have been well fed.' Karl agreed.

'I don't think you will be so well treated here.' The warder added.

'If you get the opportunity to try that meal do so, I can vouch for the fact that the way they cook them is delicious.'

'I don't understand.' Karl once more heard the German language at his elbow, and turned round to find Heinz once again occupying the space he had previously.

The warder on the other side looked over at the older man with distaste, then firmly turned his back on him and made a face in Karl's direction, he didn't care for Heinz, and he didn't care if Heinz knew it!

'Best explain what I've just said.' The warder turned on his heel, and walked in the direction of the doorway, then looked back at them both.

Karl grimaced, he found it hard to be sociable with his former commanding officer, it had taken a long time for him to forget that Heinz had been responsible for Wilhelm's death; had they surrendered straight away to the Americans, Wilhelm would still be with them now!

When they had been taken prisoner and transported to the detention centre in the USA. Karl too had understood very little English, whilst there he'd persevered by talking a great deal and listening to his captors, now he knew enough English to understand and be understood.

Heinz like a lot of the other Germans remained aloof, refusing to even try to communicate; the Americans had little sympathy for his sort of men and showed it.

Heinz looked again at Karl.

'Listen while I am talking to you.' He spat out in his mother tongue.

'Are you coming?' The warder addressed Karl turning his back on Heinz.

'I can smell the coffee.'

'Let him get on with it! His superior attitude will have to change.' He advised as he turned again and looked down his nose in disgust at the ex-German officer.

'You are the conquered he will have to realize that!' The warder said looking again in Heinz direction.

'After the coffee we can play pool for a while it will be some time before we disembark.' The warder held open the hatch that led to the stairway; Karl smartly followed.

He was going to miss these American warders who would be returning to the U.S.A. with the ship, he hoped the British wardens would be just as nice.

Karl looked behind at Heinz still at the ships rail, suddenly glad he was no longer under his jurisdiction. His superior attitude was due for a fall, they were the conquered Heinz and a lot of the others were going to have to realize that if they wanted to make the best of their present situation!

CHAPTER TWO

November 1945

A heavy iron handle on the reading room oak door groaned on its ancient hinges, before it finally yielded to Peggy's firm grasp and sprang into action.

The stiff north wind blew the dust accumulated in the corner of the door frame into her eyes making them sting, fumbling in her pocket she found her handkerchief and wiped away the resulting tears.

It was a wild night for the village meeting she thought as she swiftly closed the door behind her and drew the heavy curtains across the large windows before switching on the lights, rebuking herself immediately when she realized this was no longer necessary, the war was over and with it five and a half years of blackout.

In the gloom she quickly pulled the cords on the gas lamps that hung from the rafters on long chains and they responded with their usual plop spreading their yellowy white glow out from their snow white mantles bathing the room in light.

Peggy fished out another handkerchief from the bag under her arm; she disliked the after smell of the gas that now permeated the air, a swift smell of the Devon violets perfume she had saturated the linen with previously dispelled the pong, the relief showed in her face.

Bustling down the hall past the raised platform at the end she put her hand on a small brass door knob to the left turning it she entered a miniscule kitchen and quickly hung her coat on a hook behind the door, taking a floral overall from her bag, she pulled it over her head and smoothed it down over her dark red dress.

Her first job was to ferrying water by means of an enamel jug from the small brass tap over the shallow brown sink into the gas geyser on the opposite side of the room, observing it was full she took a box of matches from her pocket and turned on a gas tap under the geyser, gingerly putting the match to the ring she jumped backwards slightly as a small bang was produced when the flame flared up.

Routing once more in her bag she removed a clean tea cloth, proceeding to dust the cups as she removed from the small cupboard on the wall, thick white affairs, many badly chipped. Given the present austere climate it was going to be a long time before those were replaced was a passing thought.

Space was at a premium so she had to utilize the wooden draining board, no doubt much of the village would attend the meeting tonight so many would be required.

A tin tray that had seen better days she pushed into the small space alongside the cups transferring the sugar basin and teapot onto it then she looked with satisfaction at what she had accomplished.

Would whose ever turn it was to bring the tea forget it and would someone else remember the sugar she wondered?

It had been quite a shock to them all to learn that even though the war had been over for some months rationing was to remain for the foreseeable future, and the new labor Prime Minister Mr. Clement Atlee had said in a recent broadcast to the nation things were going to get worse before they got better.

Her husband Harry's comments when he heard this was 'How much worse can it get!'

They were fortunate hereabouts as it was farming country and most food was grown locally, meat in the form of rabbit and pheasant eked out the severe rationing and most people had a roof over their heads.

Peggy had read in the newspapers and heard on the wireless, that many people in the cities were living in cramped conditions; families were living in one room owing to the terrible bombing that had destroyed their homes, with no sign of release for the foreseeable future.

Hitler's bombs had mostly concentrated on the cities, it would have been very different if there had been an invasion over the English Channel in the earlier part of the war; because of their close proximity to the English channel it would have affected them locally before the rest of the country, thanks to the 'Battle of Britain' pilots this had been thwarted.

The distinct sound of a bicycle bell disturbed Peggy's thoughts and she knew immediately it was the Reverend Hounsome, he always rang it when he got to the sharp bend at the bottom of the steep hill that led from the vicarage to the village below.

She listened as the main door creaked opened, and heard him wipe his feet on the coconut matting just inside the door, then came the sound of his footsteps across the bare wooden floor of the hall

Looking up from her task she saw his beaming face in the small doorway.

'How do Vicar!' Peggy greeted him, and then the tone of her voice turned rather sharp.

'I thought Winnie Baker would have been here before you! But then she is often late. She really shouldn't volunteer for these things if she can't be on time!'

The smile on the tall figures face faded to a grimace and he raised both his hands in the air at her outburst.

'In Miss Baker's defense she has been up at the vicarage helping my wife.' His face broke back into its usual quiet smile as he continued.

'Mrs. Finch has been there also, together they have been organizing the village children's Christmas treat.' He stroked his chin thoughtfully as he continued.

'I must admit Miss Baker did leave some time ago, she should be here by now.'

He bent down to remove his cycle clips from his trousers, a tall lean man, he was dressed in his usual long flowing black vestment which made his white vicar's collar stand out even more against his scrawny neck and balding pate.

Peggy watching his action thought it more likely that the long gown would have caught in the cycle wheels rather than in his trousers, he must have tucked it up somehow. She smiled to herself at the thought.

He looked up suddenly seeing a grin playing at the corners of her mouth; completely wrong read her thoughts as he went on.

'At least we can rely on your good nature, Miss Baker knew you wouldn't let us down!'

'It's kind of you to say so' Peggy knew that he was sweet talking her to take the heat out of the situation, it was the nature of the man to do this; one of the things you couldn't fail to like about him.

Inside Peggy was seething; Winnie and Jean had been up at the vicarage organizing the children's party discussing all the ins and outs between them so that everything would be done the way Jean Finch wanted it, then everyone would be used like puppets and told what their agreed task would be!

She already knew she would be expected to do the catering; no one else would take it on! It would have been nice to be consulted first about these things before the decisions were made, no one though argued with Jean Finch! It was typical of the woman; she could manipulate Winnie like putty so that what seemed as though it was a unanimous decision was in fact precisely what Jean wanted!

Although Peggy liked the vicar she was aware of his failings, he was too weak to stand up to the likes of Jean; his wife a nervous little thing struggling to bring up seven small children in a draughty old vicarage had much the same temperament as her husband and Jean ran rings round both of them more or less running the whole village single handed.

The Reverent Hounsome had only taken this living a few months ago from the old vicar who had been here for many years and had great influence in the village; Jean hadn't been able to manipulate him he would never have allowed it!

Jean had first come to the village just before the outbreak of war when her husband Claude was given a posting with the RAF nearby, Peggy had been in awe of her then especially when she was asked to be her daily help; this attitude really annoyed her husband Harry.

'You are as good as she is.' Harry retorted on more than one occasion. 'And don't you forget it!'

Peggy often wished she could; Winnie made sure she didn't and that didn't come easily, class distinction was very apparent, despite the war. She did domestic work for quite a few of the posh houses in the village, and quite a few looked down on this state of affairs, although they were grateful for her services with the war situation little other help was available.

She was still a 'Domestic' as far as they were concerned and that was her place.

Peggy suddenly realized the vicar was still standing expectantly in front of her.

'Do you know who is supplying the tea today?' She asked looking down at his shiny black shoes and wondering how he managed to keep them so clean with all the mud about at his end of the village.

The vicar looked rather sheepish as he took a packet from the folds of his garb depositing it on the tray.

'I have just received a supply from my brother in Canada, so I have brought some along, he sends me a parcel from time to time to eke out our rations.'

Peggy picked up the unfamiliar box and opened it up; she expected to find tea leaves inside; instead she shook out a quantity of small white packets.

The Reverent Hounsome smiled at the mystified look on Peggy's face, and then he spoke.

'They are teabags; they are very popular in Canada I understand.' The corner of the vicar's eyes crinkled up in amusement. 'Don't do what old Mrs. Riddles did when she received a parcel from there the other week.' He continued.

'She snipped each bag in the corner and poured the contents into her tea caddy; then complained it didn't look like proper tea!'

'I must admit I am not surprised.' Peggy thought she might have done the same thing without the vicar's advice, although she would never have admitted it!

'My wife puts one in the pot per person; I will leave it your discretion as to how many you use.' He was so apologetic in his tone Peggy felt sorry she'd been so sharp with him; it was extremely kind of him to share his brother's gift especially when he had so many mouths to feed himself.

'Could I call on your good nature to help me put out the wooden benches for people to sit on?' His voice came with a slight stutter Peggy had noticed before when he was nervous, she guessed he was getting wound up a bit over the meeting this evening.

He made his way to the kitchen door, Peggy following him into the hall.

Each of them took an end of the long wooden benches that were around the edges of the hall arranging them in the centre starting at the back in rows.

Peggy stopped for a moment to catch her breath, looking up she realized the imposing mahogany bookcases that took up the whole end of the hall still had the sticky brown tape stuck to the Venetian glass put there to stop it shattering during the war should there have been a bomb blast.

'That will have to be sorted out.' The Vicar said followed her gaze.

'Yes I will do it the next time I clean the hall.' Peggy promised.

'Thank you. I know you can be relied on!' Peggy glowed; it made her feel that at least someone appreciated her efforts.

The vicar began to pass her some fold up wooden chairs that were to go in the front three rows just in front of the platform, and at the edge of the wooden benches.

They had just finished this task when a voice cut through the air.

'Cooee sorry I am late!' Peggy recognized Winnie's dulcet tones from the kitchen where she'd quickly returned to turn down the gas on the boiler to low.

'You always are.' Was Peggy's cutting remark.

' Winnie looked rather deflated as she looked round the door to meet Peggy's gaze.

'I thought the vicar would have told you; I was up at the vicarage organizing the village children's Christmas party with Jean.' she paused.

'You're down to organize the food.' There was contempt yet triumph in Winnie's voice as she issued this command.

Peggy sighed, she didn't expect anything else; that is what made her so cross, she wasn't consulted it was just expected, she dare not tell Harry he would be incensed at his wife being used in this way.

'Anyway I had to wait until your Harry had finished the milking, so I could bring this!' Winnie thumped a billy can down in the wooden draining board spilling some of the milk inside.

Peggy's attitude had annoyed her, she knew Peggy didn't like the fact that Jean consulted her, but that gave Winnie a certain satisfaction, who did Peggy think she was? She was only Jeans daily help after all and had no influence in the village with anyone!

'The vicar did mention you were there, he also said he thought you would be here before him as you left some time ago.' Peggy spoke softly so as to take the heat out of the situation; it was no use arguing with Winnie it never got her anywhere. She would hear all about it when she got home from her Harry, he would have filled the billy can as soon as Winnie arrived at the cow shed. Peggy was sure that Winnie had been bending her husband's ear with some idle chatter, instead of getting a move on to help get the hall ready, she and Harry knew how Winnie could chipe.

Years ago when they were all young, Winnie had set her cap at Harry; her parents thinking him lower class than they were had discouraged the union.

Sometimes Winnie harped on about this, much to Peggy's annoyance; Harry said he wouldn't have married her anyway she talked too much!

Peggy looked Winnie up and down, she knew her exact age, and they had attended the village school together, so there were no secrets.

Winnie certainly hadn't moved with the times, her parents had always brought her the best of clothing, the resulting attire had lasted, now she was caught in a time warp, she dressed in early 1920's style with high necked blouses, long skirts and button up boots which looked quite strange in today's climate, she was a source of fun amongst the youngsters of the village, although she never realized it and would have been most hurt if she had!

Her parents had owned a shop in the nearby town, when old age set in followed by the depression in the 1930's it brought financial difficulties so the shop had to be sold.

Winnie then kept house for her parents until they died just before the war broke out.

She still lived in their large house in the heart of the village eking out an existence on the small amount of money they left her, the house lay back from the road surrounded by trees and had two small deserted lodges at the entrance; Peggy always thought of it as eerie the sort of place that you hurried by in the dark.

The war had scarcely disturbed Winnie's pattern of life she had made no effort to be involved in the war effort at all, which was a shame; although she was too old to be called up, she could have volunteered for something else, it would have broadened her horizons instead of being self-centered she would have had to think of others.

Jean Finch to her credit had tried to get Winnie to be occupied in some of the voluntary organization she herself supported locally. Winnie refused, which was one of the reasons Jean asked Winnie to help organize parish events thinking it was in her best interests to have something to occupy her time.

From the noise now issuing forth from the main hall it was obvious Jean Finch had arrived.

To Peggy's annoyance the first thing she did was to tell the vicar the benches and chairs that the vicar and Peggy had spent time arranging were not right, insisted on rearranging it all making a great deal of noise in the process.

Not only was the woman large in size she was also large in mouth, it was ignore her if you dare! To her credit she was an excellent organizer for the WVS, and various other organizations that had sprung up to help the war effort, in recent years many people had reason to be grateful for her organization abilities; it was just her bossy attitude that put peoples backs up.

Jean red faced from her exertions finally put her head round the kitchen door.

'Is everything alright?' She asked.

Peggy looked up from her task at Jean, One thing you had to admit she had class; her attire was immaculate, a tweed skirt graced her hips with matching knitted twin set over the top in azure blue, the three rows of pearls around her neck were real pearls and her was hair set in marcelle blonde waves making her look as though she had just come out of one of the fashion magazines Peggy had often seen at her almost perfect home. Glancing at the two faces, Jean addressing Winnie who for the first time sprang into action beginning to pour milk into the cups Peggy had previously lain out.

'You two make a good team! You have always been a good worker.'

The last remark it seemed to Peggy was addressed to Winnie.

Peggy felt like screaming at the woman, she was the one who had done all the work and there was Winnie taking the credit as she usually did!

Peggy knew if she said anything it would fall on deaf ears; for some unknown reason it seemed to her nothing she did wasn't recognized as important by Jean Finch.

After pushing a cake tin into Winnie's hands, the sound of voices at the far end of the hall sent Jean scurrying out to greet the new arrivals.

Winnie opened up the tin examining the contents, sniffing appreciatively at the aroma that ensued.

'Jean is always so generous! These look delicious, I think she used vanilla in them; I don't know how she does it with the rationing|!' She took a large plate from the cupboard and proceeding to place the cakes on it.

'Yes I am sure they will be nice.' Peggy said not adding yes it was vanilla, she knew because she had been responsible for baking them that morning in Jean's kitchen! She even providing the carrots from Harry's garden and some other ingredients to eke out the rations; whatever she said, Winnie would give Jean the credit anyway!

By the noise outside, the hall was now filling up with Jean Finch making sure the main bulk of the villagers occupied the benches now at the back of the hall.

The voices of the two Miss Marshall's who were rather deaf and thought everyone else was as well could be heard above the general din as they were shown to the better seats.

They owned West croft a large house in the centre of the village; always in church on Sundays they had a great influence on the vicar, too much some would say especially Jean Finch who liked to think she was the Reverend Hounsome's main confident.

The shrill voice of the postmistress announced her arrival; she'd be accompanied by her husband Sydney they made a good team in the village shop, they were complete opposites, one loud the other quiet.

A few seconds later Sid popped his head round the kitchen door smiling broadly as he dropped a small brown paper bag alongside the cups with the word 'Sugar' on the side.

'Thanks Sid.' Peggy smiled at him and was rewarded by a beam in return; kitted out in a collar, tie and corduroy trousers under a Harris Tweed jacket he looked so different than he did in his usual attire of a snow white overall he wore in the shop, his hair slicked back now with brylcream he looked almost handsome.

The water began to bubble in the boiler making the lid bounce up and down. Peggy who was transferring Sid's contribution into the sugar bowls quickly turned to make sure the gas was turned off completely to prevent it boiling over.

Quickly glancing round to see that everything else was in place she removed her overall and once more smoothed down her dress over her hips before following Winnie into the main hall.

They took a seat on one of the wooden benches, just as the unmistakable tap of Captain Wilson's stick against the wooden floorboards announced he and his wife Sybil arrived; they were quickly ushered to one of the better seats at the front by Jean.

They owned one of the oldest house in the village 'Trelawney cottage' reputed to be once owned by Cornish rebel Trelawney, it was said to have a resident ghost; certain villages refused to go past it at night; Peggy thought the place eerie but didn't believe such things.

Captain Wilson's pebble thick spectacles were perched on the end of his nose, his unsteady gait a sign of his advancing years meant he used the white stick more for support that the fact that he had bad sight; he was quite thirty years older than his attractive immaculately turned out wife Sybil, her brown hair jiggled in tight curls under a felt hat, a calf length coat in a mink shade was finished off with a fox tail collar about her neck, this she threw casually over the back of one of the chairs arranged at the front.

The two of them had spent many years in India with servants before coming here to retire; because it was such a different way of life, they didn't fit in easily with the village. Perhaps it was because they sent their three youngish children to boarding school, and even in the school holidays the children were not allowed to mix with the local children, so people thought them a bit snobbish.

Just as the hall seemed full, Hugh Pemberton and his wife swept in, they were a busy couple and usually the last people of importance to arrive, they ran a drapers shop in the nearby town previously owned by Winnie's parents, many locals said they got it for a song, other said Winnie's parents were lucky to find a buyer at the time of the depression, whatever the case was they were well liked locally.

Owning 'Stocks house' a lovely rambling home at the bottom of the hill overlooking the brookland.

They had no children of their own, but did a lot for the community, Hugh was a Sunday school teacher and church warden, his wife a tall, slim elegantly dressed woman who dressed in the style of the duchess of Windsor and was very like her in looks, was brown owl and captain of the girl guides.

Peggy who 'Did' for them twice a week found them a charming couple.

It was generally accepted that with the arrival of the Pemberton's the meeting would begin, so silence descended as the vicar with Jean Finch at his heels climbed on to the platform.

Jean as she usually did called the meeting to order, she'd hardly got the words of greeting out when the oak door was flung open groaning again on its hinges.

Everyone's heads turned to see who the newcomer was.

A ripple of excitement went through the assembled people as Farmer Phillips the local landowner took a seat at the back; it was well known that he didn't come to these events unless he had something of importance to disclose to the community, people shifted restlessly on their seats wanting to know what it was!

Peggy often said the arrival of the king himself wouldn't't stop Jean Finch when she was in full flow, so they all had to sit through arrangements for whist drives, the Christmas concert, and children's parties; and whether the hall should be let out for ballet lessons, before eventually Jean invited the late arrival to the platform.

An air of expectancy filled the hall.

Farmer Phillips adjusted his Tortoiseshell glasses at the end of his nose then seemed to glare at them all.

'I will come straight to the point.' He said although no one would have expected anything else from him; he was that sort of man.

'I have been informed by the authorities the part of my land known as 'The Brooks' has been requisitioned by the government to be used as a camp for German prisoners of war.' He adjusted his weight onto the brown walking stick he held in his right hand, smoothing the other hand down his corduroy trousers.

'I have no options I have to agree to it.' His face softened somewhat as he continued.

'I honestly thought as a community we'd done our bit! He paused for breath and an audible sigh went through the audience as they digested his words.

'As you know the huts are still there from the Polish, then the Italians came after that, the Canadians and Americans used them before the invasion.' He looked a little dispirited as he continued.

'I presume the authorities feel that as they are still in place minimum work would be needed to make the site secure for the new purpose.' His spectacles had slipped a bit and he pushed them up to the bridge of his nose.

'I came here tonight to let you know the situation because it will prevent rumour spreading when you see work begin on the site. I am sure I can depend on all of your good natures just as I have in the past.' Mr. Phillips gave them a rare smile and immediately left the platform, sweeping down the hall and out of the door he left behind a stunned silence.

This was soon replaced by a babble of voices many of them in protest as people digested the news

The general opinion was one of resignation; several people were heard to say they thought as a village they had done their bit and had their fair share of comings and goings on that piece of land.

Above the general din Peggy gestured to Winnie and the two of them scuttled off to the kitchen to make the tea, they were obviously going to be very busy this discussion could go on way into the night.

CHAPTER THREE

Peggy's fingers ached with the cold as she removed the fine linen altar cloths stiff as boards from a frosty night from her washing line early next morning; going into her cottage she quickly put them onto her kitchen table to thaw ready for ironing

Looking distastefully at the blackout curtains from the small kitchen window as she drew them to let in the light she decided they really needed replacing, but with the present position with rationing this wouldn't be possible precious clothing coupons could not be spared for such things so they would have to stay put for the foreseeable future; anyway with the winter almost here they did help keep out the biting cold wind that rattled the ill-fitting sash cord windows that let in the draught as it blew across the brooks adjacent to the row of cottages where they lived.

Turning round in the small space between the kitchen range and the table she reached for the teapot, Harry left it on the table after making a pot when he went out to milk the cows at the crack of dawn, she would have liked to make a fresh pot but with the rationing at two ounces of tea per person a week such luxuries were impossible.

Lowering her ample form onto a kitchen chair and removing the tea cozy she poured the amber liquid into a cup and wrapped her fingers round it to warm them up.

Peggy loved this solitude before she began her busy day, from here through the kitchen window she could see the sun peeping over the horizon giving the promise of a lovely late autumn day that would soon melt the frost on the grey slate roofs of their cottages as it rose in the sky.

A fresh faced woman in her early fifties she was what her husband called well padded, dressed today in an enveloping overall that covered all the clothes underneath she looked exactly what she was a very efficient housewife and mother.

The clock on the mantle shelf above the kitchen range struck the half hour reminding her she would have to get a move on if she was to have Harry's breakfast ready when he came in, his break was short with just time for a short rest.

Quickly she got to her feet folding up the linen now frost free into a tight ball so that it would remain damp for ironing. At the same time she congratulated herself that she had the insight last night on her return from the meeting to realize the wind had died down and the temperature was falling, one of the many things she had learnt from her mother many years previously after boiling linen a frost on it enhanced its whiteness.

Taking a black iron from a shelf on the wall she put it on a trivet at the back of the kitchen range to heat so that she could iron it later ready to take up to the Finches when she went to work later on, glancing at the clock again she took a cast iron frying pan from the back of the kitchen range.

Putting a small dollop of dripping left over from Sundays roast in the bottom she set it on the hot plate, adding a small rasher of bacon to it she then took a loaf of bread from the breadbin and cut a thick wedge adding this to pan, carefully removing the resulting breadcrumbs she deposited these in a jar; the severe rationing of the war years had taught her to waste nothing.

Taking an egg from a batch on the marble shelf in her small larder; she thought not for the first time how grateful she was for where they lived, people in the towns were rationed to one egg every two weeks, here they kept a few hens that were good layers, which meant for them there was only a shortage when the hens stopped laying, which only happened sometimes during the very cold winter months.

Harry's employer Farmer Phillips was allowed by the government to kill an occasional pig for his own consumption. After smoking the bacon himself he generously passed some to his workers, so Harry was accustomed to a small rasher with his breakfast on most days, a thing denied to people who lived in the cities their meat ration was miniscule.

Cutting off another slice of bread, Peggy dropped the black lid that covered the actual fire on the range propped the bread in front of it on a toasting fork.

Footsteps on the path and the familiar scraping of Harry's boots on the receptacle outside the back door announced his arrival so turning she smoothed the clean table cloth on the table and put in place a knife and fork in preparation for Harry.

Peggy turned back to the stove; Harry would want his breakfast in front of him as soon as he sat down.

A small clunk told her Harry had dropped a small billycan of milk straight from the cow onto the kitchen table and the sound of water flowing meant he was washing his hands in the kitchen sink.

She transferred Harry's breakfast to a plate and turning round she was about to put it onto the table when she nearly dropped it in astonishment, there was Ned standing alongside her husband.

'I thought you were still up in your bed!' The surprise in her voice turned to affection as she looked fondly at the lad who stood head and shoulders above Harry.

Then her voice took on a sterner tone.

'Why did you get up so early?'

'I am working age now so I thought I would start work straight away!' Ned said the words almost apologetically as he turned to wash his hands at the kitchen sink.

'But you were only fourteen yesterday!' The frown beneath Peggy's brows deepened.

'You could have allowed yourself a couple of days before you began!' She sighed in resignation.

'Uncle Harry and I agreed the situation being what it is, it is better for me this way' Ned said quietly.

Peggy's jaw set in a firm line and she raised her voice an octave or two in protest,

'Well in my opinion it could have waited a day or two.'

She turned back to the range to prepare Ned a breakfast, putting another dollop of fat in the pan followed by a thick slice of bread and an egg.

Ned sat opposite Harry and Peggy quickly set the breakfast down in front of him, then she made a fresh pot of tea, putting it on the kitchen table in front of the men to brew.

Looking at the tousled head young man chasing his egg round the plate with some fried bread a proud feeling rose in Peggy's throat, it had pleased her a great deal to learn recently that he would be staying with them rather than returning to his roots in London.

'I am sure your mother could wait a few more days before she got her hands on your hard earned cash!' Peggy said in a rather severe tone.

Ned shrugged his shoulders, yet there was a new determination in his voice as he said.

'I don't want to give her the excuse to criticize anything!'

'She won't have a reason.' Peggy's voice now had a softer tone.

'In fact she should be proud of you!'

Ned blushed at this complement but before he could make a reply Harry drew his pocket watch from his waistcoat pocket.

'Time we were getting on.' He announced pulling his jacket from the back of the chair and putting it over his shirt so that his powerful muscles the result of sheer hard work were no longer visible.

Ned scraped his chair back from the table, mug of hot tea still in his hand he quickly swallowed it down in one gulp before glancing toward Harry and followed his example by taking his jacket from the back of his chair.

Then the two of them made a swift exit through the kitchen door.

Washing up the breakfast things in water softened with soda crystals Peggy stood by the kitchen window watching them pull on their Wellington boots and then march off down the lane back to work.

As she splashed the dishes around in the warm water her mind wandering back to the time when she first set eyes on Ned at the Reading Room at the very start of the war five and a half years ago.

He had been one of a batch of children who arrived after being evacuated from London as part of the government scheme.

Peggy and Harry stood at the back of the throng that assembled when the children arrived.

Her heart went out immediately to these children, many looked like little parcels with labels round their necks to say who they were all of them looked sad, lonely and bewildered,

Soon the elite of the village were taking their pick of the better dressed 'dear little girls' and fitter better looking boys who could be of use to the farming community, these were quickly trundled out of the door, gas masks slung from their shoulders, cases in their hands, to their new abodes.

Eventually just two were left; one skinny nine year old who looked decidedly undernourished; and the other small scrawny lad who didn't look more than five years old.

It wasn't surprising these two had been rejected; scruffiest of the bunch both had elbows sticking through woolen jumpers that had seen better days; it was obvious they came from poor homes. The shoes on their feet were tied up with string and all the rest of their sparse worldly possessions were tied up in a very small brown paper parcel each held in their arms probably the only warm clothing they possessed was on their backs.

These were two lads went home with Harry and Peggy.

At first it was thought the two lads were brothers, later it came to light that Ned had taken Mickey under his wing when the little lad's mother had dumped him in the line of children at the station before the train left London.

Soft hearted Ned had gone up to and comforted the little lad who was crying his eyes out and ever since then had stood up for him.

The boys were now firm friends and as close as brothers, Ned always looking out for the younger one especially when local lads set about the evacuees and Mickey was in the firing line when they first started at the village school. Ned would have none of it and made the village children learn to respect Mickey and the other evacuees. Ned had learnt to stick up for himself in the back streets of London and could be a force to be reckoned with when needed.

Without exception all the other evacuees from the village had long since returned to their roots; some of them after just a few weeks in their new abodes, a few stayed for the duration of the hostilities in the cities before returning, now in the village just Ned and Mickey remained in the care of Harry and Peggy.

Over the years at various times Ned's mother Rita had come from London to visit him.

Dressed up in high heel shoes and close fitting suits, a perky hat on her dyed blonde hair she complained loudly how difficult it was to get to their cottage; saying a disdainful voice it was too far off the beaten track and too muddy which angered her son.

'Don't know why she bothers to come if she feels like that.' Ned complained to Peggy after she left.

Peggy kept silent, not wanting to put Ned's mother down in front of him. Rita always departed with fresh produce and new laid eggs, which she gladly took; it seemed to Peggy it was all take and no gives.

She brought nothing not even a small gift for her son.

All the time she was under their roof Rita talked continuously about herself and the life she was now leading in London apparently enjoying her freedom working in a factory with no family responsibilities this life gave her.

Ned's two brothers who were older than him had been evacuated to families in the north of England.

'Don't see them too often.' Rita said, complaining in the next breath saying it was too far to go.

'They are on the edge of a small town, so fresh things are off the menu.' Rita said eyeing up the produce Peggy was wrapping up for her to take home.

Peggy smiled to herself convinced Rita visited Ned and put up with the inconvenience here for the fresh produce she could take back that was so hard to come by in London.

When Ned's father was killed during the hostilities it didn't seem to affect Rita's way of life very much, she turned up several weeks after the event to tell Ned all about it in a navy dress with bright red flowers on it; her hair newly set red lipstick polishing her lips and she reeked of what seemed expensive perfume, if she was upset she didn't show it, she just talked all the time of what seemed a good social life in London,

A couple of months ago Rita had written to her son insisting he return to London as soon as she could find suitable accommodation, Ned was needed at home now she insisted.

But Ned had dug his heels in, he loved the countryside; he told his mother he wanted to make a career out of farming and confided in Peggy that he had no intentions of returning to the 'smoke' ever no matter what his mother said!

For the next few weeks letters went to and fro between Ned and his mother; it was a real battle to get Rita to see things Ned's way.

Fortunately fate was on Ned's side, Rita's old house in the east end of London had been razed to the ground in an air raid towards the end of the war, down an underground station at the time Rita was unscathed, she was now reduced to living in one room.

The housing situation in London was dire, with no chance of any change in the immediate future.

This gave Ned great joy to point out his homecoming would put a strain on the family as his two older brothers had already returned from being evacuated, which meant there was no room for him!

Eventually it was agreed he could stay where he was until Rita found a new home, or when his older brother was called up for national service which ever was the sooner. Ned felt confident it would be sometime before this problem was solved as the three boys were each only a year apart and the eldest just over sixteen so call up was two years away.

Not to be outdone Rita insisted that if Ned were to stay and work on the farm he was to send a sum of money weekly out of the wages he would be earning.

Peggy was incensed when she heard this; Rita's other two sons were working and so was she and Peggy was sure she didn't really need the two shillings and six pence a week she insisted her younger son sent to her.

Whist an evacuee, Peggy received ten shillings a week for Ned's keep; this had stopped immediately now he was fourteen and capable of working.

This put poor Ned in an impossible situation, by the time he gave Peggy something for his keep and sent money to his mother he was working long hours on the farm for very little; but to his credit Ned made it very clear this wasn't going to deter him from what he wanted to do; in fact it seemed to make him more resolute.

Peggy admiring his spirit made up her mind that if she had anything to do with it Ned's plan would succeed and he would be able to stay here with them and for her part agreed with Ned that he should give her just five shillings a week and put two shillings away in savings, which left him a little of his wages in his pocket.

'You are just the best mum in the world.' Ned said tears standing out in his eyes.

'Nonsense, there are far better ones than me.' Peggy said ruffling his hair secretly feeling very pleased the work she and Harry had put in during the five years they had the boys was appreciated.

The water going cold beneath her fingers brought her thoughts back to the present she looked again at the clock she'd have to get on or the rest of the house would be up before she was ready for them.

Quickly removing the dishes to the wooden draining board she dried them on a linen cloth; her next task was to put porridge in a double saucepan filling the outer one with hot water she placed it in the hot plate of the kitchen range.

Then taking a small bucket from outside the back door she went through to the small sitting room and got down on her knees to clear out the ashes of last evenings fire, depositing this in the bucket she laid fresh newspapers and kindling with small pieces of coal on the top ready for lighting later on.

Giving the mantle shelf and mirror over it a quick dust she ran the duster over the Rexene suite, and then the sideboard and the small occasional table got the same treatment. The piano got a quick dust before she returned to the kitchen to wash her hands at the sink, turning to stir the porridge now steaming on the range.

Noises from above told her, the rest of the family was up and about.

A small face appeared round the door just as Peggy set two fresh places at the table.

Mickey sat himself down at the table whist Peggy reached for the double saucepan on the kitchen range stirring the contents of the pot once more pouring out a large helping of the porridge into a bowl adding a good helping of milk from the billy can she set it down in front of Mickey together with a mug of milk.

'Thanks mum.' He said as she affectionately tousled his tawny hair, before putting the saucepan back on the range ready for when her daughter made her appearance.

Peggy looked proudly at this young lad who always called her 'mum.'

Small for his eleven years he was very bright thanks to the countless hours Peggy had spent helping him with his school work since he'd come under her roof.

When he arrived he could scarcely speak properly let alone read or write, now he was always top of the class at the village school and his teachers were confident he would pass his eleven plus later this year with no difficulty, this gave Peggy a prideful satisfaction that all the work she'd done with the lad had come to good fruition.

Sylvia came in and slid quietly into her place at the kitchen table; Peggy turned from the range and looked admiringly at her only child as she once more took the porridge from the hob and poured out some in a bowl for her daughter placing it in front of her.

Sylvia tastefully dressed today in a plain green jumper over a brown tweed skirt this Peggy recognized as one of Jean Finch's daughter Bridget's hand me downs. Sylvia clever with her needle had altered it to fit her slender frame.

Peggy eyed her up and down grateful not for the first time the girl had inherited her slim build from her father's side of the family and not the thunder thighs that seemed to be her mother's lot.

Sylvia's black hair caught in the nape of her neck with a tortoiseshell clip shone from frequent brushing. Peggy recognized the clip as one she had picked up at a garden sale at the vicarage last summer, it blended well with the jumper and skirt; Sylvia had a good way with colours.

'I'm off to the pictures with Janet tonight straight from work' Sylvia announced as she chased the last of the porridge round her plate.

'I will ask dad to meet you of the bus then.' Peggy said firmly.

Sylvia grimaced, looking at her mother with her clear dark brown eyes. 'I will be alright mum.' She retorted.

Peggy put a cup of tea in front of her daughter.

'I know you work, but you are only fourteen.' She said firmly

'I am Fourteen and a half.' Her daughter replied rather sharply as she sat back in her chair to enjoy her tea.

'Dad will be there!' Peggy said firmly knowing Harry would never allow his daughter to walk the long dark lane from the bus stop to their cottages alone at night.

'All right then!' A resigned note entered Sylvia's voice; she knew it was no good arguing even if she defied her mother her father would have something to say. So she pushed back her chair and taking her breakfast things over to the sink she rinsed them quickly under the tap and put them on the wooden draining board.

Peggy sat down at the table with another cup of tea and watched Sylvia take her outside coat from the hook on the back door donning it carefully over the scarf she'd made out of an old scotch kilt picking up her handbag and gloves she waved goodbye in her mother's direction and let herself out of the back door making her way to the bus stop at the top of the lane to get the bus into work.

Her mother was she was proud of Sylvia's flare for dressmaking, when she got a job as a trainee tailor in town it was a source of great satisfaction Peggy wanted something better for her only daughter than the domestic work that had been her lot in life. In a way it saddened her somewhat that the war years had made the children into young adults a lot quicker than her own generation, although she herself had begun her working life in service at twelve years old it was still under the confines of the family. Now children expected to do as they liked as soon as they were in employment at fourteen and Peggy considered this too young for this responsibility.

A sharp knock on the kitchen door announced the arrival of Hugo from next door who called every morning for Mickey to accompany him to school.

Hugo came into the kitchen as Mickey scrambled from the table; quickly putting his dish and cup in the sink, then Mickey slung his coat over his shoulders and pulled his balaclava helmet over his head; picking up his school satchel the two boys rushed out of the door turning quickly raised their hands to Peggy with a swift goodbye salute.

Left to her own devices Peggy went upstairs to make the beds, empty chamber pots and wash basins, before returning to the kitchen.

Taking a skinned rabbit from the marble shelf in the larder; she cut it up putting it in a large iron saucepan together with fresh vegetables, then she added a couple of Oxo cubes and a sprinkling of herbs together with pearl barley, depositing it all on the back burner of the range to slow cook.

Quickly popping some rice into an enamel dish; she added some milk from the billy can Harry had brought in earlier together with a minute knob of butter; she would have liked to have topped it with nutmeg but this was no longer available owning to the war, then she deposited the dish in the oven.

Returning to the iron she had previously put onto heat, she took it from its trivet and held it for a moment in front of her face to test if it was hot enough to smooth out the fine linen, judging it was alright she spread out a cloth on the kitchen table; the starch she'd previously dipped the cloth in brought up the fine linen crisply, folding the result into neat squares she deposited it in a basket together with a clean overall.

Pulling on her outdoor coat, she closed the kitchen door behind her and began the walk to Jean Finches home.

Today because of the frost, she had chosen to walk the short distance up the hill instead of using her bike.

Nature at its best greeted her as she walked along, the evergreen trees looked as though someone had stuck sugar round the edges of the leaves, especially lovely were the holly trees with the sun glistening on the dark green leaves and the red berries.

So engrossed was she in the scenery she didn't't notice that every step she took marked the hoarfrost on the grass, spoiling the silvery green colour, it was only when she turned into Jean's gate that she noticed the pattern of her footprints stretching out into the distance.

'What a difference from yesterday.' Was Jean's greeting as she welcomed Peggy at the kitchen door.

'I was quite surprised to see the heavy frost; I thought last night's wind would have kept it at bay.' Jean took the basket from Peggy's arm, carefully removing the contents.

'These do look crisp and white; I don't know how you do it! The Reverent Hounsome will be pleased.' Peggy glowed as she took off her coat hanging it on a hook behind the kitchen door.

Praise from Jean was not a normal reaction that came her way; she revelled in it for once.

'The wind died down about eleven o'clock so my daughter tells me! Jean continued. 'I expect you were tucked up in bed by then ' She knew Harry got up at the crack of dawn for milking, so supposed early to bed would obviously be the rule in their home, little did she know that her help was pegging out the very linen she held in her hands at that particular time.

Peggy looked over to the sink which was piled high with dishes, no need to ask what her first task was to be today!

Taking her overall from her basket she donned it before beginning the chores, she enjoyed being in Jeans house you didn't have to boil water for the washing up it was on tap, such a luxury!

'Could you make a start on the pots before you bottom out upstairs?' Peggy smiled, Jean it seemed had almost read her thoughts!

The conversation inevitably turned to last night's meeting.

'I thought we'd done our share with the Poles, Italians, Canadians and Americans down at the brook lands without this!' Jean pulled out a chair from the kitchen table as she spoke sitting down she quickly lit a cigarette attaching it to a long holder, then she sat and watched Peggy scrubbing at her pots

'Well it makes sense to me!' Peggy took hold of the linen wiping up cloth.

'The huts are already there from when we had the other men here and the Americans put in the infrastructure for the roads didn't they?' Peggy looked over to Jean before she reached up to put the clean dishes in the cupboard.

'The one thing about the Americans, they built the roads in and out properly; there was no chance of their huge lorries being bogged down on that marshy bit of ground after they finished.'

Peggy saw at once the rather condescending look on her employers face.

'I suppose you might be right.' Jean said grudging; not wanting to admit her daily help was capable of such thought.

'I'm sure we shall soon see how things turn out.' The superior attitude in Jean's voice continued.

'I am due at a meeting of the WVS; so I would appreciate it if you could make sure Claude has his morning coffee before you leave.' She rose from her seat stubbing out the cigarette in a silver ash tray which she left for Peggy to clear away.

Peggy picked it up and disposed of the contents in the waste bin wrinkling her nose at the smell.

She watched Jean go down the hall; her figure encased in the distinctive WVS grey-green skirt over a dark red blouse which had an air of authority about it.

Jean picked up the uniform jacket from the hall stand and put it over her well-proportioned figure she stopping for a moment to make sure the uniform hat sat comfortably on her head, then after checking her appearance in the hall mirror she let herself out of the front door clicking it shut behind her.

Peggy heard her little Austin Seven car start up and crunch away on the gravel drive, as she made her way upstairs.

After making the beds Peggy shook the rugs out of the window, before she went into the bathroom where she lovingly polished the brass taps over the bath; looking round at the snow white bathroom suite and the electric light with some envy.

In their cottage Harry had the job of emptying the bucket in the toilet which was situated at the bottom of the garden every week, they had no bathroom and no electricity.

Friday nights the tin bath that hung outside the back door on a hook was brought into the kitchen and saucepans of water heated on the kitchen range were poured into it, then each person from the youngest to the eldest took it in turns to bath.

It always amazed Peggy that her two evacuees had accepted their primitive conditions without question, the house they lived in in London was in a very poor area, but they did have proper toilets, a bathroom and electric light, yet both the boys accepted their more antiquated way of life without question and never complained about what they had left behind.

Peggy reasoned that Mickey was in all probability a bit too young to remember much anyway.

Ned had memories of his former life; although when he spoke of it he never seemed to refer to it in a good light, it seemed his real life started when he came under their roof; that was even more pronounced after his father was killed in the war.

The two had been close, Ned had cried for weeks after his mother had visited with the sad news, quite often in the small hours of the morning quietly in his room Peggy heard his sobs and felt inadequate because she had been unable to comfort him.

As soon as she finishing her chores Peggy took a tray of coffee through to Claude's room,

Jean's husband was sitting quietly in a room at the back of the house.

Being on a hill above the village it had an excellent view of the surrounding countryside; this was lost on Claude whose sight was very limited owing to a flying accident during the Battle of Britain some years previously.

Claude greeted her with a smile, which although was lopsided due to the scarring on his face, lit up his features.

'You are in a rush as usual.' He said.

Peggy smiled down at him as she drew up a small occasion table alongside him and placed a cup she'd just poured out where it would be easy for him to reach.

'Yes Harry will be expecting his dinner at one o'clock; he has Ned with him today!'

'Has he indeed, that lad is keen!' Claude reached out for the beverage as he spoke; Peggy automatically extended her hand to stop him slopping it in the saucer.

'Thank you that is kind.' Claude said appreciatively.

Peggy blushed at Claude's reply, and was glad he couldn't see it.

'Yes I told him he didn't have to start work immediately but he insisted.' She would have loved to spend some time chatting to this man, but looking at the clock she realized her time was limited.

Claude didn't have the self-important attitude of his wife, even though he'd been decorated for his war service, he had led an interesting life as a pilot before his accident, Peggy could listen enthralled for hours when he told her about life in the RAF before the war, and how he'd learnt to fly against all the odds when he was a sickly young man.

'We will have that chat another time.' Peggy told him as she began to remove her apron.

'I will hold you to that.' Was Claude's passing shot as she quietly closed the door of his room behind herself.

Then she quickly went out of the kitchen door to begin her walk home; a midday meal had to be ready for Harry at twelve thirty and now there was Ned as well!

CHAPTER FOUR

After the euphoria of victory over the Nazi's regime and in the far east over Japan, people were brought down to earth when the Prime Minister told the British Nation that most of Europe was in dire straits and many of their servicemen wouldn't't be coming home for at least the foreseeable future, this added to the air of despondency people in general now felt.

People knew that this first Christmas after peace was signed was going to be difficult with rationing biting harder than before.

Dig for Britain notices were once more prominent, every scrap of land being used even small strips of land alongside railway embankments sported cabbages and sprouts for the table; nothing was wasted; everything was still recycled just as it had been during the war years.

Despite these difficulties, Peggy decided that Mickey and the three children living next door were due a little fun so the first Saturday in December she invited everyone to help make Christmas puddings and some paper chains to hang up in the sitting room.

Previously the puddings would have been made weeks earlier, this was now impossible because of the lack of supplies the puddings wouldn't keep as long as they had previously therefore they had to be made nearer the day with many ingredients substituted with something else.

Fortunately the children couldn't remember much before the war so accepted things as they were now.

It had already been announced that this year there would be no extra sugar to help with the festivities so Peggy had over the past few weeks carefully put a little extra aside from their meager ration so that the festive season would be more enjoyable.

Clearing a space on the wooden kitchen table the four of them grated carrots and apples together with the hazelnuts they'd gathered that autumn on the downs.

Peggy whisked up eggs mixing these together with margarine, suet, flour, mixed spice, and what currants and sugar were available added the other things to the bowl.

Then came the important part which they called 'Stir up Sunday' each child was allowed to give three stirs to the pudding and make a wish.

Peggy glanced at the four of them as they did this wondering what their wishes were, she smiled as they screwed up their faces in concentration eyes tightly closed.

Hugo gave a secret smile as he stirred.

The girls Helga and Sonja both giggled as they took their turn with the spoon the secretive look on both their faces.

'What did you wish for?' Peggy asked wondering if their wishes involved their future, as she realized it would be only another year before Sonja would be fourteen and working, with the other girl just a year younger.

Both the girls then refused to be drawn on the issue saying the wishes wouldn't come true if they were divulged.

Putting the mixture into china basins Peggy tied greaseproof piece of paper on the top before depositing them into a large saucepan to boil slowly on the kitchen range.

She scooped up the remaining apple cores and peelings the war had taught them to waste nothing; all waste went into the pig bin, or to make a mash for the tame rabbits, in turn their droppings together with any horse manure available from deliveries by horse and cart locally went onto the compost heap to be used in the vegetable garden. Peggy saved every scrap of paper, brown paper bags, greaseproof paper or sometimes colored paper all found their way into a drawer to be used again. Ash from the fire was heaped up to be used on icy paths in the winter or to use round plants to stop the slugs having their fill of precious vegetables. When the chimney sweep visited twice a year, the soot was used to cover the celery grown in the garden to keep it white.

Settling the children down at the kitchen table with colored paper and a pot of glue previously made up with flour and water, the four children began the task making some paper chains and lanterns to decorate the sitting room. Engrossed they didn't hear Gisela come quietly in through the back door until she touched her neighbour lightly on the shoulder.

Peggy turned round startled and noticed immediately an almost frantic look on the newcomers face.

'Go through to the other room.' Peggy said, quickly reaching towards the kettle to transfer it from the back of the range to the hot plate to boil.

As soon as she had poured the water into the teapot, Peggy took a tray with milk jug and two cups through to the sitting room; leaving the children to their tasks she quietly closed the door behind her.

Instinct told her Gisela wouldn't want her children to know why she was obviously upset.

Peggy looked expectantly in her direction as she took a seat next to her neighbour on the Rexene settee.

Gisela leant down and drew an envelope from her handbag as Peggy stirred the tea pot.

'I ave had the letter.' Her fingers shook as she handed the envelope to her neighbour.

'Here you read it.' Gisela's English faltered with emotion.

'Are you sure?' Peggy gingerly pulled the sheet of paper out.

'Yes please do.' Her neighbour insisted.

Peggy opened it up with more than a little apprehension, as her neighbour was so agitated was it bad news had someone died?

As soon as she had digested the contents of the letter, Peggy looked up into Gisela's eyes her face wreathed in smiles.

'Surely this is good news, isn't it?' But a frown quickly knotted in her forehead when she saw fear in the younger woman's face.

'Of course I will be glad to have Don ome, but I am so worried.' Gisela's beautiful brown eyes welled up with tears,

'I went back to Germany in the thirties because Don couldn't find a job as the engineer he'd been trained for.' Gisela announced pausing for a moment.

'It made him very frustrated and took it out on us!' Fear etched her face.

'To be honest he was violent, I had to leave, and I was scared of him and of what he might do to the children!' Tears spilled down her cheeks and she fumbled in her pocket for a handkerchief.

Peggy quickly fished one out of her apron pocket and handing it over as Gisela continued with the conversation.

'Don took this job as a farm worker because he knew this cottage went with the job!' Gisela stumbled over the words, emotion getting the better of her.

'We had to have a home when I came back from Austria.' She paused catching her breath.

'When he went into the services Farmer Phillips let us remain here because he thought Don would work for him when he is demobbed; you see from this letter that is now not part of his plans!'

Listening to Gisela; Peggy remembered how they had come to be in these circumstances.

She'd originally come to England in the 1930's as an au pair; employed by a wealthy family she met Don an apprentice engineer; they fell in love marrying very quickly afterwards when Gisela found out she was pregnant.

As the years of the depression took hold Don couldn't find work; frustrated and unable to provide for his growing family, he and Gisela argued a great deal; in the end she went back to her parents on the Austrian-German border taking her three very young children with her.

Gisela had never divulged to her neighbour the details of their split; Peggy knew it must have been something serious to send the girl all that way back to her parents, today was the first time Gisela had admitted Don had been violent.

Gisela would probably have stayed in Austria, if Adolph Hitler hadn't decided to invade that country, the first of his conquests.

Life becomes a bit difficult for the young woman with a British surname!

Her parents aware their daughter would be in a difficult position if as it seemed likely Hitler invaded Poland and Britain came into the war showed their concern, their reluctant advice because they didn't really want to be separated from their daughter was that Gisela's only real option was to return to Britain and her husband.

When Hitler invaded Poland in 1939 Gisela's parents managed to get their daughter on board one of the last trains out of Germany before the border was closed; they mailed ahead for their son-in-law to meet the train.

Almost as soon as war broke out Don's skills for which he'd been trained were recognized and he was requisitioned to help with the war effort, much in demand repairing planes both in this country and abroad; he had returned to his home very infrequently in the last five years; quite often it had been months before he could get away for the odd weekend.

For the past two years he'd been in Egypt and unable to get home at all.

'You always knew that Don would come home once the war was over.' Peggy said quietly hoped she sounded more sympathetic than she felt; she knew although Gisela looked frail, inside she was tough.

'Yes of course I did; but I thought we could stay here; but you can see from this letter that is far from what Don has in mind! Gisela looked down at her feet not wanting to meet her neighbour's eyes afraid of what she might see there; she knew Peggy had very definite ideas about a woman's place being with her husband

Peggy looked thoughtful, she didn't answer for a few moments, it was obvious to her that Don wouldn't want to come back here and work as a farm labourer after holding down such a responsible position for the last six years in the services; besides it made sense for him to use the ability for which he'd been trained so she chose her next words carefully and tried to sound enthusiastic as she turned to Gisela.

'From what Don says in his letter this Flight Lieutenant he writes about here is planning to build homes once they are demobbed, that man is obviously going places and wants Don with him!' Peggy smiled as she continued.

'The Prime Minister has announced that thousands of homes are going to be needed; so many have been damaged or destroyed by the war, it is something that people need!' Peggy tried to look into her companions eyes but Gisela still looked down, at the floor refusing to meet Peggy's gaze.

'I am sure Don wants to make good use of the skills he has; this other man has seen his potential and has the capital to accomplish this, surely this must be good news? Think of the opportunities for you all, especially for your children!' Peggy ended on an upbeat note.

Finally Gisela raised her eyes into Peggy's and Peggy registered the pain there.

'If we move people will have to know I am German.' The words came out of Gisela's mouth in a rush so at last Peggy understood the real reason Gisela didn't want to leave her present home.

The older woman took Gisela's cold hand in hers.

'Things are different now than when you first came here.' There was a positive tone in Peggy's voice.

'Things have changed, people are more tolerant now!' She gave Gisela a smile.

'When you came back at the beginning of the war the children only spoke the German tongue didn't they?

Gisela nodded in reply.

'Now they hardly remember it, so that won't be a problem?' She recalled the terrible time her young neighbour had when she enrolled the three children at the local school on her return in 1939. Because they didn't speak English, the children at school and a lot of the villagers were cruelly calling the children 'little Nazi's' To add to the misery a lot of the villagers said they didn't want their youngsters mixing with Germans!

This news quickly came to the ears of Jean Finch and she had come to the rescue, Jean to her credit hated unfairness and she was quick to defuse the situation.

Although new to the village at the time; Jean stood up in front of everyone telling them it wasn't Gisela or her families fault that Hitler had declared war on this country; she pointed out that Gisela was in fact Austrian and Hitler had taken over that country also!

As it happened shortly after this, the government as part of the war effort moved Gisela and her family to the Isle of Man together with a lot of others who had roots on the continent of Europe away from the general population where they remained for over a year.

When the family was finally allowed to return to the village, they found people had changed towards them and Gisela's past heritage was never referred to by the villagers again; they accepted her and her children as one of them especially as the children were now fluent in the English language.

The war had changed them all and broadened everyone's horizons, many people had come and gone locally, first there were the evacuees, then the land girls; later a camp was set up in the brook lands which housed Italians, Polish, and free French, then latterly Canadians and Americans, this had the effect of altering village life completely.

'It won't be nearly as bad as you think!' Peggy said consolingly

'You speak English very well and if you go to the London suburbs where it appears a lot of house building will have to take place you will find people are not as clicky as they are in villages.' Peggy hoped by being this would have the desired effect on the younger woman.

'Yes, I understand that.' Gisela shifted a bit in her seat.

Peggy looked again in her direction noting a worried frown still stood between her eyes.

'It isn't just that! Gisela's large eyes stood out in her face.

'I ask myself will Don get on alright with his children.' She paused for a moment.

'You see all their young life he has never been there! We went back to Germany when they were very young and almost as soon as we returned Don went into the services; all of us have never had any quality time together! A tear glistened again at the corner of Gisela's eye.

'It is so sad this year Sonja is a teenager and her father hardly knows her!'

'I am afraid that is going to be the case in many families! Peggy said thoughtfully.

'So many men have been away for a lot of their offspring's young lives; in many cases they are going to seem like strangers!' She was grateful not for the first time that Harry's job made him exempt from military service; he might have worked long hours but the only time he'd been missing at nights was when he was serving in the local home guard.

Peggy bent forward to pour another cup of tea from the pot passing it to her neighbour and as she did the younger women's shoulders began to shake; in moments the younger woman was distraught; her sobbing becoming louder and tears pouring down her face.

The cup rattled so Peggy leant forward and took it from Gisela's shaking hand to save it being slopped in the saucer.

'This isn't the only problem is it?' She said gently.

'No there is the other one

Kurt.' Gisela replied.

Peggy looked quite taken back and thought deeply for a few minutes before she replied.

'I thought you'd put that one behind you,' She said a bit of impatience showing in her voice.

'How could I forget? 'The large eyes now turned towards Peggy filled with tears that spilled over and ran down Gisela's cheeks.

'I loved him so much!' Gisela put her hand on her heart.

I have tried to so many times; you can't change what I feel here.'

Peggy sighed, things were so different now; emotions and morals had changed dramatically since before the war. Thanks to the influx of people into the village it was no longer the small close knit community it had been previously; it had led to so many problems here in this village and so many other places too!

The arrival of the land army girls in the village was the first thing to stir things up a bit; men began to look at the more flighty ones who were much worldlier than the local girls especially the young men; soon the able bodied ones were called up for military service so this was curtailed somewhat.

Then the site at Brooklands was requisitioned and made into a military camp

When the Polish and the Italians were billeted there, it didn't make a lot of difference they mostly kept themselves to themselves.

It was the arrival of the Canadians and Americans that really set things in motion.

The Americans in particular had been like a breath of fresh air to the war weary locals, they quickly integrated into neighbourhood. One of the first things they did was to organize a few parties for the children; with the austere war conditions the children loved it; especially when goodies were dished out that some of the younger children had never seen.

Then they began to have dances and social evenings at the camp at brook lands and at the reading room this really stirred up the villagers.

The land army girls enjoyed the attention from the arrivals but with most of the younger men away at the war, quite a few of the young women of the village, married or not also had their heads turned by all the attention the Americans bestowed on them and many were disloyal to their partners, some of whom had been away for most of the war years.

Gisela had been invited to one or two dances and to her credit at first she refused to go.

Then one day when sharing afternoon tea with Peggy she suddenly asked her neighbour if she would mind looking after her children whilst she went to what her neighbour described as social evening at the camp.

'Just to see what it is like.' Gisela explained at the time

Peggy at first refused knowing it could lead to trouble. Over a period of time gradually Gisela wore her neighbour down and she agreed to keep an eye out for the three children next door whilst Gisela attended one of the dances with another young woman from the village to see what it would be like.

To say Peggy was shocked when Gisela appeared ready to go out that night was an understatement.

She wore a maroon figure hugging dress with a sweetheart neckline which fell provocatively over her hips and highlighted the colour of her large eyes, rouge powder on Gisela's cheeks accentuated her high cheek bones; together with a bright lipstick and high heel shoes to finish the assemble she looked absolutely stunning.

It wasn't in Peggy's opinion what a respectable married woman should wear on an occasion like this; but she pursed her lips and decided to say nothing even though she felt Gisela was asking for trouble especially when she had heard in the village how the American's at the camp had behaved towards some of the local young girls.

On this occasion Gisela arrived home at a reasonable hour. Peggy did notice a bright glow in her cheeks and a glint in her eyes, she had rarely seen before in her neighbour, this disturbed her somewhat but she asked no questions and Gisela gave no indications as to how the evening had gone.

Late morning the following Monday, Peggy was standing in her yard putting her washing through the mangle when a very good looking American officer approached her enquiring where Gisela lived. Taking him to Gisela's door; her neighbour insisted Peggy stayed with her when the man was invited in for a cup of tea.

From the start it was very apparent that there was a spark between these two people, eventually Kurt became a frequent visitor although sensibly Gisela insisting Peggy was always present on his visits aware of talk in the village about men from the camp who frequented the houses of married women.

Kurt well in his thirties made no secret of the fact he was divorced and that he had children; it was also very clear he was smitten with Gisela.

It was thought that soon the Americans would be spearheading an onslaught on the French coast and it was known that the order could come at any time; the uncertainty of the situation meant every day these two spent together was very precious, so it was no surprise that Kurt spent every opportunity he could with Gisela.

Even though she knew how close they were growing, Peggy was appalled when Gisela asked if she could look after the children so that she could go away for one night with Kurt.

Everything in Peggy shrieked 'don't get involved in this.'

Gradually Gisela wore her neighbour down.

'It may be our only chance ever to spend some time together.' She implored Peggy adding

'It's only for one night!' Her large eyes looking into Peggy's pleadingly.

'But how do I explain your absence to Harry? 'Peggy asked hoping this statement would make Gisela think about the situation, and put her off the plan.

'Say I have gone to relatives.' Came the curt reply

'Harry knows you don't have any relatives in this country?' Peggy protested, adding.

'I could never possibly tell him the truth he would never understand, or accept it!'

'Say I have been invited to an old neighbours wedding back where I lived before the war and it is too far to go and get back in one day; he wouldn't be able to dispute that!' Gisela pleaded again.

'What do I say about why you are not taking the children?' Peggy asked rather tetchily she didn't like lies or dishonesty, really not wanting any part of this charade.

"Harry knows Hugo suffers from travel sickness, he would accept they would be better off with you for just one night.' Gisela's large eyes once again entreated her neighbour.

'Would you think it over?' She asked.

Peggy didn't give a definite answer, but she did mull it over in her mind for several days, and Gisela's pleading eyes played with her mind giving her several bad nights.

Before the war she wouldn't have entertained such a proposition; now things were different, Kurt was going away to war and everyone everywhere now lived for the moment with little thought of tomorrow, if there was a tomorrow for them!

In the end Peggy was spared having to make the decision; the weekend away never happened, suddenly all leave was cancelled.

No one actually saw the departure of the American troops, they seemed to be spirited away at the dead of night; there was silence from the camp with just a skeleton crew remaining there.

Within days the radio was announcing the invasion of France had begun.

For weeks afterwards Gisela watched the post, but nothing came; it was as though the time she had spent with Kurt never happened at all.

Gisela grew listless; the large eyes had dark shadows underneath through many sleepless nights.

There were reports of many deaths in battle and Gisela was convinced he must have been killed in the first onslaught or she was sure he would have contacted her.

They were never to know the real truth, his family were in America, and they were his next of kin; there was no way the authorities would let someone in England who had known him just a few weeks know what the position was with regard to one American soldier.

It was presumed his family in America knew nothing of his few weeks' dalliance with an English housewife; particularly as she was Austrian who spoke German how would he explain that away?

It took a long time for Gisela to recover, she lost interest in everything and cut a sad figure with her high cheekbones became even more a feature in her thinning face, her clothes hung on her once hourglass figure.

'You can't change the past.' Peggy told her, bringing the conversation smartly back to the present.

'No you can't.' Gisela admitted a faraway look still in her eyes.

'My father always said people are more precious than possessions. I wonder if he still thinks that way now they have lost so much thanks to the war' she said sadly. Gisela had recently heard from her family to say things were very bad there, the rationing in their country and the damage to the interior being even more severe than here.

'I am sure he does!' Peggy paused.

'But if you think about it he must have always had your best interests at heart otherwise he wouldn't have insisted you came back here before the war started.' Peggy's words seem to go home and Gisela gave a slow smile which didn't reach her eyes.

'Look how people here have accepted you here after that initial problem; you have been happy here haven't you?' Gisela's smile at last lit up her face.

'With friends like you and Harry how could I be unhappy?' She said quietly.

'Well!' Peggy looked into her neighbours eyes thinking deeply again before she spoke.

'Well you may be surprised to know that Harry is very anti-German.'

Gisela's eyes narrowed with shock.

'But he has always been so kind to me!' The words came out almost in a whisper.

'To be honest I think that Harry looks upon you as Austrian even though your national language is German.'

Then a guilty look crossed Peggy's face.

'Perhaps I shouldn't have told you that! Harry actually never shows the resentment he has inside to many people, only those he is close too.' Peggy stroked her chin thoughtfully.

'I know for sure if Sylvie brought a German home he wouldn't't like it at all; he always blamed the fact we never had the son he would dearly loved on the fact we waited so long to marry, after Sylvia was born no more came along!' Peggy paused for a long moment.

'It really all stems from losing his father in the Great War. Harry was only a little older than Ned when his father was killed in the trenches in 1917; His mother was left with seven young children to bring up alone.' She caught her breath before continuing.

'Times were grim. Harry and his brother Bill had to work really hard to help bring up the other younger members of the family.' Peggy paused, not certain whether or not to continue with the conversation but she realized Gisela was listening intently.

'Did you know Harry then?' She asked.

Peggy averted her eyes as though ashamed of what she was about to say.

'I knew Harry from school, we started walking out when Harry was just nineteen but it took years to get him to the altar. Eventually we got married when he was just over thirty!' She put emphasis on the last word, as her neighbours eyes widened.

'That's a long time to wait.'

'Harry gave a promise to his father before he left for France to look after the family if he didn't come back.' Peggy continued.

'Harry always keeps his promise that's the type he is!'

'But he promised to marry you.' Gisela protested.

'Yes well he did, didn't he—eventually.' Peggy looked up a wistful look in her face and her eyes misted over.

Gisela took in the change in her neighbours face before she replied.

'I didn't realize you had such a long engagement!' She said sympathetically. 'That must have been a difficult time!'

'Yes it was ten long years; I came to think we would never be married.' Peggy brushed away a tear at the corner of her eye.

'Although I respected Harry's position as far as the family were concerned it was very hard at the time. 'She added very quietly.

Gisela now extended her hand to Peggy's knee.

'I'm sure you did.' She said with real feeling in her voice, adding.

'I am surprised Harry's mother didn't say something; she seems a lovely lady.'

'She is!' Peggy agreed.

'There were many times that she tried to intervene; Harry however was adamant, he is the oldest by just eighteen months and very stubborn, he would not change his ways or opinions even though Bill his brother lived at home and wasn't about to marry.' Peggy shifted her weight on the settee to a more comfortable position.

'His youngest sister Ruth was a baby when her father was killed; we got married when she went into service at fourteen.' Peggy sighed. Then the resigned tone that had been in her voice lifted a bit as she said.

'Of course no one could ever be sure we would have had the son Harry wanted and that is why in lots of ways the evacuees have been a blessing, A smile fleeted for a moment at the corner of her mouth.

'They are like the sons we never had and are we not fortunate they are such lovely boys.'

'Yes they are and a credit to you both.' Gisela agreed.

'I have tried to make this their home.' Peggy's eyes misted over again.

'One thing is for sure I would miss them so much now!'

'I have often listened when your lads have spoken to my children; they would only return home under the greatest protest; of that I am quite sure.' Gisela put the emphasis on her last words.

That made Peggy's face break out into a real smile.

'You don't know how glad I am to hear you say that.' The smile extended to her eyes.

'Both boys have said the same to me; it is good to hear they are saying it to their peers which must mean they really mean it!' There was no mistaking the happiness in Peggy's voice now.

It was now Gisela's turn to comfort the older woman.

'One thing I have learnt about children, they often tell each other their true feelings; in Mickey's case you are the only mother he cares to remember, he was such a little lad when he came here! As regards Ned he has said quite openly you have looked after him much better than his own mother ever did! 'She paused for a moment.

'He admitted he was often left to run the streets at home whilst his parents were in a public house. You and Harry have given these lads a real purpose in life.' Gisela took Peggy's hand into her own.

'You can be very proud of that!'

'That it is a great comfort! Ned is settled for now; although I am sure his mother won't allow him to remain on a long term basis. Its Mickey I really worry over, nothing has been heard of his mother for a couple of years; there is always this fear at the back of my mind that she will turn up one day and demand the little fellow go home with her.'

'I hope that does't happen!' Gisela said a horrified look on his face.

'It would break his heart!'

'Mickey has the occasional nightmare, he wets the bed sometimes lately; I thought he'd grown out of that. I am sure it's because he is so uncertain about his future.' The worried look came back into Peggy's eyes.

'One thing I do know; it would break my heart also to part with him now!'

There was no mistaking the horror in Gisela's voice as she said.

'If his mother was alive surely she would have been in touch by now? I know I would have to know where my children were!'

'You are different Gisela; Mickey's mother is the type who only cares about herself, that was very apparent on the few times she did visit.' Peggy broke off the conversation as the door between the living room and the kitchen burst open and four faces appeared in the doorway holding the finished paper chains and lanterns in their hands.

The two ladies got to their feet to admire the results; Peggy went straight into the kitchen to get the drawing pins so that they could festoon the children's' handiwork around the small sitting room.

She came back to see Gisela standing on a chair holding up a chain whilst Sonja stretched it across the room to see how far it would go.

Taking a drawing pin from Peggy's outstretched hand Gisela firmly put it into the chain and then into the picture rail, before stepping down to admire the children's handiwork.

'Thanks for the tea and talk.' Gisela whispered to her neighbour, when they had finished decorating the sitting room and the younger woman was preparing to take her leave.

'I can always rely on you to make difficult situations seem more bearable.' Gisela fondly squeezed her neighbours shoulder.

'It is my pleasure.' Peggy quietly spoke in reply, as she saw her visitors out of the door, with a special smile for Gisela to let her know her sympathies were with her.

CHAPTER FIVE

A fierce wind blowing across the Pennine hills found all the cracks in the wooden buildings that nestled in a dip on the bleak moor, it ratted the ill-fitting windows, Karl fought to open the door it almost pulled it off its hinges.

Outside he stood for a moment looking around. whipped along by the blustery wind snow flurries began to sting his cheeks making them burn; wrapping his arms around his body he pummeled his fingers into his back hoping to get the circulation going, although it had little effect, so he walked briskly around the perimeter of the high fence standing between the prisoners and the outside world stamping his feet to keep them warm.

The PoW camp he'd been told was at on a high point in the Yorkshire moors, he wasn't really sure where Yorkshire was, just that it was in the north of England.

They had arrived late at night when an army truck had deposited them here from the troop ship after their disembarkation at Liverpool docks, and that was all they had seen of the area where they now living.

He looked out at a rather desolate scene below, the bare moors stretched out into the distance; he wondered if all of England was like this, with their bleakness already covered with a snow he was reminded briefly of his homeland across the continent where the winters could be very severe; there quite often the snow could hang around for many weeks with temperatures well below zero.

His homeland wasn't as bleak as this, a big difference was the thick forests of pine trees, perhaps there were some here, he thought he could spy some lower down from this vantage point.

Karl hoped the snow wouldn't last, it was bad enough not to be able to wander freely in this cheerless place without being snowed in also, the very thought filled him with dread.

During the last few weeks the ache in his heart was echoed in his face making it pale and drawn; a haunted look hung about his eyes, his once muscular body, sadly lacking the exercise he'd been used to felt out of sorts.

Never before in his life had he felt so lost and alone, the past was fast becoming a distant memory and the future to say the least a blank canvas; frustration was building up inside, he felt he'd lived a lifetime with nothing to show for it, what the future now held he couldn't dare even think about.

He wasn't alone in this; the majority of the men imprisoned here couldn't wait to go home to their families. They knew their beloved homeland and their loved ones were in a terrible situation; yet here they were on this island with just a strip of water between them and the mainland of Europe with quite short train journey on the other side yet unable to do anything about it.

So near yet so far from their loved ones who needed their help so desperately, it hadn't been so bad when he and some of his comrades had been imprisoned in America for those few months; their guards there had been more sociable and there was no possibility of a quick way home with the Atlantic ocean between the captives and their loved ones, although they had no freedom in their prison camp in Pennsylvania they were treated very well.

Here there was a mixture of prisoners, as well as those who had been captured by the American's some had come straight to England after their capture on the European mainland by the British forces and their allies.

The food situation was also very different here; a larger variety had been available in America where no rationing existed. Here the rationing was very severe so food supplies were curtailed with no choice available, you either ate what you were given or went without.

It had been made clear to the PoW's they would be growing crops on the spare ground around the compound when the weather got warmer which would give more selection, that's if they were here long enough! Talk was they would be moved on to another camp shortly, possibly to the South of England, for some of the men here it would be the third move in as many months.

Karl hadn't been moved around as much as many of the other men, he had been here since this camp had been opened up for the prisoners which was when he first arrived, then there had been a lot of work to do to make this place more habitable.

Most of the men, Karl included had been glad of this, occupation was a great therapy even if it was only slapping distemper on the walls of huts that were very run down, and painting the doors a dark shade of green. It kept minds occupied for a short period of time.

One or two of the men who were skilled in working with wood were still employed patching up the door and window frames where this was required this was very necessary to keep out the winter fast encroaching upon them now.

Karl preferred to work on the land, at the present time this wasn't allowed; hopefully the situation would change when the weather improved, and already some of the officers in charge hinted that it would be soon. Most of the men hoped so too anything was better than the way they were cooped up now!

When volunteers had been requested for work in the kitchens Karl had gladly put himself forward for this although this meant peeling potatoes and various vegetables till his hands ached, it was better than being idle although it didn't stop his mind working overtime.

Karl looked around at his surroundings again, the lecture they had been given that very morning kept going round and round in his head, and once again it had been drilled into them the appalling things done by the Nazi regime, they had these lectures and films every day to show them all the terrible things Hitler did, it was repeated many times to make sure that the message got across to the inhabitants of the camp.

The tragic news about the Jews the most difficult to stomach; that an organized attempt by their beloved country to destroy a whole section of the human race actually happened was appalling.

When they first learned of it most of the men had been terribly shocked; and a good section of them refused to believe what they were being told saying it was lies to make them believe bad things of Hitler.

Today's films and revelations had been about the concentration camps, showing how many Jewish people, gipsies, the mentally infirm, and others that had refused to follow Hitler and his ways had been systematically slaughtered.

The dreadfulness of the film he had just seen pounded again through his brain, nothing prepared the men for it was dreadful to the extreme; the horror of what had been displayed; thousands of dead bodies piled high in trucks was much worse than anything anyone of them could possibly have imagined.

The film had gone on to show stick like figures their skin pulled so tight to their skulls they were hardly recognizable as human beings; great heaps of corpses testified to the callousness of the S.S. guards it was a pitiful sight,

Then there were the poor souls who had been found alive by the former enemy if you could call it alive so dreadful was their condition, which was even worse! Many were suffering from typhus, typhoid and tuberculosis amongst other things, covered with lice and so sick the film stated they had no chance of recovery; 40,000 they were told made up that number alone!

Karl shook his head trying to get the picture out of his mind; it wouldn't go it just kept flooding back making him feel sick to his stomach.

Heinz still with this contingent refused to believe the evidence, saying it was British propaganda; he advised his fellow prisoners not to believe what they saw.

There was still a small minority that still even with all this evidence refused to consider anything Hitler did was wrong, Heinz even tried to incited the men to try and escape, but the heart for this had gone out of the majority of the men, many of whom had seen the defeat by the allies and realized there was no way back.

It was especially hard for Heinz he'd been a Nazi officer for a long time and as such was indoctrinated with so many of the Nazi ways; after the lectures he spoke to the men at the camp about many of the Nazi rallies before the outbreak of war; spending time describing to anyone who would listen about the Fuehrer and his stirring speeches and he went on about the fervor that came from the Nazi party and the euphoria that accompanied Hitler's rallies; going on to describe the marches that were held with flags everywhere with everyone giving the Nazi salute, it was noticeable how all of this was so ingrained into Heinz's mind it wasn't going to be easily removed.

Heinz could be very convincing, many of the prisoners listened sympathetically to him not knowing whether to believe him or the people that now held them captive who were trying to teach them the opposite.

Heinz also tried to convince them all Adolph Hitler was still alive and would lead a revolt soon against their present captors.

'It will come any day now, you will see.' He declared.

One or two of the prison warders who spoke good German listened in on what he had to say and reported it to the higher authorities.

Fortunately Karl and most of the other men here had different thoughts about the situation because there was evidence that the truth was being told to them.

A letter one of the other prisoners sent from his family in Germany was passed round for others to read, its contents had really stunned them all. The ex-Panzer's family had been asked to go to a nearby concentration camp now evacuated to see for themselves how bad things were because so many people didn't believe the truth about how cruel the Nazi regime had been.

Through the pages of the letter the men saw for themselves that the writer was terribly shocked by what had been seen, describing piles of emaciated bodies and the gas chambers where people died, confirming what the British authorities were telling them, with evidence from one of their own most of the men here agreed it was obviously the truth.

When the letter was shown to Heinz he still refused to believe it, but any authority he'd previously exercised was severely curtailed by the men who now believed what their captors told them was the truth.

Karl thought back to his home town before the war and recalled the Jewish families he had known there, although these families kept themselves very much to themselves with regard to their religious beliefs several of the young boys had been his friends and good friends too. There had been a time when many of these Jews had been people of standing; persons who were looked up to in the community, most people felt absolute horror when these Jewish families were forced to wear a yellow star on their clothing and then sent into ghettos. Karl had personally seen a few of them marched away by the Gestapo but many had just disappeared at the dead of night never to be seen again and when enquiries were made as to where these people had gone the authorities told the enquirers they had gone to encampments to aid the war effort.

No one at that time ever dreamt the Jews had been systematically killed it was only now these men knew from the evidence put before them what really happened to those people and how they had been so cruelly treated.

Today they had seen a film of damaged and mentally retarded children being systematically killed by Hitler's henchmen just because of their problems and Karl recalled a small child he'd known in his home village who was damaged by her birth; the authorities advised her parents to let her go into an institution then told them not to visit it was obvious now she had probably been put to death as this also was part of Hitler's policy.

He shook his head in disbelief, there was nothing he could do about the past now, he just had to hope that the future would be better; it could hardly be worse!

Karl had been so proud of his German heritage at the youth camps he'd attended during his boyhood, there he had a glimpse of a world he didn't know existed, he and Wilhelm had enjoyed days at summer camp, bathing in the sea and taking part in all sorts of activities and sports; it had been a charmed time how could it have all gone so horribly wrong?

To take his mind off unpleasant thoughts he looked again at his surroundings; the bleak moors hereabouts it did nothing to enhance his mood or the thoughts going round and round in his mind.

His feet felt like ice blocks in his leather boots as he stamped them on the frozen ground a bit like the ice that seemed to be deep in his heart that nothing seemed to diminish.

The big worry for him was that Germany had been recently divided by the Axis powers; Karl's home was now in the Russian sector, something that also brought a certain dread to his mind as he recalled his father's words.

'Stalin was a man to be feared much more than any other enemy that faced this country.' His Father had said as he feared for his son when Karl had left home to join the army at seventeen

Karl's brother had been killed during the German armies advance on Russia in 1942; this made his father even more afraid of the Russian threat; rumour had circulated for years in their part of Germany about the way Stalin treated his people, it tore at Karl's heart now to think his family if they were still alive were in this regime's clutches, for them there would be no way out; they were in a worse position than he was himself, at least here he had a measure of safety.

He sighed at least most of the men here knew they had families to go back too; for him personally he wouldn't feel nearly so bad if he knew if his family had come through the war alright; he had heard nothing from his parents or his sister; the silence told him perhaps they were no longer alive.

He had heard that many had escaped from his home town to the other sectors of Germany and talk was this loophole was in the process of being sealed; his father suffering from problems with his chest after being gassed in France in 1917 would find escape especially difficult; and his mother would never leave her husband so it was almost certain they were now in a horrible situation if they were still alive. Then there was his sister where was she?

Karl wrung his cold hands in silent despair before putting them in his pocket to warm up, if only he knew what had happened to them; he was sure they were probably equally as worried over his fate.

At least his childhood memories in the 1930's were good even though it saddened him to know that his best friend Wilhelm with whom he'd shared so much had been lost in France.

His father had a hard time to eke out a living as a farm labourer especially during the very harsh winters in their home country. His parents had provided as well as the could for their family, during the torrid summers they'd all work hard to prepare for the winter; Karl, his brother and his sister bringing wood from the nearby forests; helping with the harvests during the summer holidays was fun and meant food would be stockpiled for the colder months ahead when his father's chest complaint often meant he couldn't work.

When they came home from school there was always warmth indoors and the delicious smell of cooking; the smile on his mother's face as they came through the door, the love she had for them tore at his heart now that he wasn't sure that he would ever see her again.

Karl glanced again at the moors, the light was beginning to fade; far down below a village was just putting on their night lights, he'd noticed out of the flaps of the lorry that brought them to this place the British too stockpiled for the colder weather, logs were piled against houses, hayricks in the fields for animal feed during the winter, just the same as they did at home; these people probably didn't want the war, they probably were mostly just as poor as his countrymen, and hated the food shortages and rationing.

The stars began to twinkle in the sky, he glanced at the crescent moon peeping over the horizon; the same moon he'd seen at home, he had no money to turn over in his pocket which is what his mother would have told him to do! So he just prayed silently to himself that his parents and sister were watching the same moon too.

He turned glancing again toward the huts; the men inside were just lighting up the oil lamps, he could see some of them bent over a table writing or whittling away at a piece of wood, many of the men had made some really nice things from small logs and pieces of wood the guards had brought in to them.

Today the guards had brought in a fir tree ready for the Christmas celebrations in a few days' time, that again evoked memories of his childhood, every year his father would bring in a tree from the forest for them to decorate usually with homemade bits and pieces; his mother he recalled fondly had some lovely glass decorations that she had kept from her younger years these were brought out every year to be admired as she hung from the dark green branches by her work worn hands.

Christmas had always been a magical time but the best time was when they got together with people in the local community for dancing at the largest house in the village on the 6th of January to celebrate the arrival of the three wise kings at Jesus crib; mostly very poor people, everyone brought something along for all to enjoy, someone would play a tune on a squeeze box or an old fiddle and that would set everyone dancing, then they laughed, joked and sang folk tunes far into the night.

The snow was falling heavily now and it was almost dark so Karl made his way to the hut door; stamping the snow off his feet on the concrete path he went inside, the warmth and the smell of stew for supper hit him as he opened the door making him realize how hungry he was.

Talk was they were to be moved again early in the new year; he hoped it would be far away from this bleak place, talk was it might be in the south of the country would it be better than here?

Soon the New Year would begin and winter become spring, and with it perhaps renewed hope for all the PoW's

CHAPTER SIX

The church bells echoed their peal around the countryside the first time they had been rung at Christmas for six years.

Today began for Harry like any other, there were cows to be fed and milked and the rest of the farm animals attended to before joining the family for a later than usual breakfast which for once they spent together before the family got ready to go to church for the morning service.

When Sylvia came down to join the family she wore an eye-catching cherry red suit made from a piece of corded velvet found on shelf at the shop where she worked; it had been there since before the war and her employer knowing how clever she was with her needle had generously given it to her. Her shiny dark hair held in a clip her mother gave her as a Christmas present she had brushed behind her ears and this added to the effect so she looked strikingly lovely; Harry looked up from his breakfast with pride at his daughter as she took her place by his side where her mother put a breakfast in front of her before sitting down herself with the family.

Sylvia was in the church choir and Harry playing the organ so it was necessary for them to leave the house ahead of the rest of the family to be in their places before the rest of the congregation arrived.

Sharp tears sprung into Peggy's eyes when she saw the look on Harry's face as he took his daughters arm to escort her up the hill to the church; watching them from the kitchen window laughing together at a private joke Peggy was glad not for the first time she and Harry at least had one child of their very own.

Earlier on she had watched Ned take his leave this time dressed in his first grown up suit.

He was one of the bell ringers so he also had to be at the church early, the suit was another acquisition from Sylvia's boss who discovered it tied up with string in a brown parcel when he was clearing out.

Put in during the early years of the war for alterations it had never been collected by its previous owner and although she was aware the suit probably belonged to someone who was a victim of the conflict, Sylvia closed her mind to this as she unpicked seams and spent some time adjusting it to fit Ned.

Peggy left the house fifteen minutes after the others with Mickey holding her hand, she had made sure the last minute preparations for their lunch later in the day were all in place before she closed the back door

Mickey's firm grip was very comforting as they ascended to the church on the hill together, he was equally well turned out, with knee length grey trousers and a jacket; a hand me down from Gisela's son Hugo who although slightly younger than Mickey was much taller and broader, long grey socks made from wool recycled from an old jumper that Peggy had meticulously unpicked and re knitted on four needles graced his legs; he'd found them in his Christmas stocking that morning together with an orange, apple, a few sweets and a coloring book with some crayons. Peggy had picked up an old book on History at a jumble sale which she added to the gifts.

The smile she received from the lad gladdened her heart he was so pleased you would think he'd received the crown jewels.

She'd briefly gone next door to Gisela to wish her a happy Christmas just before she left. her neighbour shunned religion so Peggy made no mention of the services on the hill

Gisela had stood in her doorway still in her dressing gown; Peggy noted the sad look and the lack of lustre in her neighbour's eyes and guessed she was missing her family in Austria.

'Come round later for tea we can have some games and a piece of Christmas cake.' Peggy invited when she saw the three children disconcertingly playing cards at the kitchen table looking as though they needed some cheering up.

'Thanks we will.' They all answered in unison.

The hill to the church was steep and the two of them were puffing by the time they reached the lynch gate after passing the time of day with some of the parishioners they took a pew half way down the aisle.

Playing softly Harry was quietly seated behind the organ; he didn't really like the task of organist, only obliging the vicar when the original man had been requisitioned by the war office to move to a different part of the country to aid the war effort.

Harry couldn't read a note of music; he played by 'ear' which he did so well very few people would have guessed. He was always hopeful that the original organist would return now that the war was over and release him from the task; so far there was no news of this happening.

Glancing around Peggy saw not for the first time since the war ended the church was now noticeably emptier; many of the families still had their men folk on active service and any evacuees that had remained till the end of the war had departed back to their homes together with most of the land girls but she realized it wasn't just this before the war the village life had revolved round the church. All that had changed now, people didn't think it necessary to go to church on Sundays or any other day for that matter.

There were one or two sad families grouped about, those whose husbands and sons hadn't return from the war; they were putting on a brave face but times were particularly difficult for them, any money they did receive for the loss of their breadwinner was sparse to say the least and in a lot of cases the women had to work to make ends meet.

Looking towards the altar Peggy saw that the elite of the village had returned to the front pews they had occupied before the war, she sighed; it was obvious now the class distinction that had prevailed before had returned to the village.

During the hostilities, the vicar had reserved the front three pews on both sides for the people billeted at the Brooklands camp and it had been good to see them march in dressed in their uniforms.

Now Captain Wilson and his family gone back to the front seats on the side Peggy was sitting together with Winnie Baker and opposite sat the Misses Marshall, Jean Finch and her daughter. It was excusable with Jean, she had brought her husband into church in a wheel chair; his place at the front was the most sensible because this meant he wasn't obstructing the aisle.

The Reverend Hounsome seemed to catch this mood in his sermon which was all about people being the same in the eyes of God, he told the congregation how things were going to be very different now the war had ended, with so many displaced people all over the world who had to pick up the pieces of their lives after the turmoil of the last few years, people would have to learn tolerance.

Peggy wondered how this was going to hit home here; it didn't take long to find out!

Before the war after the service those in the front pews would sweep down the aisle ahead of the rest of congregation and press their hands into the vicar's monopolizing him so that the ordinary people passing by on their way outside had to skirt round these people and had no contact with the minister at all!

Today this didn't happen, the vicar starting at his end of the church shook hands with each parishioner as they rose from their seats so attention was given to each one.

Peggy chuckled as she saw the look on Captain Wilson's face; obviously he was not amused by this turn of events, after wringing the vicar's hand he smartly leant on his walking stick and marched out of the church with Sybil in tow, behind followed their three children at present home from boarding school.

The vicar obviously practiced what he preached; not taking into account what some of his parishioners thought, after his attitude with Jean Finch the other week Peggy found this very heart warming.

She had thought him weak obviously she was wrong!

Peggy and Mickey waited by the lynch gate for Harry, Sylvia, and Ned to join them before they all made their way just down the hill together ready to stop off at Jean Finch's home for a traditional glass of sherry and a piece of shortbread made in preparation for today by Peggy in Jean's kitchen the day before.

Winnie was already handing round amber liquid in dainty glasses when they arrived, she graciously gave two into Harry's outstretched hand with a sweet smile before turning her back to attended to other arrivals.

Harry pressed one glass into his wife's hand sipping slowly from the other before making his way over to a group of men talking together in one corner.

Peggy smiled to herself she was used to that sort of treatment from Winnie.

She looked around at the large crowd already nudging each other in Jean's sizeable lounge and partaking of the beverages provided. The Finch's always seemed to have a plentiful supply of everything despite the shortages everywhere else! Peggy knew Jean had many connections in America and Canada and regularly received parcels to eke out the rations and to her credit Jean was always generous with everything she had.

Remaining on the edge of the group Peggy felt out of her depth; she disliked crowds, and small talk. Draining her glass she swiftly picked up two more sherries from the tray that Winnie had deposited on the small hall table and balancing them carefully in one hand she edged across the hall and turned a small brass knob on a room opposite once inside she caught sight of a figure sitting quietly in a chair by a long window that overlooked the village.

'Hello there.' She said softly.

Claude turned his face towards her, a smile playing at the corner of his mouth as he recognized her voice.

She couldn't miss the joy in his voice as he said.

'Always a pleasure to see you Peggy.'

A former pilot he'd been badly injured in the early days of the war; although he'd had extensive surgery on his face he was very conscious of his scars and his almost sightless eyes so he often hid himself away when company was around.

'I was glad you were able to make it to church. 'Peggy pressed one of the small glasses of sherry into his hand; he gripped his long fingers around its stem.

'Thank you that is kind. 'He held the glass tightly in his hand.

'As you know I'm not one for company but I don't like to miss the Christmas service.' He raised the golden liquid slowly to his lips savoring the taste before continuing.

'I thought the vicar did it very well didn't you?' He motioned for her to draw up a chair alongside his specially adapted one, which Peggy did gratefully glad to take the weight off her feet for a bit.

I'm sure you are not going to bustle about with a duster today!' Claude teased.

'So for once you can talk to me without rushing off.' His face became serious again as he took another small sip from the glass.

'I'm only allowed one small glass of alcohol a day, so I make sure I enjoy it.' He licked his lips.

'That will I hope change when I have one more operation which my surgeon assures me will do away with some of the pain I have, it will be good not to have to rely on painkillers so much. Then I can enjoy a tipple once more!' He turned his almost blind slate blue eyes towards the window.

'Tell me have you seen any sign of activity at the PoW camp? It is nearer your end of the village than here.' Peggy was sure she could see a glint in his almost unsighted gaze.

'I could ask Jean, but to be truthful she seems to get little spare time; between us I think that is how she copes with what has happened to me! She is really very sensitive beneath that bossy exterior.' Fleetingly his face was edged with pain as he shuffled his legs slightly.

'Jean never mentions anything.' Peggy said softly.

'No I don't suppose she does!' He smiled as he often did when his wife was mentioned.

'That really isn't her way.' His face took a serious expression again.

'She has had to put up with a lot! Jean comes from a Yorkshire family; her father was a barrister, she belonged to a horsy set with a social life that went with it when I first met her.' Claude's voice dropped an octave.

'We had a good life before the war, life as an officer in the RAF wasn't a bad little number, quite a good existence, you know what I mean parties and fun!' He said.

Peggy smiled to herself.

'Not really the sort of life I have led!' She said.

'No I suppose it isn't.' Claude replied.

There was a short silence as Peggy thought for a moment, before her marriage even with her long engagement the only social life she ever enjoyed was the odd tea dance in the local town on a Saturday afternoon, but it was obvious that Claude and Jean came from a different class. She had seen pictures of Claude and Jean scattered all over the house when she did the cleaning it was obvious that they were enjoying themselves at various social occasions, she'd often noted how fashionably dressed Jean had been and how devastatingly handsome Claude was before his accident.

Peggy had to admit Jean was still a good looking woman with a bubbly personality even if it did border on being domineering at times.

Claude didn't seem to notice her negative comments as he continued the conversation.

'With the war everything changed. When I was so badly injured I knew nothing would ever be the same again; Jean gave up the life she loved so much to nurse me; there is nothing more that she can do for me now so she spends her life helping others in the community; she comes from good north country stock, they are the type that always put their heads down when the going gets tough, it's in her genes.' He paused for a moment and there was no mistaking the pride in his voice as he went on.

'That is why she has been so splendid during the war years, organizing the local WVS; helping in so many other ways! People don't realize quite what the WVS did during the dark days when it all seemed so hopeless; someone as dedicated as Jean was invaluable then.' He paused for breath.

'She cooperated so well with the ARP Wardens. Organizing lectures for women in first aid, staffing ARP Canteens, you name it Jean did it! You would be surprised how many times she was called out to feed civil defense workers after raids; supervising people who were making sandbags and running communal feeding centres. I have every reason to feel very proud of her!' He sank back into the cushions of his chair with a small sigh.

'I sometimes wish that I hadn't become such a burden, I feel I have held her back.' A small tear glistened at the corner of his eye.

Peggy rather taken back by Claude's revelation didn't really know how she should reply she hadn't realized before how Claude's accident had affected Jean; and saw her for the first time in rather a different light; at a loss for words so she decided to steer the conversation back to the PoW's

'I walked the dog down by the PoW camp the other day; nothing much seem to have been done I don't think they have any prisoners yet in the enclosure, there has just been a stronger fence erected with barbed wire on the top.' She paused for a moment to get her breath

'The huts seem to be neglected they could do with a lick of paint.' She continued.

Claude smiled. 'You are probably right! Farmer Phillips dropped by the other day, he admitted much the same, he told me the prisoners would need work to do so perhaps they will start by bringing the huts up to scratch.' He tapped the side of his nose knowingly as he leant forward and pressed his empty glass into Peggy's hand.

'Mr. Phillips seems to think some men may be transferred here just after the New Year.' Claude's chin was set firm.

'I spoke to a few people when I went for my assessment at East Grinstead Hospital last week. I understand some prisoners that have been shipped in from America will be interned here together with some that have been detained from France and other countries. My source tells me all prisoners will have been processed before being sent on to other destinations, whatever that means!'

'Really that's interesting.' Peggy said knowing that people Claude mixed with at East Grinstead were people who had held high positions during the war, if anyone knew about the future of these Germans they would!

'My source also told me they will have to integrate into the community to help restore the infrastructure damaged during the war before returning home. The Prime Minister has already said as much and rightly so in my opinion.' Claude declared.

'Do you think people will accept this, they will have to mix with our people?' Peggy thought fleetingly of Harry.

'I am sure they will in time; you would be surprised what short memories most people have, especially when good comes of it!' Claude sounded very reassuring.

'I am not so sure; some people find it very hard to forget!' Peggy's tone was unusually sharp taking Claude by surprise; he wished he could see her face clearly to interpret her real feelings, but decided say no more on the subject, it obviously upset her and that was the last thing he wanted.

They were both quiet for a few moments and Peggy glanced out of the window; the view from this vantage point was quite spectacular you could see over the whole village right down to the sea shimmering with the sun on it in the distance.

Looking again at Claude she thought it a great shame that he would never again see the lovely countryside hereabouts, East Grinstead might be able to patch up his scars, unfortunately they could never give him back his sight.

Claude broke the silence 'I miss the view.' He said it seemed he almost read her mind!

'Yes I think I would find that hard.' She said hesitantly.

'I have my memories; it's surprising what one can see in their minds eye.' She realized he was following with his limited sight to where she was looking and she looked in the opposite direction.

'The weather looks as if it's about to change, there is a dark cloud coming over the downs.' A worried tone came into her voice.

'I think it is cold enough for sleet or snow I was frozen this morning when Jean pushed me up to the church, although I would never admit that to her as she would be very upset if she knew.' Claude said with feeling.

'Yes I felt for you.' Peggy thought it nice that he spoke of his wife with such feeling,

'It isn't easy when you are sitting in one place not able to move.' There was a small catch in his voice,

'I can understand that. It must be very frustrating. 'Peggy touched his knee sympathetically.

She looked out of the window again eyeing the dark cloud that looked more ominous.

'I think it might be a good idea for us to make a move home before the bad weather sets in.' Peggy said as she quickly rose from her seat, their row of cottages were a good fifteen minutes' walk and she certainly didn't want to get her best coat wet; it would be a long time before she had enough clothing coupons for another!

'Yes that would be sensible; it's been lovely talking to you, it's so seldom you have the time!' Claude smiled appreciatively.

'I will try to make the effort more often!' She said as she bent and gently kissed Claude's cheek; immediately blushing to the roots of her hair, this sentiment was foreign to her.

'I shall hold you to that when you are rushing around doing the chores. 'He rewarded her with another smile.

Peggy looked at him, she was sure few people realized what a brave man he really was, his concern was always for others he rarely drew attention to himself.

'Before you go please could you turn the knob on the radio for me, I do like to listen to Avar Liddell read the news.' Claude said.

Peggy walked over to a small table and twiddled a small black Bakelite knob, hymn music issued out.

'Another ten minutes for the news.' She said looking at the clock.

'That's alright; I like to hear this music.' Claude admitted.

Leaving him and closing the door to his room quietly behind her, she slipped into the hall where she had every intentions of quickly rounding up the family to go home, noticing the boys were deep in conversation with several others of their age group she looked round for Sylvia and Harry they were nowhere to be seen.

People were thinning out a bit and glancing through to the kitchen, she saw a pile of dirty sherry glasses on the draining board, then she noticed Winnie adding another tray-full to the pile before donning her coat and making a swift exit out of the back door.

Peggy sighed, that was typical of Winnie offer round the drinks then disappear especially when the washing up needed doing! She simply couldn't walk away leaving dirty glasses to be washed up after the hospitality extended by Jean to her family, besides it was likely she would have to do them when she came to Jeans to work tomorrow, she was only given Christmas day as a holiday.

Having completed this task it was a good half an hour later that she eventually rounded up everyone for the journey home.

Harry was reluctant to finish his conversation with Sid making Peggy feel very guilty. He worked nearly every day of the year with very little time for fraternizing with neighbours and in the past few years with most capable men away fighting any spare time had been taken up with the home guard leaving little time for himself; even today when most people were enjoying a public holiday Harry was still expected to do necessary things on the farm.

As the family left Jean's house together the black cloud that had been threatening was now overhead as they started down the hill.

Fanned on by a sudden howling wind freezing sleet bit into their faces; huddled in their coats and warmed by the sherry at Jean's they made their way quickly down the hill to their home in the village.

Harry had to shout so that he could be heard above the wind.

'I will have to go and see to the animals.' He declared.

'There are some I can't leave out in this weather!'

'Not in your good suit!' Peggy chided.

'Don't worry I will do it!' Ned suddenly put on a spurt and ran ahead, his long legs quickly covering the ground; it seemed just minutes before he was at the cottages in his best clothes and outside again in his working gear taking off up the field to see to the creatures out in the bad weather.

Harry's face was a picture as he grinned from ear to ear.

'Well that is a first!' He said adding.

'I think I am going to enjoy having Ned as my working companion!'

As soon as they opened the door of the cottage the warmth from the kitchen range and the smell of the chicken roasting in the oven for lunch hit them, reminding them how hungry they were. Roast chicken was a rare treat, most chicken were kept for the eggs they laid, an old one that had stopped laying was boiled for a stew on occasions, but for today Harry had selected a young one to roast, a few days ago he'd killed it, plucked and cleaned it in the shed outside and hung it up.

Peggy took her overall from the hook on the kitchen door getting busy straight away putting the vegetables she'd previously prepared on to cook whilst Sylvia got busy laying the table, putting the few crackers round the plates that mother and daughter had made over the past few weeks in preparation for this day.

Harry went into the sitting room to bank up the fire with some logs and for a rare smoke before his dinner, he enjoyed a pipe on the odd occasion, Mickey went with him settling down to enjoy his Christmas gifts.

'That smells good!' Peggy turned from stirring the gravy to see Harry's mother pink cheeked and happy as she was escorted through the kitchen door by her son Bill who had never married and still lived at home with his mother.

Peggy was all smiles.

'Come in!' She greeted them as Sylvia quickly found a chair for her grandmother to sit on to take the weight off her cold and swollen feet. The elderly lady gratefully collapsed into it, then quietly watching the final preparations for the meal

It was a jolly party that sat down to Christmas dinner; the chicken had been stuffed with chestnuts picked in the woods that autumn and it was delicious, baked potatoes with spouts, Swede, parsnips and leeks from the garden were served with gravy made from the giblets and an Oxo cube.

The Christmas pudding was voted a great success despite the shortages; they all found some silver three penny pieces in the mixture, Peggy had put in after boiling them up that very morning before leaving for church; she saved them each year for this event.

After washing up they all retired to a well banked up fire in their small sitting room which had a festive air, the paper chains the children had made hung from the ceiling; sprigs of holly and ivy were twisted round the mirror over the fireplace and round the few pictures.

Yesterday Harry brought in a fir tree from the garden putting it in a bucket; it was one they had since Sylvia was very small; it would be returned to the garden as soon as the celebrations were over.

Mickey trimmed it with the decorations Peggy had brought down from a box under her bed, many were glass baubles she'd had before the war and carefully preserved, on the edge of the branches candle holders held little candles.

Harry lit each one with great care to make sure none of the branches caught fire he'd seen the damage that could be done with candles; just before the war a thatched cottage locally was burnt down because of carelessness with Christmas tree candles.

Later in the afternoon Gisela and her family joined them, they played ludo, snakes and ladders then charades; the elderly couple who lived the other side of their cottage came in to join them for a piece of Christmas cake which Peggy had managed to ice thinly with some precious sugar out of their ration, then a toast was made with Peggy's homemade cowslip wine.

Harry found a small bottle of whiskey that he shared with his brother then he played some tunes on an old piano accordion; they sang out old songs with real joy, the room echoing to the sound of their voices, Sylvia accompanied him on the upright piano that took up nearly one wall of the sitting room.

Later Harry and Ned left to attend to the animals and do the milking, whilst the rest of the assembly baked chestnuts on a hot shovel over the coals, all agreed it had been a very pleasant day.

As dusk fell Bill took his mother home in her bath chair, and the couple next door left, leaving just Gisela and her family with Peggy, Sylvia and Mickey to enjoy a pleasant evening round the fire before Ned and Harry returned.

The next day was a normal working day which meant being up early as cows were milked at daybreak so the party broke up about eight thirty.

Peggy was the last to retire around ten thirty after she had cleared away and made the house tidy ready for another busy day tomorrow, blowing out the candle she had used to light the way up the narrow staircase of the cottage she then glanced out of the bedroom window.

It was nice at least not to have to pull the blackout curtains over the windows so you could look out at the night and observe the ink black sky and twinkling stars. The clouds had now moved away and it had grown increasingly cold; Peggy was sure there would be a sharp frost by the morning.

To the left the whole village panned out before her; to the right was the brook lands the wired fences of what was to be the new prisoner of war camp standing out glinting in the rising moonlight which already gave a silvery glow to the rest of the countryside.

She mused to herself what affect it would have on the village when the PoW's arrived; it had been announced they would have to work to help the economy round here, this probably meant work on the land there was precious little else for them to do!

She was worried how Harry coped with that, or would he have more empathy towards these men when they were amongst the villagers most of the time?

She looked up at the church standing out like a ghost on the hillside above the village, it had looked out on generations of village life during its long history, the front tower with its slits of windows looked like a face, solid and dependable.

Jean's house nestled just to the left from this angle reminding Peggy of her conversation with Claude earlier on, she was really pleased he'd told her the reason behind Jean's bossy ways, deciding she would try be more tolerant of her employer now she knew why Jean acted that way.

Peggy passed a weary hand over her forehead shivering a little, there was no heat in the bedroom, and a fire here was only lit in cases of sickness.

It had been a busy day, all she could think of now was warmth and sleep; holding onto the brass knob on the bedstead she climbed in beside her husband's comatose body, asleep almost as soon as her head touched the pillow through sheer exhaustion.

CHAPTER SEVEN

1946

Peggy waved to District Nurse Eileen Hudson as the two passed on bicycles going in different directions.

Eileen was going in the direction of the junior school; Peggy was heading for the lane that led to her cottage.

The strong March wind blowing almost a gale helped Peggy on her way; whereas Eileen was battling her way into it, her navy blue gabardine coat flowing behind her, her navy nurses hat perched firmly on her head held on with a hat pin covered her dark blonde hair firmly caught in a bun at the nape of her neck.

Peggy had been at the school just last week for Mickey's medical, as he was due to change schools in September, and she guessed Eileen was either attending medicals with a doctor today, or looking for nits in the children's hair; she smiled to herself as she thought of Mickey and Gisela's children's nick name for the nurse 'Nitty Norah.'

She had known Eileen since they were children at school; eldest of a large family of girls, no one would ever have believed the then scruffy little child would grow up to command the respect by all in the village and beyond, many local people had especial reason to be grateful for her tireless work as a district nurse during the dark difficult days of the war when she'd gone out on her bike in all weathers in the darkness to deal with any emergency.

Eileen had pointed out to Peggy how small Mickey was for his age when she was present at the doctor's examination, Peggy in his defense had pointed out he wasn't actually eleven years old until the last day of August which being the last day of the school year made him the youngest in the class.

The doctor suggested was he was given an issue of cod liver oil and orange juice to build him up, this was normally supplied at the clinic to children less than five years of age; Mickey had been horrified when told of this prospect and asked Peggy not to tell anyone in case someone poked fun of him because it was normally only available to babies.

Peggy was quite sure the supplements wouldn't make any difference to Mickey; she reasoned that he had a particularly small bone structure and nothing was going to alter that!

He was a wiry lad and in Peggy's opinion healthy enough even if he was a bit of a fussy eater.

He only drank the third of a pint of milk supplied to all school children under eleven under protest and he absolutely hated the cod liver oil and the orange juice which even when it was mixed with water was very sour, precious sugar from the rations failed to make a lot of difference, Peggy resolved to buy him Virol if he wouldn't take the supplements or perhaps cod liver oil and malt which she heard was very good for children.

At the clinic whilst waiting for the supplies a little while ago; Peggy laughed at the grimace on a babies face when offered a bottle of the orange juice, obviously Mickey wasn't the only one who thought it sour!

Peggy rode her bicycle to the village shop she had in her bag the families' new ration books which she had queued for earlier in the day at the reading room together with most of the rest of the village.

Collecting flour, cheese, tea, and various other basics to keep them going for a while from Sid's shop where she deposited the ration books, the basket on her bicycle was piled so high it made her cycle wobble a bit as she rode along,

Turning her bicycle off the main road she came to the concrete the Americans had put on the lane that led to the PoW camp further down; it had been put there to stop the Lorries using it getting bogged down in the mud when they were here, the same lane led to their cottages.

Two enormous Lorries turned in behind her; dismounting as the lane was narrow and she didn't want to lose her precious cargo, she stood on the grass verge whilst the convoy passed her by.

Out of the canvas covered rear some young men peered out at her; one with piercing blue eyes and a lock of blonde hair smiled at her and she smiled back as she watched them go on down the track to the Nissan huts surrounded by a wire fence at the end.

In the past few weeks there had been much activity on the site; talk in the village said the PoW's would be arriving soon; perhaps this was the first of the batch.

She didn't bother to mount her bicycle again, the rough lane that led to their cottages branched off and was filled with ruts she was sure she would lose some of her precious cargo out of the basket if she rode.

A little dark green Austin Seven car passed her by, stopping by their gate.

The occupant wound down the window of the car and a rather thin hard faced woman poked her head out Peggy recognized her at once as the person in authority dealing with Mickey.

'I thought it was you! I have caught you just right!' She said in a sharp voice.

'I'm Miss Perkins, if you remember.' Peggy nodded in agreement, how would she forget that!

Peggy stood her bicycle against the back wall of her cottage.

'You'd better come in.' She invited with more graciousness than she felt as she took basket from the handlebars of her bicycle and went through her back door depositing it on the kitchen table.

Miss Perkins was the last person she wanted to see!

'You know I am here about Michael.' Miss Perkins had followed her in and now stood in the doorway; Peggy looked her up and down, She had an overbearing attitude as if she was of a better class, although she knew the woman reasonably well from all the times she'd visited the cottage about Mickey's case, the two of them were not first name terms. Miss Perkins wasn't that approachable! Dressed in a navy blue suit with a white collar falling over its lapels, she had on her head a distinctive rounded hat that all officials seemed to wear, with her round metal spectacles that sat firmly on the high bridge of her nose, Peggy thought she looked like an owl

Peggy saw her visitor through to her small sitting room, everything had been thoroughly cleaned that morning but she noted the distasteful way the woman looked about her surroundings as though it was beneath her, her attitude made Peggy feel rather cross, it was just as well Harry wasn't here, he hated class consciousness offend or please he would have put their visitor in her place.

Miss Perkins removed her hat putting it down beside her, her hair a titian shade firmly pulled back in a bun made her look even more stern,

Peggy decided she would be quite pretty if it was in a softer style around her face

'I will put the kettle on the fast hob if you'd like a cup of tea.'

Not waiting for an answer Peggy went through to the kitchen to remove her outdoor things taking her overall from a hook on the back door she put her coat and hat in its place pulling an overall over her head tying it at the back.

The kettle left on the back of the stove was already hot so it didn't take long to boil; in minutes she was setting a cup of tea in front of her guest; sitting herself down in the armchair opposite.

Miss Perkins looked at her over the rim of the teacup; her glasses rather misted up by the hot tea made the beady eyes that gazed out seemed a little less foreboding, a little smile played around her mouth as she spoke.

'First of all I must tell you I have been along to the school to have a word with Michael.'

'I see!' Peggy was a bit put out at this announcement, always one to speak her mind she immediately asked the first question that came into her head.

'You could have spoken to him here!' There was a note of indignation in her voice.

'Not in this particular instance, you see we have traced Michael's mother!' Miss Perkins didn't take in Peggy's obviously shocked reaction, to Peggy's amazement there was almost a trace of glee in her visitors voice.

'I really had to know how Michael felt about that piece of news without any outside influence.'

Peggy looked down into her cup so that her visitor couldn't see the pain in her eyes; her heart sank to her boots, this was news she really didn't want to hear!

Mickey's mother had only come here twice to see him before she disappeared; Peggy never forgot the terror in Mickey's eyes when he'd been called in from play to confront her the first time.

His mother tried hard to give a good impression but it was obvious to Peggy this woman had been cruel to her son. Insisting on staying the night as it was late in the afternoon when she arrived, Mickey got into a panic when he was told and Peggy never forgot the look of relief on Mickey's face when his mother announced the next morning the countryside was far too quiet for her and she was glad to be heading back to London.

The second time she came a few months later it was to announce that Mickey's father had been lost at Dunkirk; it quickly became obvious she was enjoying her life without the responsibilities of her child, dressed in fashionable clothes, hair in newly set she looked as though she'd stepped out of a fashion magazine.

At that particular time whilst the battle of Britain was raging, there had been talk that children locally were to be evacuated to the northern counties owing to their close proximity to the English Channel.

Although many left Harry and Peggy had no intentions of allowing Sylvia to go, they had seen too much locally of how badly many people treated the evacuees that had been here, it was suggested to Mickey's mother it was up to her whether or not her son remained where he was when she came to see him, all Peggy got was a shrug of the shoulders and a dismissive attitude before she again took herself off to London, that was the last they had seen of her, fortunately no one seemed to worry over their evacuees, the boys were allowed to remain where they were even when many local children were evacuated north.

The authorities insisted that evacuees wrote regularly to their parents, Mickey wasn't enthusiastic about this; he always had to be reminded about keeping in touch. Codes were given by the authorities to use so writing was easy, the letters said very little except that he was still in at Peggy and Harry's home and that he was well.

At first the letters seemed to be delivered, although Mickey's mother never replied to them, then after a while they were returned as undelivered. The feeling was perhaps she had been killed in the blitz, when Peggy got in touch with the authorities, they said Michael's mother had moved on and left no forwarding address. With the war and all the problems with the bombing no one was going to try and find one woman who seemingly didn't want to be found!

'I have to tell you.' Miss Perkins went on in her formal way, as she broke into Peggy's thoughts 'Michael's mother doesn't want him back!'

For a moment Peggy wasn't sure she'd heard the woman right.

Miss Perkins sniffed.

'The war has done a great deal of damage in a lot of ways.' She said.

'Michael's mother has a good job and a lifestyle that doesn't include a child.' Miss Perkins took in the astonished look on the other woman's face.

'If you had seen some of the things I have, nothing would shock you anymore!' Miss Perkins face softened somewhat as she said this

'Although Mickey is the only case I have on my books of parents who have shirked their responsibilities; several of my colleagues have similar cases; these women are earning good money, and enjoying their freedom, they like it that way and don't want it to change.' For once there was feeling in the Miss Perkins voice as she continued.

'Some of these women have successfully disappeared. During the blitz so many people moved about, in many cases it has been impossible to know whether people are dead or alive!' Miss Perkins gave a deep sigh.

'It was only by chance we were able to trace Michael's mother! She certainly didn't want to be found.' Miss Perkins paused obviously not going to relate just how she'd discovered Mickey's mother's whereabouts.

'I must admit very few parents have flatly refused to have anything to do with their children this one is just an exception.' She sniffed in obvious disapproval.

Peggy sitting on the edge of her seat felt her hackles rising with indignation; how could a mother treat her child this way?

Surely a normal person would want their child back particularly as her husband had been lost during the war and Mickey was all she had of him!

Pulling herself together heart in her mouth, she pulled her overall down over her knees; something she always did when nervous, yet she had to know what the future was for Mickey!

Peggy asked the question that had been in her thoughts ever since she'd seen the woman pull up outside her door.

'What will happen to Mickey now?' She asked tentively.

'We-ll, if you are agreeable, he can stay here for the time being.' The woman reached down for her bag and drew out some papers as she continued the conversation.

'Of course it isn't down to me what happens to him long term. Only my superiors can say how long he will be here; long term fostering is one option, and you must realize there other decisions to be taken. I can tell you this with the situation so bad with housing in the cities it will be some considerable time before any permanent decisions are made.' She glanced around the living room.

'I shall put in my report that Michael is well cared for here; if you are agreeable I will recommend he stays with you as a foster child for the foreseeable future, are you are agreeable to that?' Miss Perkins face took on a softer look.'

I shall say that I feel it isn't in the boys best interests to be uprooted again.'

Peggy felt choked up; she couldn't believe what she was hearing!

It was several moments before she could speak, she didn't want to seem too keen because it might give the impression she wanted Mickey here for the small amount of money that would be forthcoming if she fostered him, fortunately Miss Perkins was sorting through the papers in her hands so didn't notice the other woman's obvious delight at this piece of news.

'I must say to you though the final decision doesn't rest with me; I can only recommend.' She ferreted in her bag for a fountain pen and then proceeded to write a note on one of the bits of paper.

Peggy at last found her voice.

'I hope you will make it clear to the authorities Mickey is happy here. We are united family unit and he is very much a part of that! And we would always consider adoption.'

'Yes that I can see! Michael made it clear that is the case when I spoke with him earlier.' Miss Perkins looked around the small sitting room again with just a glimmer of a smile as she took in the gleaming brass fender and the rows of photographs on the mantel piece several of which were of Mickey and Peggy felt perhaps she had underestimated her guest's attitude when she first came into the room.

'Of course I can't say whether you would be considered for adoption. Miss Perkins paused and took a deep breath.

'We shall continue to pay you the ten shillings per week you have been receiving for the care of Michael, until we sort out the arrangements for fostering, if that is agreeable?' Miss Perkins voice now became rather patronizing as she looking at Peggy over her spectacles.

Peggy nodded in reply as Miss Perkins eyes went down to her papers, her tone now annoyed Peggy she would gladly have kept Mickey for nothing Miss Perkins made it sound as though ten shillings was a lot of money, whereas it barely covered expenses for a growing lad, but then Peggy had been used to making do during the years both the evacuees had been under her roof, she was glad to continue if it meant Mickey's happiness.

When the boys had first come here the only decent clothes they possessed were the ones they were wearing, even these were full of holes including their socks and shoes, she recalled her horror when she opened the small brown paper parcels tied up with string both boys carried, which were supposed to contain a change of clothing; she had better bits of cloth in the rag bag she kept for cleaning!

Fortunately people of the village were very kind passing on outgrown clothes from their own children; Peggy had unpicked jumpers she brought at jumble sales making them into sleeveless pullovers and socks; before very long both boys had been reasonably turned out, as reasonably as clothing coupons and the war restrictions would allow, one thing was sure the boys were fed well and happy.

'Perhaps you could attend to these before I go.' Miss Perkins took out some papers from her large bag, holding them out for Peggy to look at.

They sat in silence for a while whilst Peggy scanned them, Miss Perkins watching closely as she did so. Then Peggy led the way back to the kitchen to sign the papers at the kitchen table. Miss Perkins picking up her bag followed behind putting her hat back on her head ready to leave.

After the papers had been signed to Miss Perkins satisfaction she almost snatching them from Peggy's grasp and transferred them to her copious bag, then she held out her hand which Peggy shook firmly as she made her way out of the back door with scarcely a backward glance.

Peggy watched from her kitchen window as her visitor climbed into her little car smiling to herself as after some minutes Miss Perkins had to climb out again it obviously wouldn't start.

Miss Perkins removed the starting handle from the back and gave it a couple of turns as Peggy watched from the window, feeling a bit guilty because she made no attempt to help.

It seemed the lady was quite strong, a few turns on the handle and the little motor purred into life; Peggy knew little about cars but she did know that this operation could be quite dangerous when the handle sometimes 'kicked back' Harry had told her it could break an arm if they were not careful, her visitor managed it successfully.

Settling herself into the motor, Miss Perkins revved the engine then bumped off down the rough path to the main road.

Turning from the window to attend to the shopping still in its basket on the kitchen table, Peggy hoped it would be sometime before she saw that visitor again!

CHAPTER EIGHT

Peggy had a spring in her step a few days later when she quickly closed the latch on the back garden gate that led to the Pembertons' house, going over to the kitchen door she turning the brass door handle letting her into their spotless home.

As she did so Rover the Pemberton's aged collie skipped past her running out into the garden to enjoy the late spring sunshine she turned and watched him go, wagging his tail which was a burnished copper colour in the bright sunlight he laid down on the green lawn and rolled over and over in sheer delight.

Peggy loved the two mornings a week she spent cleaning the Pemberton house, the master and mistress left early in the morning for the local town and the draper's shop they ran together, so she usually had the place to herself.

'Stocks House' was beautifully situated at the bottom of the hill that led to the Vicarage and the Finch property, although not elevated in the same way as the other two properties and the church; it had a unique position on the edge of the village a little apart from the main road.

An old high flint stone wall surrounded the property on two sides these mostly faced east; here espalier apple, pear, and peach trees wound round the rough texture of the stones, full of pretty blossom now they gave promise of a fruitful harvest later in the year.

Peggy went straight through to the large lounge, which ran the whole length of the house from North to South commanding lovely views of the South Downs from the front and an unrestricted view over the brook lands at the back, on a clear day you could see the English Channel shimmering in the distance.

It was here today that Peggy began the tasks that lay ahead of her.

After cleaning out the fire grate she lovingly stroked wax polish into the beautiful oak and mahogany furniture that graced the room, removing the lovely Indian rugs Hugh Pemberton had brought back from a visit to that country many years ago when he was quite a young man, she took then outside and threw them over the clothes line, beating them with a carpet beater she had taken from the kitchen cupboard.

Fortunately there was little dust as this chore was done twice weekly, the occupants were more often out of the house than in it, and the only one who really made a mess was the dog with a few dogs' hairs.

Puffing and panting with the effort of beating the mats she paused for a moment to catch her breath, and watched Rover still rolling over and over on the lawn obviously enjoying his freedom, he the pride and joy of his master, was an old dog, and although at present in good health, Peggy had wondered from time to time recently how Hugh was going to feel when the inevitable happened and Rover succumbed to old age.

Hands on hips Peggy looked down towards the Nissan huts where the PoW's were housed, then beyond to the sea sparkling in the distance, legend had it that smugglers years ago brought contraband up through the brook lands to this house and up the hill to Jean Finch's house which was one of the oldest in the village.

It was said there was a tunnel from Jean's house to the church, and years ago the smuggled goods were kept in the bowels of the church, it was probably hearsay Peggy kept an open mind on the matter, knowing the French coast wasn't many miles across the channel.

Straightening her back she pulled the rugs from the clothes line to take back into the house, going back again to the lounge she got down on her haunches to lay the fire with paper and a few sticks with a few pieces of coal on the top, ready for the mistress to put a match to when she returned, tired after her busy day at the shop in town.

Peggy then buffed up the brass and copper fire irons until she could see her face in them, putting them back in position, getting to her feet she stood for a moment admiring her handy work, feeling well satisfied with her efforts, she then fetched a mop from the kitchen cupboard, rubbing it over the oak boards on the floor, before returning the rugs to their place.

She was just about to buff up the furniture she'd previously waxed when the sound came of the back door opening, and Rover bounded into the room so she left her task to see who had arrived.

'Bill, Hello! I did wonder who it was when Rover bounded in.' Peggy said as the Pembertons gardener stood in the middle of the kitchen removing his hat and looked expectantly in her direction.

'Did't expect you today, don't you usually do the Finches garden on a Thursday?' Peggy enquired.

'Yes, I genially do, but they had some new fruit trees delivered to'ther day, which needed to go straight in so I swapped the days over this week.' Bill paused and smiled at her.

'Is there any chance of a cuppa? I could just do with one!' He pulled one of the chairs from the kitchen table and sat down expectantly.

Peggy grinned; she knew when Bill first appeared that this was what he was after! Picking up the kettle she shook it, gauging that there was enough water in it for a pot of tea without refilling it she lit the gas on the stove with a flint gas lighter the Pembertons had left on the side and quickly put a tray with cups, saucers, tea pot and sugar basin onto the kitchen table, then fetched a small tin marked tea from the cupboard putting it alongside the other items.

'Speck you'd like one of these.' She watched Bill's face light up as she took a small biscuit barrel from the kitchen top where Mrs. Pemberton kept it for occasions such as these.

Opening it and looking at the contents before put it on the kitchen table in front of Bill, she deduced from the variety inside that her employer probably went into Woolworths during her lunch break from their shop when she was in town and got the biscuits from the tins arranged round one of the counters where you put them into brown paper bags and paid for them by the pound, she did it herself when in town.

Never one for being idle, Peggy went to the kitchen cupboard and removed the ironing board, and iron guessing there was just time to heat it up before the kettle boiled.

Bill scrutinized her actions.

'Sit down for a moment.' He ordered. 'The ironing can wait.'

He pulled out another chair from beneath the table and patted it invitingly.

'You need to take the weight off your feet for a spell.'

Peggy plonked herself down on the proffered seat; only to rise just a few minutes later when the kettle announced it had reached boiling point.

Adding a little water to the teapot to warm the pot, she threw the water into the sink before reaching for the tea tin, the Pembertons' had a good supply, so she put two heaped teaspoonful's in the pot before pouring on the water, stirring it thoughtfully and not feeling in the slightest bit guilty as she would have at home for being extravagant because of the rationing.

Hugh Pemberton had relatives abroad who sent a good supply and he was never stingy.

Bill tapped the side of his nose knowingly

'I have some information you will find interesting!' He saw at once the reaction to his words by the twinkle in her blue eyes; Peggy liked to know what was going on locally.

She passed a cup over to him, all ears now he'd whetted her appetite.

'I was talking to Claude yesterday up at the Finches; he says the vicar goes down there.' Bill pointed to the Nissan huts in the distance. 'He goes to talk to the prisoners!'

'Next thing you know, they will soon be attending church with the rest of us!' He finished then not able to disguise the triumph in his voice, he added.

'Then you never know what they'll be doing next!'

Peggy was taken back at his words but didn't want to show it so Peggy waited quite a few moments before she replied.

'What do you mean? She demanded. 'I would have thought they'll be going home to their families before long.' She paused for a moment

'Surely that's the next step isn't it?' She queried

'Dun-no about that, Claude seems to think that won't be for some time yet.' Bill gave a wry smile before he continued.

'Can't keep those men cooped up behind that wire forever, what about if they are allowed to mix with us?'

Peggy didn't really know what to say. 'We-ll if it happens!' She trailed off, the thought was too disturbing.

'Dun-no how the village will take that, do you?' Bill continued he didn't seem to notice her discomfort.

'We shall have to wait and see, speck some in the village will be put out.' Bill helped himself to another biscuit from the tin, and passed his cup over for a refill of tea.

Peggy was silent whilst she poured out the amber liquid and passed it to him.

A thought going straight through her mind, some will be put out! Including my Harry! But that information had to be kept to herself she did not want Bill to know Harry's thoughts on the Germans; it would be difficult to explain it to anyone even the vicar, and certainly not Jean,

Winnie or Claude, you would have thought if anyone had reason to dislike the Germans it would have been Claude injured as he was, but Claude just wasn't that type of person!

Her mind went back to an argument she and her husband had on the subject last night, some of the prisoners from the camp had been sent to work on the farm under Harry's supervision, Peggy overheard Harry telling Ned not to trust them, unusually for her she felt she had to intervene.

'There are good and bad in all people.' She had told Harry crossly. 'You can't tar them all with the same brush, it isn't fair or just.'

Harry raised his voice as his quick temper got the better of him.

'You would change your mind if young Sylvia wanted to marry one wouldn't you!' He snapped

'If Sylvia loved him, I wouldn't object, and I am sure you wouldn't either.'

At this point Ned retreated from the room, he knew Harry's temper!

Harry had crashed his fist down on the table in frustration, so Peggy said no more, she had hoped that Harry had begun to mellow on this particular subject, but it seemed it wasn't so.

Fortunately Harry wasn't the sort to harbour bad feelings and all was put right when she brought him in a cup of tea later on and was greeted with a smile, but the conversation niggled at the back of Peggy's mind for the rest of the evening, surfacing again now after the conversation with Bill.

She drained her cup, and got up from the table.

'I suppose I had better get on or I will be late home for Harry's mid-day meal.' She said pointedly.

'Guess I had better too. 'Bill scraped his chair back and struggled to his feet, pulling himself up he rubbed his back.

'It's the screws. 'He told Peggy as he made an effort to straighten himself up.

She smiled, most likely rheumatism she thought scrutinizing him up and down, well past retirement age, Bill did jobbing gardening and odd jobs around the village to eke out his tiny state pension.

He was much in demand with many able bodied men still away with war effort, any available agricultural workers were required to grow food desperately needed for the nation so there were very few men available who could cultivate the flower beds and ornamental gardens of the 'Posh' houses in the village,

Bill filled this gap in the market.

Peggy watched him go out of the door, with Rover sniffing at his heels as he followed him into the garden.

She plugged in the iron, it was luxury here at the Pembertons she didn't have to heat up the black irons on the kitchen range; they like the Finches had electric irons.

Peggy didn't personally think they were really any better than her 'black' ones just easier to use, she loved ironing, relishing the fresh scent of the snowy white linen, boiled in the copper then left to dry in the sun and wind.

Putting the laundry away in the airing cupboard she glanced into the lounge just to make sure everything was in its place, then she went through to the kitchen to wash up the utensils she and Bill had used for their mid-morning break, taking off her apron she donned her coat letting her out of the back door

With a cheery wave to Bill now cutting back in the rose bed, she patted Rover on the head before letting herself out of the back gate, and going off on her bicycle.

A few minutes later she was in Sid's village shop.

Sid his white overall enveloping his portly form, was serving Winnie some cheese, cutting it from a large round block with a wire.

'Don't give me too much of the rind.' Winnie ordered. 'It's bad enough we get so little with the rationing without getting rind that I cannot use.'

'Do you want some cheese Peggy? This round is fresh in today.' Sid deliberately brought her into the conversation, so that he could shy away from Winnie's sarcastic manner.

'Yes ok Sid.' He cut a large slice weighed both pieces then put them down side by side.

Winnie sniffed, Peggy knew exactly what she was thinking, as she had five in her family her rations were considerably more than the 4 ounces a week allowed to Winnie, farm workers were also allowed extra cheese in their rations from the government, which made the size of her block look massive beside that of Winnie's

'I do miss being able to make cheese dishes.' Winnie whined, as Sid turned his back on them both to wrap the cheese in greaseproof paper before turning round and handing it over to them.

'Is there anything else I can get you ladies?' Sid asked.

Peggy picked up a brown paper packet of pudding rice and put it on the counter, whilst Sid attended to the ration book Winnie gave him, carefully cutting out one of the coupons before returning it to its owner, he didn't need to do the same for Peggy she had deposited her books with Sid previously as did a lot of the local people who used his premises exclusively for their rations. Winnie didn't trust anyone preferring to see what rations she was entitled to, although she did most of her shopping at Sid's

Sid took the cash both Peggy and Winnie offered for their wares, then the two of them walked out of the shop together, just as Dorrie Mann came scuttling up, her high heels clicking against the brick pavement.

'Ow's the little one?' Winnie called to her, Dorrie smiled sweetly as she levelled with them.

'At home with me Grandma, and that's where I shall be as soon as I have finished my job!' Dorrie then tottered speedily along to open the gate of a nearby cottage not giving a backward glance as she let herself through the brown door now in front of her.

'I wonder that girl still has the gall to show her face round here.' Winnie sniffed as soon as she was out of earshot.

'I bet that stocking seam is painted down the back of her legs with gravy browning.' She added rather unkindly, and then continued.

'No doubt she will soon persuade her grandparents to play host to those prisoners if and when they are allowed to share our hospitality.'

Peggy grimaced at Winnie's remarks; she like Winnie knew all about Dorrie's past and although she didn't approve of the girls actions, she had a more realistic view of 'live and let live' than her narrow minded friend.

Then just for a moment a real shiver of fear ran down Peggy's back as Winnie said.

'I don't suppose you would say the same if your Sylvie brought one of them home!'

Peggy chose to ignore that remark. Sylvie had been too young to go to the American dances, but if Bill was right and those men now at the camp were allowed to fraternize with the young people it could be a different story.

'Quite likely it is gravy browning, I wouldn't't fancy doing it myself, but the young un's all do it.' Peggy said glancing sideways at her companion.

'Sylvie does it because she keeps precious clothing coupons for other things, although I did hear the other day clothing coupons will be the first thing on rations to be done away with.'

'She's jolly lucky the old couple took her in.' Peggy realized Winnie had completely ignored what she said and continued the conversation as though Peggy hadn't spoken at all, a disapproving look now outlined Winnie's features.

'Most people would have shut the door on her after what she did!' Peggy sighed to herself, she wondered if Winnie had ever been young; thinking back to her school years she had always seemed old beyond her years.

'I agree they would.' Peggy privately felt very sorry for Dorrie, although most people would have said she got what she deserved; it wasn't as simple as that.

Peggy had seen trouble brewing when the American and Canadian service men had occupied the Nissan huts when preparations were being made for the invasion of France.

The Americans had been very generous, especially in helping the village people and it was very popular, their rations were far more adequate than the British ones and the children enjoyed such treats as cakes with real chocolate, nougat and chewing gum, not seen by some since the commencement of the war and unobtainable with the present rationing.

Dorrie had led a very sheltered life, her mother had died when she was very young leaving her grandparents to bring her and her sister up, a very plain girl with a long face she wasn't endowed with the good looks of her sister who had left the village to marry an English service man; so when an American took an interest in her at of one the dances her head was turned

'I think we would be amazed how many babies those Americans left behind.' Winnie continued.

'That's human nature for you.' Peggy hoped her quiet reply would take the heat out of the situation.

'Yes I suppose so.' Winnie's tone was grudging then the tone turned spiteful again as she said.

'You have to be inclined to behave that way!'

Peggy tried to hide a smile, how could this confirmed spinster, who to her knowledge had never even had a boyfriend say such a thing!

'Yes.' Peggy replied. 'I have often thought the war has been responsible for a lot of heartache one way and another.' Peggy knew several older women whose husbands were away fighting in the services had a liaison with these men, her neighbour for example.

There was talk that some had back street abortions and some children born had been fostered or put up for adoption before the husbands returned from overseas service.

Peggy though of Gisela and her situation, not that she had ever discussed that with anyone, and certainly wouldn't with Winnie, she was too judgmental and narrow minded to understand the position but she knew also of at least one woman in the village whose husband was going to come home quite soon after some considerable time away to a young baby who couldn't possibly be his own.

Recalling the stiff opposition from her family and the church she said.

'One thing I would say for Dorrie, she didn't have the child adopted, and in a way she is to be admired for taking that stand.' Peggy added gently, she knew how much her little girl meant to Dorrie, and how well she cared for her.

'Not if you take into account the affect it has had on her family.' Winnie sneered.

Peggy shifted the bag on her arm to a more comfortable position.

'Yes I agree with you, it is not fair that for a couple of that age to look after a toddler, but what other options are open to Dorrie?' She queried.

'She has to work to support herself and the child, her grandparents can't help on their pension can they?'

Peggy had watched the old couple who were in their 80's struggle with the lively little girl, they had already brought up Dorrie and her sister when their daughter had died young and their son-in-law had deposited the two girls on their doorstep many years ago.

Winnie sniffed again; she had no answer to that one!'

'I had best get on. Ned and Harry will want their lunch.' Peggy reached for her bike propped against a wall, and put her bag on the handlebars, with a quick wave she peddled off down the street, grateful for once to have had the last word with Winnie.

Dorrie looked out of the cottage window that served as the hairdressers where she worked and saw the two women part company; she knew she'd been the topic if their conversation. She had learnt to ignore it, it came with village life but it still hurt. Peggy she knew to be a kindly soul but the other one! Winnie Baker was in her opinion a judgmental old spinster twisted because life had passed her by!

Dorrie looked at her reflection in the mirror, knowing only too well she was no oil painting; her long horsy face was the bane of her life which no makeup could change, but one thing she was sure of was that Luke had loved her, if he hadn't been killed in the offensive, she was convinced he would have come back for her.

She remembered so clearly their first meeting,

Her sister Olive had gone along to the dance the Americans gave at the 'Reading Room' taking Dorrie with her, mainly because they'd heard there would be plenty of food there; with the austere rationing this was a treat and they didn't want to miss out.

They arrived to music blaring out, so different to what they were used to, this music had beat, and it made your toes want to start tapping.

Dorrie remembered looking up from her laden plate into the most incredible black eyes she had ever seen; from that moment she was lost, Luke held her heart.

They spent as much time as they could together after that night; aware time was precious.

With some difficulty she'd kept him at arm's length; no one knew when the call to action would come, life was at a fast pace, no one knew what tomorrow would bring.

She remembered so well that last day they'd spent together, they sat on the downs looking out over to the sea, at first she had refused to give in to his request, but caught up in the urgency of the moment she had given into him and they'd made love just as the sun was going down bathing everything in gold, the next day he was confined to barracks and overnight the Americans were gone.

For weeks afterwards she thought everything was alright, her period though scanty arrived and she felt really well, Luke's letters full of love flew across the channel, the news was positive, the allies were winning, the future looked good.

Suddenly Luke's letters stopped; Dorrie was desperate, then a letter came from his commanding officer to say he'd been killed in action, hardest of all back came her letters to Luke that she had sent over the past few weeks, which he had never been able to read.

Heartbroken she went to work every day wishing she could join her soul mate, feeling unwell she sought the advice of her doctor, and was really shocked to find she was well over four months pregnant.

With the truth out, she was sent to a home for unmarried mothers, where pressure was put on her to have her child adopted; she resisted this despite intense pressure, how could she part with the only thing she had of Luke?

She knew it wasn't fair on her elderly grandparents to look after Susan and she tried really hard to make other arrangements; the situation was dire everywhere, housing was at a premium, she had no money and had to work, eventually she did the only thing open to her she brought Susan home to her grandparents who she knew would mind the child whilst she worked, there was no other way, she was determined no one was going to take the only thing she had of Luke away. Susan was too precious.

CHAPTER NINE

Summer 1946

The Reverent Hounsome caught his breath as he looked out at the young men's faces now stretched out before him and the familiar nervousness that had always been part of his makeup began to bubble up inside.

By nature a shy man, he had always found public speaking hard and had never fully understood why his father had insisted he entered the church as a vocation when a young man, what he did not realize that his father had recognized despite his shy manner he had a natural empathy and kindness towards people which is a far better quality.

He knew he would have to speak slowly to control the stutter that threatened to surface at times like these, not realizing that this was probably going to be a help to these men who might have difficulty understanding the faltering German he'd been taught as a school boy and it would especially help those who had different dialects from some areas of their country.

Looking out over the sea of faces in front of him he saw most of the men now looking expectantly at him were in the bloom of youth, made to grow into men at a time when they should have been free of the horrible responsibilities that the war had brought on them . . .

He always found it comforting to concentrate on something in the room when he was talking to people, so he looked at a picture painted on a wall at the back of the dining area which had been cleared for this occasion, hand painted it was an alpine scene, he wondered briefly if one of the men who were now facing him were responsible for the painting, as it was recognizant of their homeland.

The camp commandant who was at his elbow clapped his hands to bring the assembly to order, and a silence fell over them all as the cleric cleared his throat just as the camp commandant announced in German.

'This is the Reverent Hounsome who has come to talk to you.' He gave the cleric a slight nudge forward.

Pulling himself to his full height, the Reverent cleared his throat and in a quiet voice delivered the speech he had prepared in his study a few days earlier which in essence said to the men that as England was a mainly protestant country like their own it was right that the church offered help both physically and spiritually to their German brothers, he went on to say the church would help where ever possible; and he himself would give a service here at the camp on Sunday afternoons inviting all faiths to attend.

The address it seemed had been understood by the majority as a quiet clapping by the men accompanied the end of his speech.

When he had first read about the prisoners of war's position in a British Council of Churches pamphlet, it had said in part that the PoW's were in a difficult psychological situation, being on the side of a calamitous war they had lost they were beset with special difficulties which clergymen could help address.

It went on to say a handshake in German is the same as in English, stressing these men needed the help of the church.

The Reverend Hounsome although shy was never one to shirk responsibility, as soon as he was able he applied for a permit to visit the men in their accommodation, this he had received just a few days ago and this was the first opportunity to address the men.

After his address the Camp Commandant steered the minister off the platform to introduce him to some of the inmates.

The Reverent shook the hands with quite a few before the commandant introduced him to Karl who had been hovering behind them both. This young man will be of great help to you he told the cleric, he has quite a good command of the English language.

'That is good.' The Reverent Hounsome opened out an outstretched arm to shake warmly the handsome young German now standing before him, looking into the blue eyes and open face he immediately liked what he saw.

After this Karl stood near the Reverent Hounsome's elbow to help with some of the German words the vicar found difficult as he spoke to the men.

Later tea was served and the discussion continued the older man was really amazed to learn later that Karl had only picked up the English language during his yearlong detention in America as a prisoner of war and he congratulated Karl on his mastery of it in such a short time.

After this initial visit the vicar spent as much time as he was able away from his duties with the men at the camp, he came to know many of them well and gained the respect of most of them.

Over time the men began to trust the Reverent with their problems and one thing became very clear the men were very resentful of being kept as prisoners when their own country was in a mess, an often repeated grumble was their situation was nothing short of forced labour.

Although sympathetic towards them the Vicar endeavored to be impartial, but his help was appreciated in other areas, he used his expertise to help reunite families with the aid of the Red Cross also acting as negotiator between the men and any problems that arose with the village population.

Sometimes the men were moved to work elsewhere where the need was greater and a new intake came in, this saddened the vicar somewhat as he had built up a rapport with a lot of the men who were transferred but he made an effort to get on with the new intake, succeeding well with his genuine kindly manner.

Karl much to the Reverent Hounsome's delight remained at the camp so he was able to continue to be of use to him translating difficult German words where necessary.

As time passed, restrictions were relaxed slightly and the Government deemed it right for these men if they wished to attend church for morning service on Sunday morning instead of it being held at the camp.

As association with the general public wasn't allowed, the vicar thought it best that they came in to the church during the singing of the first hymn.

It had been the object of much discussion by the dignitaries in the village when the subject had first come up at a meeting of the village, and the usual occupants of the front pews in the church were highly annoyed when it was suggested that these men should have their customary places.

Jean Finch had gone along with what the vicar suggested and order was restored after she pointed out it was the best place for them as they were to come in after the service started and leave during the singing of the last hymn so that association with the villagers would be avoided. In the end after much discussion and some sour comments this was agreed upon.

The first Sunday that the men were led into church by their warders their hobnail boots echoed round the stone walls above the singing of the congregation as they took their allotted places. Dressed in their distinctive dark brown uniform with blue patches on the tunics and trousers they stood out amongst the variety of clothes the rest of the congregation wore, after the first few weeks people soon got used to this arrangement and accepted it.

On this first Sunday Sylvia, from her advantage point in the choir stalls watched as the men filed into the allotted space. Because the song they were singing was a well know one and she knew the words off by heart, she was able to take her eyes from the hymn book and gaze out at the collection of handsome young men in the prime of life standing to attention just a few yards away.

Right the end of the first row a tall man with fair curly hair that looked as if it defied the brushing it presumably had that morning had Sylvia's heart pounding in her chest as he looked up straight into her eyes and her hands shook as she watched him pick up the hymn sheet prepared by Jean Finch in the men's national language. Averting her eyes with some difficulty she looked back to the hymn sheet in front of her.

Jean had approached one of the teachers at the village school she knew to be well versed in the German language, and persuaded her to type out the hymn sheets so that the men could follow along the service in their native tongue and the vicar had thoughtfully chosen some of the hymns with the German Prisoners in mind.

'Glorious things of thee are spoken Zion city of our God.' was sung in the church most Sundays it was the same tune of the German national anthem and the Reverent Hounsome hoped it would help the men feel more at home.

On this first Sunday the sound of masculine voices filling the church as it was sung was electric bouncing off the ancient stone walls and echoing round and round as the voices reached a crescendo adding to the melody that burst forth from the rest of the congregation.

Everyone sat quietly when the vicar delivered his sermon; it seemed to Sylvia from her advantageous position the prisoners were listening intently to his words although she did wonder how much they actually understood.

She took little sideways glances at the men before demurely lowering her eyes again to the wooden shelf in front of her that held the hymn sheets and the Book of Common Prayer, she raised her eyes once again just as the blonde man in the front row raised his looking directly into hers, she was mesmerized, and couldn't look away, deep down inside something stirred within her, a powerful feeling so intense it frightened her yet went into the depth of her being somehow filling her with great joy and a longing to get to know this man better.

Karl for his part couldn't take his eyes from the sloe eyed dark haired girl that caught his gaze, deep down the feelings also ran deep, making a supreme effort to take his mind off this he concentrated on the Reverent Hounsome who was finishing his sermon from the pulpit.

When the vicar approached the prison authorities about the men attending church on Sundays Karl like a lot of the other inmates had felt it was a no go area, although he'd been brought up as protestant in Germany, he'd rarely attended church although his parents had. Religion wasn't something Karl found easy especially as they were expected to shoot people if commanded during the war offensive who like themselves were Protestants or catholic, even if they were of a different nationality.

Most of the PoW's present today had come to church because they admired the man who now stood before them, quietly in the weeks he had attended their camp the Reverent had spoken to each one of them drawing them out and taking time to listen to their troubles and helping where he could, he had been especially helpful to Karl who still hadn't been able to trace his family.

After the success of getting the PoW's to the church services the vicar organized a small concert at the camp to be given by the people in the village; although the men were still not allowed to fraternize with the locals on a permanent basis this concert was designed to give the men a bit of entertainment that was allowed.

It was a welcome respite to their restrictive living which consisted of little more than work, eating, and sleep. The men left every morning in a working party to go where they were instructed, Karl mostly worked on the land often at a local farm which Farmer Phillips owned so he quite often he worked in direct contact with Harry and Ned, conversation was not encouraged between PoW and other farm workers and to begin with wardens were often in attendance. It was a very lonely life and especially difficult for those who had wives back at home with just the other inmates of the camp for company.

Outside the huts the men cultivated the ground, sowing seeds so a variety of fruit and flowers flourished, some of the men obtained wood and spent many hours carving it into toys and other articles.; because the men were restricted and not allowed freedom most set about making the Nissan huts that were now their home more habitable, paint was found, mostly green, cream, or brown, doors were painted and the walls distempered, the more artistic painted pictures on the walls mostly reminiscent of their homeland

Things improved between Heinz and Karl, Heinz had to admit after many films and lectures how bad the Nazi regime had been and he now accepted Hitler was a bad men. Karl wasn't the sort to bear a grudge and had long since forgiven Heinz over the death of Wilhelm, so the two of them became firm friends, they were often sent on working parties together.

Heinz still only spoke a few words of English so he relied on Karl to help out when problems with the language surfaced; neither of them were moved from this camp like a lot of the other men. Karl privately thought it was because they had experience of farm work and were useful in this mainly rural area.

.As time passed the British government gave no hint as to when they could be repatriated the men's moods grew very sober as long days and nights seemed to stretch out with no relief in sight. For Karl it wasn't quite as monotonous as it was for the rest of the men, almost all of them had heard from their families, yet for him personally it seemed he had nothing to look forward too at all.

By nature a mild tempered man he didn't let his inward thought show, inside he felt dead with no plans or hope for the future.

CHAPTER TEN

February 1947

The snow which had been falling for hours on the already frozen ground lay heavily on the Nissan huts and the wire fences surrounding them, drifting in the bitterly cold north wind.

Glancing out of the window Karl was reminded nostalgically again of his homeland as it had when they had been in Yorkshire at this time of the year, at home snow and frost often covered the ground for months before spring finally broke through in a sudden burst of warmth.

The coke burning stove in the corner of the large communal room where the men spent most of their time when they were not working was quite inadequate for this harsh weather, it didn't do more than take the edge off the penetrating cold, but with the severe rationing it was all there was and the men were told they were lucky to have any heating at all with shortages throughout the country. Power cuts were prominent and food shortages accentuated by the severe weather meant they like the rest of the population of Britain they had to put up with these conditions, farming was impossible on the frozen ground and thousands couldn't work, so the PoW's went out in working parties to clear roads, and pavements with shovels to keep them busy.

Once the sun went down, the evenings were long and dark, an oil lamp with its dim light lit the huts making it impossible to read or even whittle at wood or paint, so time dragged.

Karl stood and beat his arms across his chest to try and get a bit of warmth into his body; he glanced out of the single pane of glass in the ill-fitting windows that were not meant for this sort of weather, the wind rattled them when it was at its fiercest and ice built up on the inside making patterns that just stopped short of the centre so you could see out, this side of the huts faced north, so the sunshine didn't penetrate enough to melt it,

Although the wire fences still surrounded the enclosure, the gate was open now on a permanent basis and the men were no longer confined to the huts as they had been previously, yet they were still restricted quite simply because they had nowhere else to go.

Repatriation home has begun at last but was very slow frustrating most of the men somewhat. A trickle had now returned home, and the promise for this year was many more would follow; a ripple of excitement went through the men when this was announced.

For Karl this rang hollow, he still hadn't heard whether or not his families in what was now the Russian sector of Germany were alive or dead.

The Reverent Hounsome had been very kind to him trying to help by getting in touch with the Red Cross on Karl's behalf but so far there had been no joy from there either.

Karl had come to accept that perhaps he would never see his parents and sister again and whenever thoughts about this surfaced he tried to put it at the back of his mind concentrating on something else, something he did right now.

Looking through the window over the brook lands and fields surrounding them spread out before him, he could just see the snow covered roofs of the cottages where Sylvia lived, watching the tendrils of grey smoke from the chimneys snaking away into the atmosphere he looked beyond to the rest of the village stretching out, the land rising up to the church and some more houses on the hill; straining he could just see the house where the vicar lived in the distance its stone walls grey against the white covering of snow.

Karl had been invited to his home just before Christmas with some of the other PoW's there he met his wife and family and were made very welcome. Later back at the camp some of the men carved toys out of wood for the Reverent Hounsome's children to show their gratitude for the kindness the minister had shown to them all during the last few months, most of the PoW's had great respect for this man.

Karl looked again at the cottages where Sylvia lived and a warmth rose in his heart, nothing had changed the feelings he'd felt for her since he first saw her in the church in the autumn of last year.

Over the Christmas period just passed, the government for the first time allowed the PoW's to fraternize with the villagers.

Jean Finch with her usual flair for organizing, and with the help of the vicar thought it would be nice for the men to share the festivities on Christmas Day away from the Nissan huts and with some local families.

The first thing she did was to arrange a concert at the 'Reading Room' for everyone in the village so they could all meet the men. Once the villagers were assembled the heavy boots of the men clomping on the wooden floor announcing their arrival and they were shown to the seats reserved for them at the front of the hall.

Jean had thoughtfully arranged things which she felt would help the men feel at home, so she arranged a Christmas tree in one corner lit with small candles and had paper chains festooned from the rafters.

First the village children were invited to do some singing, followed by a nativity play.

Miss Ducker thumped out the tunes on a piano almost as ancient as herself and the whole village joined in the songs.

Then the men were invited to the platform, dressed in their prison garb, their boyish faces were scrubbed clean as they rendered 'Jesus shall reign' in good English thanks to coaching by Jean Finch, their masculine voices raised the roof.

The audience were delighted and clapped wildly then all went quiet as the men broke into their rendering of 'Silent Night' The villagers were enthralled as the hymn was sung in its original language the clear rich sound of the mens voices echoing round and round the hall. It was quite a few moments after the final chorus was sung that the audience broke the spell with spontaneous clapping.

As soon as this was over, tea and biscuits were served and the men were invited to mingle with everyone, shy at first the villagers stood in small groups but soon the men were talking to their hosts companionably.

A little later Jean Finch called them all to order and with the Reverent Hounsome at her side she suggested families who were interested could take a PoW. to share their Christmas celebrations in their own homes, warmed by the occasion most people immediately agreed.

Jean was at Peggy's elbow a few minutes later.

'Will you take one or two?' She asked her daily help; Peggy hesitated for a moment;

'We could manage two.' She gave Jean a smile which didn't reveal the havoc going on inside, knowing Harry's attitude to the German's. He was busy with work on the farm so unable to be present so the decision was up to her, knowing an argument between her and Harry would probably result, she was in a tricky situation, aware Harry wouldn't thank her for letting people know how he felt and the people here would think it very strange if she didn't take one or two of the men, because it was second nature to her to help others she hoped she had made the right decision.

Jean Finch gave her a smile before she went back to the vicar who had begun to hand out a different colored spill to each of the Germans

Jean gave each of the villagers a spill from a different container these were also different colours, each person would match the colour of the spill they received with the colour the prisoners received and this would be the man they would take for Christmas day. She deemed this was the fairest way to deal with the situation, so there was no favoritism.

Karl received a pink spill, he looked over to where Peggy was sitting; he'd seen her previously when he'd been in the back of a lorry taking him back to the enclosure one day last autumn talking to Sylvia as the two of them made their way back to their cottage, and he knew she was married to Harry who he often worked for, because he was able to speak to Ned about it on odd occasion during working hours.

Would Peggy get the pink spill he wondered? Then he could see Sylvia on Christmas Day!

Karl looked over as Peggy took her spill, it was yellow! Drat he thought!

Heinz standing next to him was holding his spill behind his back, Karl took a quick look. It was yellow!

Quickly he put his spill into the hand of the other man, Heinz understanding little English wasn't really aware of what was going on so didn't take any notice of the swap.

When the men were invited to meet their prospective hosts for Christmas day matching the spills they had drawn, Karl went over and gave his prospective host a wide smile he then looked over his shoulder to see who Heinz was going to, it was Jean Finch!

That pleased Karl Jean had been up to their enclosure helping them write letters to their relatives and generally helping to make life more comfortable for them, all the men liked her, so he was sure Heinz would have a good time in that household, so any feeling of guilt left him.

Immediately Karl knew he was going to like Peggy as she extended her hand in greeting, she reminded him of his mother, he tried to listen attentively but the excitement of knowing he would be spending Christmas under the same roof as Sylvia meant he couldn't concentrate on what Peggy was saying so he just nodded as pleasantly as he could as Peggy chatted on about the festive season in their house and who would be there.

Inside Karl was euphoric the only person he cared about being there was Sylvia, being so close to her even for a few hours would be bliss.

Peggy was to take two men for Christmas day and Karl was pleased to see the other person now standing beside him was Hans who came from the same area of Germany as he did; he knew Hans had a fiancé back home and couldn't wait to go back to her, so there would be no opposition for Sylvia's charms.

Christmas came up to Karl's expectations, the PoW's attended the morning services, then Jean invited them all to her house for the very smallest glass of sherry that she could provide with the rationing.

The house was so crowded with people that they spilled outside into the garden, the sherry warming them against the freezing cold wind; Jeans thoughtfulness broke the ice for the families, who afterwards took their allotted men to their homes for the rest of Christmas day.

It had been the best time Karl had experienced in a very long time, Sylvia's family were very close and he felt drawn to their simple way of life which he realized was very similar to his own back ground.

The best part for Karl and Hans was the really nice home cooked meal which Sylvia's mother produced with aplomb, she really excelled herself for the two men and her family knowing canteen cooking wasn't the same as home cooking.

Karl loved feeling part of a family again, and the two men got on well with the evacuees whilst enjoying the company of the rest of Sylvia's family, especially her grandmother and her uncle who joined them over lunch, it was a jolly time and Karl realized how much he had missed family time, quietly hoped his parents and sister were still alive and having a good time together where ever they were.

Harry and Ned had left later in the afternoon to see to the animals on the farm, and then Gisela and her family joined them for tea. For Karl and Hans it was so nice to be able to talk to someone in their own native language, to realize also how the war had affected Gisela and to learn how she came to be here so far from her homeland. They could both see the sadness in her eyes as she opened up to them and Karl could tell she wasn't that happy at the prospect of her husband's return in the new year by the way she spoke about it, his heart went out to her. He wished he could help her but knew that it wasn't possible; they did however discuss the plight of the people back in their homeland.

Gisela had heard from her parents and what she spoke about sent a sinking feeling into the very depth of Karl's being.

'If we think things are bad here.' She told the two men. 'They are ten times worse there.'

Karl watched Hans face blanch as Gisela told them about the division of Germany and the plight of those now in the Russian sector, news about the plight of families in their homeland was slow to filter through to the PoW's; what information there was, was mostly gleaned from letters sent to the men in the camp, so both Karl and Hans were glad of the information which they would be able to share with the other men when they returned to camp later that day.

Gisela went on to tell them how she sent a few parcels to her parents when she was able, including some of the things her children had grown out of, and went on to say how gratefully these things had been received by people who had literally nothing. Gisela went on to say how kind Jean Finch had been when she explained the situation to her, how she had gone out of her way to organize locally for parcels to be sent to her people in Austria, although with the severe rationing it was difficult for much to be sent.

'That seems like her.' Karl told Gisela; as he went on to explain how kind the lady had been to them all up at the PoW camp.

Gisela was sympathetic when Karl told her about his parents, more than anyone else she understood how hard it was to be in what was now the Russian sector of Germany,

'Many got out.' She said sadness ringing her large eyes. 'Before Germany was divided, but now it is almost impossible.' She extended her hand to his as tears filled his eyes; going on to explain to Peggy and the family assembled the position as Karl loudly blew his nose into a large handkerchief.

They were just discussing how Hans's family had managed to escape over the border before the Russians took control when the living room door burst open and Harry returned so the conversation turned immediately to other things as Harry announced one of his sheep was lambing.

'It's a bit early.' He said, 'So Ned is staying up there to see that all is ok.'
Karl and Hans immediately got to their feet.

'We will go up to Ned; I expect he could do with a bit of company.'
Karl reached for his warm outside coat, both men being glad to get out of
the emotion packed room and think their own thoughts.

Beside this Karl was really pleased not to have to spend any more time
in Harry's company; he felt very uncomfortable with the older man's eyes
constantly boring into him every time he looked up, over dinner in an
unguarded moment he felt he saw hate there as he looked Karl's way.

He had tried very hard to get on with Harry but he remained aloof,
which was quite a surprise as Karl hadn't found much hostility from any
other English people; he had heard it said that English people could be
rather unapproachable especially those who lived in the south of England,
so he put Harry's manner down to this.

Looking back at the cottages as he made his way to the sheep pens
Karl's face softened as he thought about Sylvia, he'd glanced in her direction
in church that morning as she sang in the choir, he could see now in his
mind's eye the shape of her face with its pointed chin and the brown eyes
that gazed so honestly into his making him feel warm and comfortable
inside. Analyzing his feelings as he walked along he realized that there was
now no doubt in his mind he was in love with her, and from the way she
looked at him he was sure she felt the same.

It had taken him by surprise when Harry had announced pointedly
over dinner that his daughter wouldn't be sixteen until the coming May,
Karl had thought that she was at least eighteen, Harry had directed this
statement at him personally even though everyone else was round the
table at the table.

It fazed him somewhat that Harry seemed to have taken such a dislike
to him, because he had not given a hint to any one not even to Sylvia that
he was more than a little attracted to her, perhaps Karl reasoned it was
a fathers sixth sense about him that made him wary, Karl was unaware
that the feelings he had for Harry's daughter shone through his eyes for
everyone present including her father to see.

One thing Karl was sure about if he had to wait for many years to
make Sylvia his wife he would, time didn't matter to him as they had their
whole lives before them, he only hoped Harry would see that in time.

Hans interrupted his thoughts and the two men chatted in their native tongue as they walked along, especially about Gisela and the information she had imparted about their native land.

They found Ned in the lambing shed, and both men dropped to their knees in front of the sheep pen as they examined the new arrival.

'Had a good day?' Ned asked.

'Yes!' The men said in unison making them both laugh.

Ned looked them both, and then directly at Karl.

'Harry's bark is worse than his bite; he's a bit sensitive with regard to his daughter.'

Karl smiled at him, he had an affinity with Ned they laughed together especially in the work environment over some shared joke, the German learnt a lot from the evacuee about the English, and the English farming methods that were in some ways quite different to the ones they used at home, and Ned had a great deal of empathy towards the PoWs, even though Ned's father had been killed in the war, he bore no grudge towards the Germans realizing they were not directly responsible for the German dictators actions. Karl appreciated this especially when he caught the younger man defending him against one of Harry's outbursts about the German race one day.

Harry was difficult with all the PoW's and particularly with Karl because he was the one who quite often had to work in close proximately with him, at times it was nearly an impossible task, just when he thought he'd broken the ice with the older man, he would change back into the bit of an ogre, Karl fortunately was of a placid disposition so he shrugged it off finding the best way was to keep his head down and get on with his work when Harry got difficult.

Karl looked again through the small window; the snow had stopped at last but it was still bitterly cold; he felt very restless and making a quick decision he picked up his outside coat which was slung on his bed and went outside for a walk around the enclosure hoping to get some heat into his limbs before the long winter evening closed in; outside he once again beat his arms across his chest to get some warmth into them.

Swirling snowflakes from the drifts brushed along by the strong wind tickled his cheeks making them sting, people were saying it was the coldest here in years; if it was like this here it must be horrendous in his homeland known for its cold and penetrating winters, he had heard that all over Europe the weather was bad.

Looking at the sky he note it still had a greyish colour with that yellowish tinge that indicated more snow to come, at least the wind which had been quite ferocious in the last few days had died down somewhat that would prevent the new snow falling from drifting, the drifts had been very deep for some weeks now.

'You know what our job will be tomorrow!' Karl looked round to see where the voice came from saw Heinz standing a little away framing the door.

'Yes shifting some of the white stuff!' Karl laughed.

'Well I don't really mind do you?' Heinz smiled.

'No its better to be busy don't you think? It takes your mind off other things!' His friend nodded in agreement.

'Yes and I have had good news. 'Heinz was now beaming from ear to ear.

'I will be going home soon!'

Karl gave his companion a sideways glance, his voice incredulous.

'When? He exclaimed.

'Have you got a date?' Karl felt a sinking feeling. Heinz was one of the few people who had stayed in the same camp with him throughout his time in England; it would be strange without him around, even though they hadn't really got on when they were together first as PoW's. He scarcely recognized this man as the hard faced German officer he had been, he now spoke enough English to be understood which he'd made an effort to learn, strong muscles in his once bony arms were clearly visible and he had also filled out a bit which made his facial expressions less severe. Most importantly of all his personality had completely changed, it had taken time but even he had come to realize how wrong Adolf Hitler had been, and was now looking forward to a peaceable future back in his homeland.

'Well I haven't actually got a date yet.' Heinz replied.

He couldn't hide the joy in his voice as he said

'The camp commander says it is definitely going to be in quite soon.'

Karl looked a little disconsolate, the news made him feel so lonely.

'I will miss you!' He declared.

Heinz picked up on his friend's downcast look.

'I hope there will be good news about your family before long!' The genuine feeling in the older man's voice was something the old Heinz would never have had; obviously the lectures and work here in England had worked miracles.

Suddenly there was a sparkle in the older man's eyes as he said.

'Once this cold weather clears away, the camp commander says we will be allowed to go to the village dance on a Saturday night. That can only be a few weeks away. I might as well have a little fun before I go home, what do you think?' There was a sparkle in Heinz once lusterless eyes.

'Yes that will be nice, especially as we can go together!' Karl put his arm about his companions shoulder, his spirits lifting, the chances were Sylvia would attend the village hop and nothing was going to stop him being there also, now that it was allowed.

Heinz smiled at his companion.

'My feet are frozen, let's go inside, perhaps we could manage a game of cards before the darkness sets in?' Arms round each other's shoulders they went into Nissan hut together.

CHAPTER ELEVEN

Girlish giggles greeted Peggy when she let herself in through the back door of her cottage, a good feeling that Sylvie and her friend Janet where having fun preparing for the dance at the village hall later that evening brought a smile to Peggy's face. Janet had spent a great deal of time at their home this winter, with the particularly severe and penetrating cold they hadn't been able to go out very far except to work.

Because of coal rationing and power cuts caused by the bad weather the family had been forced to share the one small sitting room at Peggy's house for any activities, not that power cuts affected the small tied cottage occupied by Harry, Peggy and the family, there was no electricity!

In this respect they had fared better than some other people in the village because lighting was by gas lamps positioned on the wall with a wick and a glass dome, although the light that shone forth from them wasn't as bright as electricity it was quite adequate for most of the family activities.

The coal rationing meant that the sitting room fire could only be lit in the evenings this commodity had to be reserved for the kitchen range which was essential for cooking and at least it meant that one room was always warm.

Upstairs they had was no lighting at all oil lamps or candles were used, the ill-fitting sash cord windows in the bedroom had newspaper or cardboard squashed into the gaps and quite often ice that gathered during cold spells on the inside of the glass remained all day.

The two girls had spent the winter adjusting dresses worn by their mothers to tea dances in the early 1930's into something more modern for the joys that lay ahead for them both.

Sylvia's little hand sewing machine had been busy whirring away all winter as the girls worked on their costumes, Sylvia had made a pale green satin affair her mother wore into a very fashionable piece for herself adding frills in a darker shade of green; Janet had also adjusted a lemon dress of her mothers, although not good on the sewing side, she pinned up seams and did some of the hand finishing work.

Janet was just a couple of years older than Sylvia and the two had been firm friends since babyhood.

Peggy pushing Sylvia in her big coach built pram into the village park, met with Rose who was Janet's mother doing the same thing, the pair had known each vaguely from the tea dances they had attended in the early 1930's at the local town, but hadn't been real friends at this time, Peggy being several years older than Rose moved in a different set, now they both had small daughters they found more in common and took the young ones in their prams to the park most days.

Rose and her husband Len married when Rose was just eighteen, although it was never discussed Peggy was aware that Rose was already pregnant at the time; it wasn't something you could hide in a small village where everyone knew everything about everyone else.

Len and Rose now lived in the red brick council houses near the reading room with their family, Len had joined up early in the war, leaving Rose pregnant with her second child. Whenever Len came home on leave it seemed he always managed to leave his wife pregnant again, and as a result, Janet now had four little brothers with scarcely a year between each one, although there was talk in the village whether or not the youngest one was actually Len's!

It did seem that Len had been away for just over a year when this lad was born and not only was he darker skinned than the rest of the brood but there was also the fact that Rose had gained a reputation by being prominent up at the camp particularly when the Americans and Canadians had been there; it was said in the village that she had entertained the men sometimes in her home.

All seemed well at the family home now that Len had been demobbed, although he did frequent the public house more than most men, who usually only had a pint on Friday or Saturday nights.

'Hi mum, we are ready.' Mickey tumbled down the stairs and opened the door at the bottom into the kitchen disturbing Peggy's thought pattern. With his hair brushed and plastered down with water in an effort to stop the curls that usually fell over his forehead he looked quite smart, Peggy looked with satisfaction at the fair isle pullover painstakingly knitted out of odd bits of wool she had made for him during the winter months, thought how well it sat well over his short grey trousers that finished just below his bony knees leaving a gap between them and his knee high socks.

Hugo followed close behind, the two boys although firm friends where complete opposites in every way; Hugo dressed much the same as Mickey with trousers just above his knees, revealed them scabby and covered in grazes, nonacademic it was well known he was a bit of a rebel at school and quite often in a scrap with other boys, what Peggy didn't know was he was fiercely protective of Mickey who being a bit of a swat, was often ridiculed and being small in stature wasn't good at defending himself

The two lads were off to the reading room where a youth social had been organized for the young ones, this was to be followed by the dance for the older youth scheduled to commence after the interval when refreshments would be served.

Usually this was an annual event held about a month after Christmas to brighten up the village, one Saturday for the young ones and the next for the teenagers, this year with the dreadful winter they had just experienced it would it have been difficult getting through the snow which had drifted deep in places and the water pipes in the reading room had frozen up so it was unusable. Then there was the question of heating, fuel wasn't available for the paraffin heaters used heat the hall and it was put off again because the vicar didn't like the idea of social occasions during lent, with Easter now behind them, and now the better weather had arrived it had been decided that the two youth events could be held together.

The boys pulled their coats from the hook on the back door wrapped scarves tightly around their throats before raising their hands in a goodbye salute as they made their way to the back door.

Just a few minutes after Mickey and Hugo departed, Ned came crashing down the stairs, looking very grown up in a white shirt and flannel trousers, he was escorting Sonja and Helga from next door to the first half of the social they would come home with Peggy after she and Winnie had served the refreshments and cleared away. Both girls had been highly annoyed when their mother insisted they attend the young ones event and not the older gathering.

Gisela had insisted that as Helga was not yet a teenager and Sonja only just one, they were to do as she asked so Ned had kindly said he would go along with the girls; Peggy knew he had a soft spot for Sonja

Harry had taken on the late milking today so that Ned could be free to get ready and enjoy himself, he stood now preening his hair in the mirror that stood above the kitchen sink and Peggy sitting at the kitchen table observed his muscles moving through his crisp white shirt, with all the heavy work he was involved up at the farm he had filled out a bit, now fourteen and a half he looked much older, especially as he was nearly six foot tall.

'You'll do.' Peggy teased him, looking proudly at his long lanky form and thinking what a nice young man he was becoming.

He smiled in reply, picking up his jacket from the chair where he'd flung it before his liaison with the mirror; slinging it over his shoulder and made his way to the back door, whistling as he went.

Minutes later Peggy saw the Ned, Sonja, and Helga pass by her window giggling at some joke she was sure Ned had composed; Sonja tall and willowy with her mother's lovely eyes, reached above Ned's shoulder. Helga just a little shorter was thicker set favoring her father.

Gisela voicing her doubts about the girls going to the social was reassured when Peggy offered to bring the girls back with her before the dance for the older ones began, which would also mean Ned could join in this element also so he wouldn't miss out.

It was some time later that Sylvia and Janet chattering excitedly appeared from upstairs, looking up from her knitting as the girls entered the sitting room Peggy took a deep intake of breath as they stood before her; dressed in their finery they both looked stunning.

'Will we do mum?' Sylvia said giving a quick twirl, the green dress she'd fashioned to fit her slim figure fell beautifully from the waist the frill at the bottom giving it a lovely full effect over her slim legs and high heeled shoes.

'You look really nice.' Peggy quickly reached for her handkerchief blowing her nose; so that her daughter wouldn't see the tear that appeared in her eyes.

'You look lovely too Janet, that colour really suits you.' She enthused as she turned her attention to the other girl admiring the lemon dress that sat equally well on her.

Janet, taller than Sylvia with bright blue eyes had a rather angular face with sharper features than her friend; a dimple featured when she smiled, her main beauty was her naturally blonde curly hair which she had caught at the side with a pretty clip to match her dress and then hung in curls down her back.

Peggy looked at the smear of lipstick on their lips and the tiniest bit of rouge on their cheeks, glad that Harry was at work so as not to witness this, he would never have approved!

Sylvia paused over the fireplace looking at her reflection in the mirror that hung there, brown sloe shaped eyes glanced back as she pulled her straight dark brown hair which was parted in the middle and hung thick over her shoulders into place, then she pinched her cheeks to add a little colour. Both girls clasped a small bag in their hands, more lipstick and powder in there to be applied later Peggy ruefully thought before remembering she would have done the same thing at their ages.

There was niggling thought at the back of Peggy's mind, the bloom of German youth was just down the road in the Nissan huts; as these young men were now officially allowed to associate with the local people she was sure some of them would be at the dance. She quickly thought back to Christmas when the young man Karl had shared their day, she noticed with some uneasiness in an unguarded moment the look he gave her daughter, and how that look was returned by Sylvia. The glances between the two reminded her of her own demise when she had waited so long to marry; she wanted the best for her daughter, yet didn't want to see her throw away her youth too soon and again there was the question of Harry!

If Peggy was honest she had to admit she liked Karl, he was very polite and had explained to them at Christmas in his really quite good English the war wasn't the German soldiers fault just like the English who were called up and had to fight.

Peggy watched Harry's eyes narrow visibly as he digested this piece of news. She knew her husband well enough to know he wouldn't say anything about what he was hearing at the time, he would save it for later in the day when they were alone and he picked out the bones of the day as they prepared for bed.

Before the war she wouldn't have worried so much about this present situation, the war had changed things so much, then it would have been unthinkable for two girls to go to a dance unaccompanied; freedom these girls enjoyed was now seen as a right, and with that freedom had come a lapse in morals.

Harry in particular had tried to instill strict morals in all the three children under their wing which included their evacuees. It was one of the reasons when it was offered they wouldn't allow Sylvia to be sent north as an evacuee when it became apparent the south of England was under threat from an invasion over the channel.

Both Harry and Peggy had seen firsthand how evacuees had been treated by many people here in this village that had arrived at the outbreak of the war, it had been a unanimous decision and nothing would induce them to let their daughter suffer the indignity that that some of the young ones had suffered here when they arrived. It was true there were people, who had treated the evacuees very well, but neither of them was going to take a chance that Sylvia might find a good place; they decided they would rather take a chance of an invasion and keep their daughter safe under their wing. At the time both Harry and Peggy had been very surprised the authorities hadn't sent Ned and Mickey up north, they along with several others in the village were allowed to remain here. Peggy was extremely grateful for this another move would have been a bad upheaval for Mickey in particular just when he had settled down so well and put his trust in them.

The two girls put on their outdoor coats preparing to leave, Sylvia's dark locks contrasted well with Janet's blonde ones, both wore reasonably high heels, with 'fully fashioned' lines painted down the back of their legs with gravy browning, they smelt of perfume too, Peggy had noted the California Poppy on her daughters dressing table which had now obviously come into play!

Peggy watched them go down the lane from the kitchen window; she now had about an hour to herself before she'd make the same journey to serve the refreshments, she and Winnie had already spent a good deal of time that afternoon preparing everything in advance at the Reading room.

As the two girls hung their coats on a hook in the small vestibule to the left at the entrance of the Reading room Jean's daughter Bridget came through the door and the three of then entered the hall together.

Sylvia liked Bridget although educated at a private school and boarded there, she didn't mind associating with the locals when she was home; she was at present on extended Easter holidays.

The Wilson family had tried to monopolize Bridget to make them like their own brood who kept themselves apart from the village children; Bridget would have none of that, she was very gregarious like her mother, good at organizing, she wasn't as domineering as Jean, her nature being quieter and more patient like her father, whose slim fine boned looks she favored.

The sound of music bursting forth from a wind up gramophone greeted the three of them as they sat down at one of the small tables strategically placed at the back of the hall; they had come early because both of the girls had promised the younger element in their households they would watch some of their entertainment.

Before the war it would have been Harry with his squeeze box as he called his accordion there to provide music, but now people led very busy lives and Harry worked long hours.

Miss Phillimore an infant teacher at the local school had stepped in with her machine and was organizing the younger ones with games. They were playing musical chairs with Ned obliging the school teacher by putting the music on and off. Sylvia smiled as Mickey made a run for the last one, to be beaten by another youngster.

Sonja and Helga came over and pulled up seats at their table, at once getting into conversation with Bridget, who wanted to know how things were with them, and when their father was to be demobbed.

'He should have come weeks ago.' Sonja said.

'I don't know what the delay is.' There was a sad tone to her voice.

'But I must say I don't mind.' She sighed. 'Mother tells us he has plans to move away.' A perplexing look in her face she looked down at her shoes.

'Helga and I like our school, and it isn't really a good time to move, I for one shall be leaving in a year.'

'Really' Bridget looking suitably sympathetic, although Sylvia knew she didn't understand the position Sonja was in, with her sheltered upbringing she had no idea how the situation was for these village children who left school at fourteen and were expected to work a 45 hour week immediately they found a job.

Bridget was already sixteen, Sylvia had heard her mother say Jean had told her it was expected after the next summer term when Bridget was seventeen she would to go to finishing school possibly in Switzerland, which had remained neutral during the war and was unaffected by the terrible devastation on the continent.

'You know the Reverent Hounsome will have told the men at the camp about this dance.' Bridget said as she changed the subject.

'Perhaps some will come, I do hope so some of them are really dishy!' Bridget gave an impish grin.

'Now they are free to come and go, it must be nice for them.' She added with a gleam in her eye.

'Yes that is true.' Janet broke in adding.

'My dad says he wonders what the position would have been if Hitler had invaded us!'

Bridget shuddered. 'It does not bear thinking about.' She declared. 'Just let's be thankful that didn't happen.'

'Yes thanks to your dad and mine!' Janet said with feeling.

'But you know I do feel sorry for these men.' Bridget continued.

'I don't like the restrictions at boarding school but at least I know that at the end of term I can go home, it is been much harder for them.'

Janet nodded in silent agreement.

Sylvia said nothing her heart began to thud in her chest—perhaps Karl would come!

The feeling of sheer pleasure went to the very depths of her being at the prospect.

CHAPTER TWELVE

Heinz was lazing on his bed staring at the ceiling after a hard day's work in the fields as Karl came into the room.

'Going to the dance tonight?' He asked

'I don't know I am so tired.' Came the reply.

They had been especially busy these last few weeks after the thick winter snow had melted; suddenly spring planting became vital to ensure the maximum growing time so they worked long hours on the farm.

Heinz lowered his eyes slowly from the ceiling into the eyes of the former panzer soldier, and slowly a smile lit up his features.

'Well I have thought about it.' He declared as he slowly swung his feet from the bed to the floor.

'Tomorrow is Sunday so there is no work so yes I will come!' He pulled himself up on his feet stretching to his full height.

'Good.' Karl immediately reached into his locker for his shaving gear, taking a towel from the top he put it under his arm and quickly made his way to the washroom.

'I leave the soap for you when I have finished, I still have a slither left.' He called over to Heinz as he left the room.

'Thanks I have used my supply for this week.' Heinz said adding.

'It will be good when that stuff comes off the rations!'

A short time later a small contingent of the former prisoners left the encampment together. The men were in a good mood, they laughed, cajoled and teased each other in their native tongue as they walked along; the news that this year most of them would return home had a good effect on their mood, and the fact that they were now not restricted brought a new spirit to them all.

It was quite a long walk to the village from the camp and they kept to the roads built by the Americans, the fields either side were waterlogged because the heavy snow they had experienced that winter had melted and this taking its time to drain away.

Karl was more than a little apprehensive about this evening, he was sure that Sylvia would be there Ned had indicated this when the two of them had worked together earlier that day

Karl liked Ned, over time during the many hours they worked together the younger man confided in Karl about his background and the way things were with his mother; Karl found it very difficult to understand how a mother could treat her son in this way.

In turn Karl told Ned about his own family and Ned sympathized with his predicament

Ned also explained how Peggy and Harry had been surrogate parents to him and how grateful he was that he'd been evacuated to their house, he went on to tell Karl about his life before the war and how hard it had been in the back streets of London. Going on to explained to Karl why Harry was so hostile to the German prisoners.

'But the First World War was years ago, like the English, few of the German men who fought in this last war really wanted too. Surely it is time to let go of any grudges?' Karl had retorted after this conversation unusually sharply for him.

'You would have thought so.' Ned's quiet reply took the heat out of the situation; Ned was wise beyond his years perhaps as a result of being evacuated at a young age, also having to make a stand against his mother.

'Just thought I'd warn you about Harry.' Ned said as they finished the task they were doing, he was conscious of the spark between Sylvia and Karl, he had observed over the dinner table at Christmas, and thought it could only bring trouble. Sylvie had been like an older sister to him and Mickey, they'd spent so much of their formative years together under her parent's roof and like a brother Ned as going to look out for her.

'I should just be careful.' Ned warned with real feeling as he prepared to leave.

'Harry can be very protective of his daughter, and he has a quick temper which he can lose very easily.'

'Yes I will be.' Karl was rather shocked; he had never mentioned his interest in Sylvia to anyone, was it that obvious he had an interest there?

'Well just remember what I have said.' Ned tapped the side of his nose knowingly.

'I wouldn't want you to be on the receiving end of Harry's temper.'

'Thanks for the advice.' Deep down Karl felt a certain foreboding, although knowing one thing for sure it wouldn't stop what he felt for Sylvia!

Peggy and Winnie had just put out the trestle tables and brought out the bridge rolls filled with egg and cress together with fairy cakes and biscuits when the contingent from the camp made a noisy entrance in the Reading room, their noisy boots echoing on the wooden floorboards above the children who were singing at one end of the room.

A buzz went round as they now stood rather hesitantly in the centre not knowing where to go.

Over a dozen in all Peggy reckoned doing a swift count, hoping there would be enough refreshments to go round.

With the young men from the village over eighteen away on national service the local lads seemed mere boys in comparison with these men they really stood out. No longer in prison garb they had been made to wear until recently, they were nicely dressed, many extremely attractive, tall and broad shouldered and this hadn't gone unnoticed by the local community, most of whom were concerned about the affect this would have on the young girls in the village.

Bridget immediately went over to the men and commenced introducing herself in their mother tongue; taking the men round to meet the locals she suggested they sat at the tables scattered about the hall, and then she invited the locals to help the men to the food and drink on offer, with this she broke the ice.

Out of the corner of her eye, Peggy noticed Karl had sat with Muriel and her heart lifted; Muriel was a bit on the flighty side so she was hopeful that would be a good thing!

Karl was none too pleased to be at a table with two young ladies he didn't know, fortunately Heinz was with him, so the two of them sat quietly whilst the girls at Bridget's request fetched them some refreshments; these they ate in silence.

Having cleared up the tables and washed up, Winnie and Peggy got ready for their departure; Peggy immediately going round to the younger ones she had promised to take home with her; these included Mickey, and Hugo.

Sonja and Helga were fooling about on the fringe of a group of older ones and very reluctant to leave especially as Ned was allowed to stay on; Sonja complained loudly that she was almost fourteen, and under much protest collected her coat marching along in the rear of Peggy's small party.

'Dad will be along for you at nine thirty sharp!' Peggy called to Sylvia as she and Winnie went towards the door with the younger ones in tow.

Sylvia grimaced. 'I could always walk back with Ned!'

'Dad will be here!' Peggy's voice had a definite air about it.

Sylvia looked over to Janet, who shrugged her shoulders, her father would probably be down the pub and she would have to find her own way home, which admittedly was nearer the hall, and not down a dark lane like Harry and Peggy's cottage, and she was nearly two years older.

Bridget took in Sylvia's expression and smiled sweetly.

'Never mind you will be sixteen this year, won't you?' She said.

'Yes in May. But that won't stop my dad. He is very protective.' Sylvia didn't add he will want to see who I am with, even though the thought went through her mind.

'Well thank your lucky stars he is, I have always had to stand on my own two feet, with my Pa an invalid and my mother always busy with committees and things.' Bridget looked down at her feet as if not wanting to meet Sylvia's eyes.

'Besides at boarding school there is very little freedom that is why I enjoy it so much here.' She raised her face her cheeks pink.

'Yes, sorry I should have thought!' Sylvia suddenly felt very guilty, remembering Bridget's dad's terrible injuries.

'Mum will be here later though.' Bridget said.

'She wouldn't let me go up that dark lane to our house alone, so I don't think my situation is much different from yours really.'

'No of course.' Sylvia's gave a rather terse reply, thinking in her heart her situation was very different from Bridget's sheltered life!

Miss Philimore who was also the local infant school teacher had now wound up the gramophone and put the music in a dance mode, and a waltz belted out across the hall.

One of the PoW's came up bowed low to Bridget indicating his hand towards the dance floor. Bridget went off on his arm, chatting away in German.

Sylvia was envious, she wished she had the sort of education that Bridget had where other languages were taught. Then immediately she felt ashamed of her thoughts, Bridget was a kind hearted girl who never put on airs and graces for all the advantages of her privileged background which her parents could afford to give to their only child.

Sylvia watched Bridget on the floor, then she turned her eyes in another direction and saw Muriel brazenly sidled towards an assembly of men now grouped together at the edge of the dance floor and single one out easing him towards the dance floor, Sylvia couldn't believe her eyes.

Muriel was dancing with Karl!

Sylvia felt fury rise inside her, she had never liked Muriel, a silly giggly girl who was in her opinion much to forward for her own good, and she tried to look away but found she couldn't.

Karl's face turned Sylvia's direction and she could see the grimace on his face, it was clear he wasn't enjoying the experience of Muriel's charms, but was obviously too polite to say so.

As they turned in the waltz he looked again in Sylvia's direction and he could see the hurt in her eyes, he hated the position this girl had put him in!

Muriel was everything he disliked most in a girl, silly and giggly; he had wanted his first dance to be with Sylvia, indeed the only one he wanted to dance with was Sylvia! Why had this silly girl singled him out?

The record finished on the gramophone and with it a lull, Karl firmly escorted Muriel back to her seat, just as Heinz came up behind him, giving Karl the perfect excuse to turn and talk to his friend.

'What do you think about that blonde girl over there?' Heinz asked his friend.

Karl followed his gaze.

'She looks very nice.' He told Heinz, taking in the fact that she was sitting alongside Sylvia!

'Do you think we could go over? Heinz looked doubtful.

'I don't see why not, we are free agents now remember?' Karl said.

'Anyway I know the other girl, I spent Christmas at her parents' home, and so let me introduce you to her friend.' Karl led the way walking smartly over to the girls table.

Sylvia looked up from her lemonade she was drinking straight into the eyes of Karl; her heart missed a beat as the two men drew up chairs and sat down at the girls table.

'This is Heinz.' Karl introduced his friend as he tried to draw his eyes away from Sylvia's that were mesmerizing him.

'This is Janet, my friend.' Sylvia said turning her face away, she didn't want Karl to see her hot cheeks.

Heinz took Janet's hand and held it for a long moment, it was obvious from the start that Heinz found this lady attractive and by the look on Janet's face it seemed the feeling was mutual

The two couples passed the evening in deep conversation with intermittent time for dancing.

Karl often having to intervene when Heinz found a certain English word hard to find or pronounce, this added a bit of fun and laughter to the conversation, in fact later when they compared notes later neither girl could remember having such a good evening for a very long time.

So engrossed were they that Sylvia got quite a shock when she looked at the clock high on the wall and discovered it was almost nine twenty five.

She got up from her seat in a hurry, her dad was due at nine thirty and he was always a punctual man, it wouldn't do for her to be sitting here with Karl!

Karl concerned, took in the fearful look that had come over Sylvia's face.

'Are you alright?'

'Yes. I have to get my coat; my dad is coming for me at 9 30 and he is always sharp.' She was flustered now.

'Alright I understand.' Karl said softly understanding completely now the reasons for her change of mood.

'I shall see you again.' He added softly touching her on the cheek.

'Yes.' She added shyly, although her thoughts saying to her this was definitely going to happen!

Sylvia walked on air as she made her way to the cloakroom, Karl's last words ringing in her ears

'I shall see you again.' Too right he would if she had anything to do with it.

'Oh there you are.' Harry who had obviously just arrived stood framed in the outside door.

She took her coat from its hook, and Harry tenderly wrapped it around her.

'Do it up it's a chill wind tonight.' Her father told her as he took her scarf and wrapped it round her neck.

Sylvia didn't give a backward glance as the two of them made their way out of the door; she wasn't going to rock the boat just yet by giving her father any inkling of how the night had gone and who she had been with.

CHAPTER THIRTEEN

Gisela had woken really early just as the sun had appeared over the horizon turning the pale green distempered walls of the bedroom a pale shade of yellow.

Stretching out her arms, she hit her elbow on the wooden headboard making pins and needles run down her arm. 'Drat' she said to herself as she drew the limb back beneath the warm sheets massaging the sore spot until the feeling came back; then she extended her fingers over the vacant space by her side, rubbing the cool linen there with her hand.

At last the day had arrived, from today Don would occupy this vacant place, he had been away for most of the five and a half long years of war.

She had expected him to come home several months ago; then suddenly with no real explanation this had changed, it was difficult to understand this because Don had written and said that his planned work with someone in authority in the RAF was all set up to commence quite soon after the original discharge date he had been given.

'It is the way forward.' Don had written at the time full of enthusiasm for the project of prefabricated houses this man wanted him on board to help build, using his expertise as an engineer.

'So many houses have been destroyed and so many have to be built.' He had enthused in his letter.

Recognizing that this was true, Gisela had to agree this was the case, although very few houses in this small village had been destroyed by the bombing, she knew all too well how bad the situation was in the large towns and cities.

Gisela wasn't unhappy that Don had this enthusiasm for a good job for their future. BUT and it was a big but, at the back of her mind there were always thoughts about the way she had been treated when she first came back from Germany at the beginning of the war, people had been so unkind to her and to her children. She was still a German, admittedly an Austrian German but most people didn't know the difference and the upheaval again when they were settled so comfortably here with good friends and neighbours like Peggy was hard to take.

And then there was the question of Don's present job here on the farm. Farmer Phillips had let them have this cottage which was a tied cottage on the understanding Don would return to work on the farm on his demob, Gisela knew this was the last thing on Don's mind; he had no intentions of working on the farm any longer than he had too.

Gisela felt bad about letting this benefactor down.

One thing had made her feel a lot happier, was that Don hadn't mentioned work or what he intended to do in very recent letters so she thought perhaps he may have had second thoughts about the housing project she hoped this was the case because perhaps it meant the family could stay here! So could she look forward to the future with renewed confidence putting problems in the distance and recent past behind her?

It seemed she and Don would never be separated again with the exception of going back to be officially demobbed it was important they built up a life together. In a way she found this prospect exciting, yet deep down was a fear of what lay ahead, so many things had changed in both their lives they were now two very different people the war had seen to that.

She knew without a doubt there were going to be some difficult days ahead as they all adjusted to family life again.

Gisela put her fingers through her long blonde hair already peppering slightly with grey at the temples then she raised herself up on one elbow and looked at her reflection in the mirror attached to the wardrobe door opposite her bed.

She smoothed down her nightdress, a pretty shade of pink made out of parachute silk by young Sylvie next door then dyed this shade by herself, the colour she decided flattered her complexion.

She looked at her reflection again, perhaps she didn't look too bad, Kirk certainly hadn't thought so, but he wasn't Don!

How would HE feel? That was a question!

Her thoughts turned again to Kirk; he had liked what he saw, and that at the time it had made her feel better about herself, a real woman who was desired, it sharpened her senses now as she thought of him remembering the shape of his head and deep eyes that seemed to probe the very depths of her being as she pulled the bedcovers round her neck it was almost as if she could feel his warm arms about her.

She lay in this position for quite a few minutes savoring her memories. Then with a big sigh she firmly pushed these thoughts aside, they just had to stay at the back of her mind forever; they couldn't be allowed to surface ever again if she was to give this marriage a chance.

Don could never know about this liaison even though nothing improper took place. He wasn't the forgiving type and he had a terrible temper if he ever found out she would never be allowed to forget it!

There were more pressing problems to deal with, the most important one was Don's relationship with his children, nearly all their entire lives, and she had virtually brought them up alone, now they had to learn to be a family again.

Even when Don had leave over the war years it had been for a very brief time and not enough time to build up a rapport with his children, during the last two years he hadn't been home at all.

Would the children get on with their father was the query that gone round and round in her brain for months now. Sonja was almost 13 and in another year would be ready to go out to work, Helga was 18 months younger, and just a year separated her and Hugo, as things were now they were a happy family unit the children were well behaved, and most people said they were a credit to her, how would the family life pan out now with Don here all the time was the question.

Gisela looked towards the bright sunlight coming through the window, shielding her eyes she could just see the edge of a red, white and blue union jack as it fluttered from the top of the window just out of reach; Hugo had put it there yesterday with a huge welcome home sign for his father.

She brushed her hand over her forehead, it was Hugo she worried about most of all. To date he had never actually known a father figure in his life, in fact he had never really spent any quality time with his father at all!

Don had welcomed his daughters, but Gisela was horrified at Don's attitude when she found herself pregnant just months after Helga was born, he told her to get rid of the baby as they couldn't afford another child, abhorrent to Gisela, she just wouldn't do that. Don was adamant and made sure she knew that the baby wasn't welcome when he arrived, because it was a son, it seemed to her he resented the new baby even more.

It was a particularly hard time, the depression that existed at the time made it impossible for Don to get work. Hugo was a very grizzly baby and Gisela got no rest, Although he couldn't get work and was at home a great deal of the time Don didn't lift a finger to help her all he seemed to do was complain about the crying baby.

Desperately unhappy and worn out attending to three small children Gisela became depressed and short tempered; she longed to go home to her parents where she knew help would be at hand within her extended family,

The clincher came when she observed Don with some of his nephews, she abhorred the way he treated them, realizing then her husband had a cruel streak in him; she immediately made a decision, she wasn't prepared to live with this and see her children especially Hugo treated that way.

There was a particularly bad quarrel between the two of them which resulted in Gisela packing her bags and going back to her homeland, there she would have stayed, if it hadn't been for the war.

Now her hopes rested on the fact that perhaps time had mellowed her husband, if it hadn't she really wasn't sure that she and Don had a future; sadly she also knew what had been staring her in the face for a long time. Don wasn't only a virtual stranger to his children he was almost a stranger to her!

Sleep was now elusive with so much buzzing through her mind, she felt cold and decided to go down stairs perhaps a hot cup of tea would help. Swinging her slender legs out of the snow white sheets onto the white cotton counterpane she made sure her feet landed on the small slip mat by the bed and not on the cold brown linoleum that covered most of the bedroom floor. Feeling for her slippers with her feet under the bed, she slipped them on her feet, and then crept down the narrow stairs so as not to disturb the rest of the family.

The kettle soon boiled and she sat for a long while warming her hands on the sides of the cup, raising the brown liquid to her lips it slipped down into her stomach warming her through and making her feel more comfortable.

She heard a sound from outside and got to her feet looking out of the kitchen window; Peggy was already about, putting her washing through the mangle that stood in the yard, the water from the rollers rattling into the galvanized small bath resting underneath, Gisela stood for a moment gazing fondly at her neighbour, such a hard working lady put her to shame.

Spurned on Gisela began her daily chores going to the meat safe on the wall outside the back door, waving briefly to Peggy who was still turning the mangle.

Don had complained often about the 'bully beef' that seemed to be the main stay of their meals in the services; so Gisela decided she was going to prepare a goulash which she was sure he would enjoy for his first meal at home,

Putting some skirt of beef she had managed to get from the butcher into a large pan, she covered it with stock, congratulating herself that she'd been prudent enough to save her ration coupons for this occasion. Then sitting down at the kitchen table she prepared the vegetables whilst the kettle she had just refilled buzzed merrily on the stove. Putting together other ingredients which included some herbs from the garden she stirred it all together before adding it to the pan on the stove to stew quietly on the back burner, from experience she knew skirt of beef could be very tough without a long slow cook.

She heard the kettle splashing its contents onto the stove so she quickly removed it to stop a white ring appearing on what had recently been black leaded. Quickly pouring the water over just a few more tea leaves she added to the pot, she sat with another cup of tea savoring the peace, realizing possibly this would be the last time for a long time she would actually have time to herself without Don demanding attention if he was in his usual form.

Don dropped the two khaki duffle bags to the ground after scrambling out of an army lorry which screeched to a halt on the main road at a point closest to the village.

George who had prepared to jump down with him was having his usual banter with his army mates who had yet to arrive at their various destinations; it was a few moments later that George dropped down by his side bashing the side of the truck indicating to the driver to draw away.

Within seconds came the sound of the revving up of the engine before the lorry moved speedily away.

The two men waved to their comrades hanging out of the back of the lorry until it was out of sight; then picking up their duffle bags they threw them over their shoulders and set out on the short walk down the stony pathway that led to the homes.

They were unusual companions George was squat with broad shoulders, Don a tall thin man, his shoulders seeing narrower than they were because of his height, both men had been in the services for most of the duration of the war.

The difference didn't end there. For George it was a real wrench to part company with his comrades, he loved the camaraderie of his fellow service men and the freedom it gave him as 'One of the Boys.' he admitted he didn't like the fighting during the offensive and was glad that was over but he did like being in the thick of things, a change to life in civvy street was going to be far from easy transition for him.

Don on the other hand as an NCO, thought himself in a different class from other servicemen, he wasn't particularly liked for it.

There was another thing the two men did have in common and that was an eye for the ladies, this was the reason why they were both returning now quite a few months after most of their units had been discharged, they both caught a nasty case of Pox in Egypt so they had been kept behind until it had hopefully been cured; they were not the only ones to fall victim to this malady. It was covered up by the British army, but it was rife amongst the men who found the delights of the Kasbah hard to resist with its call girls and loose women; being far from home the lure of this was almost endemic amongst some of the servicemen.

As Don and George walked together on the rough stone road that led to the village Don glancing sideways at his companion saying in a firm voice that had just a trace of doubt in it.

'We must be sure as we have previously agreed that the truth is never told as to why we have not been discharged before this.'

George smiled confidently as he took a cigarette packet from his breast pocket and passed one of the white sticks inside to Don which he lit up immediately.

'Well as only you and I and the army know about it, it can remain our secret.' George said as he drew deeply on a cigarette now firmly between his teeth.

'It will, won't it?' Don turned to his companion and sounded even more doubtful, he trusted George, but, and it was a big but he wasn't sure he could trust him; George was fond of his ale which had the habit of loosening his tongue on certain occasions. George also thought a lot of things a joke which Don a more serious minded person didn't find funny, and it was possible the truth could come out this way?

Don frowned he had a lot more to lose than his erstwhile companion. George's wife was a long suffering woman putting up with George's many infidelities even before the war, and he had no real ambitions for the future like Don did; which was why in Don's opinion George was still a private in the army after six years of service.

Don rounded again on his companion, repeating the message.

'So much depends on my wife not finding out, it could affect my whole future. You understand how important that is?' He had to get this message through; this was the last chance they would be able to talk about it before they reached their homes.

'Yes of course!' You have my word, I won't tell anyone!' George gave Don a sly smile, he didn't really like Don George had the opinion the fellow thought too much of himself, but circumstances had decreed they had been in this situation together, under a normal situation there paths would never have crossed except perhaps to share a pint down the pub on a Saturday night.

It was a terrible shock when Don first found out that he had picked up the malady after a night out, and worse was to come when he found out it would mean that he would have to stay longer away from home until he'd been cured especially as it meant his plans for the immediate future had to be shelved.

He'd been going to the special unit a few days for treatment when George made an appearance.

Don was really shocked to find him there although he was from the same village Don didn't have a lot of time for this man. Previously their paths had crossed a few times, it was known although he was married he was also a bit of a philanderer and in the past only time Don had actually had any real contact with him was at the village pub on a Saturday night before they had both gone into the services soon after the commencement of the war.

Don hadn't lived long enough in the village to get to know anyone much at all he'd taken the job with Farmer Phillips as a stop gap until he was able to get a job in the profession he had been trained for.

The fact that a cottage went with the job was an added bonus when Gisela had unexpectedly returned from Austria, since joining up, he could count on two hands the weeks he had spent at home since.

This time partly because of contracting this problem he hadn't been back for over two years.

Don had big plans for his future they didn't include working on Farmer Phillips land in a remote village, he wasn't going to stay long, he knew though it was imperative that his secret was kept, not only for his marriage but also for his future job prospects, the officer with whom he'd planned to work with was a religious man and wouldn't take too kindly if he knew the truth about his delayed absence.

Don had been absolutely furious when he'd contracted the Pox because the job he had lined up was to commence almost as soon as he was to get his discharge; the delay had meant it had been a great embarrassment to have to admit that he wouldn't be available when the project began at the starting date, the officer unaware of the real problem behind the delay had kindly said he could put a job Don's way when he did became available, and that Don was to get in touch when he was finished in the services, now Don was hoping that it wouldn't be too long before he heard from his officer friend, it irked him that he would be unable to be in at the start of what was to him an important job, but there was nothing he could do about that now however much it irritated him.

The two men came to a sharp corner in the pathway and the village now panned out before them the first thing they saw were three small figures sitting on a wall looking in their direction, they waved their hands enthusiastically in the air as the men approached and as they drew closer the figures dropped from the wall and started running towards them.

Don rubbed his eyes; for a just a moment he stopped rooted to the ground in astonishment, the tall slim girl the largest of the three now hurtling towards them could be Gisela, yet the person was far too young. Then it dawned on him, it had to be Sonja his eldest! He couldn't believe how she had grown! She was almost a young woman, so the other two had to be Helga and Hugo he hardly recognized them either.

Don guessed he'd changed very little as he held his arms wide and the three of them hurtled into them; tears streamed down faces as they hugged each other close.

George stood to one side taken aback by these advents, he had no children and wasn't to know they had been given the day off school to welcome home returnees from the war.

When they had all recovered their composure they set off to walk the last few steps to the village, all five of them companionably arm in arm when they parted company at the main village road.

Don and his children making their way down the farm track to their cottage, where Gisela was anxiously waiting.

CHAPTER FOURTEEN

The smell of stale cigarette smoke and beer hit Don's nostrils as he pushed open the door of the 'Gardeners Arms' and made his way to the counter.

'A pint please' He instructed the barman who came up to serve him.

As soon as it was put it down in front of him Don took a long swig at the foaming liquid before putting down the money that he held in his hand in payment.

'You look as though you really needed that.' The barman retorted as he put the money in a wooden drawer resting under the counter.

Don's smile in reply didn't meet his eyes, but he did felt some relief as the ale passed through to his stomach, it seemed to hit the tight coil that seemed to be bound up permanently inside of him these days relaxing him somewhat.

A voice rang out from his left.

'Hi there Don do come and join us.'

Don felt a sense of dismay as he recognized George's dulcet tones; he wasn't really in the mood for company and especially not George's company! He liked his former army colleague, but his effervescent manner could sometimes be more than he could take when he wasn't in the frame of mind for it, and he wasn't in that frame of mind today!

Don glanced over in the direction of the voice and his mood sunk even lower when he saw that George had Len sitting with him at the table; he shot them both a steely grin. However much he didn't want to socialize, there was no way he could avoid their company without appearing rude.

So he picked up his pint and shuffled over to their table deposited his ale on to it before pulling up a wooden chair which he lowered his thin frame on to.

George was his usual cheery self.

'Don't see you too often in the week!' He said as he pulled a cigarette from a packet in front of him, offering the packet to the other two men who both refused.

George then he lit the cigarette in his hand and took a hard drawl, issuing the smoke from his mouth slowly.

'I was going straight home, but then changed my mind.' Don said by way of explanation.

'I needed a boost tonight, so I reckoned a pint of ale might help.' Don picked up his ale and took another long swig.

Len got suddenly to his feet, and picked up his glass.

'I am having another, do you two want a refill.' He asked

'Might as well.' George drained the small amount had left and Don did the same, passing the two pint pots over to Len to join the one he held in his hand.

'Have you any News?' George enquired when the other man was out of earshot.

'I wish there was, but I have to answer, sadly no!' Don knew exactly what George meant, it was about the job he'd been promised by the flight lieutenant which the two of them had discussed when they were confined in Egypt together.

'I watch for the post every day hoping it will come; of course the post usually arrives when I have left for work.' Don sighed. 'It is so frustrating, I thought things would have moved on in the right direction by now, you hear so much about the dire housing situation, this plan of the flight lieutenant was so promising, but nothing seems to have come to fruition yet! I want so much to get on with the project instead of wasting myself doing what I am here. And I do blame myself because if I hadn't caught the pox in Egypt I would have been in at the start of the scheme, now I have to wait until there is a place for me.'

'Yes I can see your point, but remember though what you are doing now is helping the country. Food is urgently needed as well as houses!' George said loudly.

Don looked around to make sure no one else was in earshot, and then said quietly.

'It isn't just that I have not heard, it is also the fact that Gisela has been so difficult about moving away from here, she makes the excuse that she doesn't want to uproot the children at this time.' Don sighed.

'She is more than pleased that the letter has yet to arrive. 'Don ran his fingers through his hair.

'But there is more to it than that! She likes the people here.' He looked downcast.

'And would you believe she is more than willing to put up with the basic things in that tied cottage rather than move to a home with all modern conveniences!' What do you make of that?'

'Hum well, these women have their own ideas.' George said.

'You would have thought she would appreciate us after being away for all those years. Especially when you are so ambitious, ready to put your family first and build up a good future for them'

Don gave a long sigh before he replied.

'Yes I agree, but you know sometimes I feel a stranger in my own home; it's as though I am not wanted back, I have tried to get on with my children but there is a barrier between us, and Gisela doesn't seem to be the same any more either.'

Don looked at his companion again, George really wasn't the sort of person who would understand about his wife and children, not only did he have none of his own, his wife was a quiet little thing that did just as George asked.

'Well at least she was faithful to you whilst you were away; a lot of the wives were not!' George observed trying to change the subject to a positive note.

Don raised the tone of his voice and thumped the table in front of him,

'She better had been. I have got no time for these wives who were running around after anything in a uniform!'

Just then Len came up behind him ready to put the three pints held precariously in his hands on the table.

'Here Steady!' Len admonished as he put the ale down.

'You'll spill the beer if you do that again.'

Len stood motionless for one moment then with a trace of annoyance in his voice he said.

'AND I should watch what you say! I got the end of that conversation! 'His brows knitted together

'There was nothing personal, 'George replied trying to take the heat out of the situation.

'Well, I did take it personally, what my Rose got up to at the camp when the Americans were here she told me about.' Len looked in Don's direction, the frown beneath his brows deepening, his eyes flashing.

'I think you should ask your wife if she has been as honest!'

George took in the look on Don's face and his heart hit his boots, he had bad memories of Don's temper tantrums when they had been in Egypt.

Don scraped his chair away from the table and almost threw it across the wooden floor of the pub then slinging his jacket over his shoulder he marched to the door, he slid on a wet clot of sawdust grasping the doorframe to steady him before going outside.

George rose from his seat quickly following him.

'Hey take it easy! Len is a bit sensitive about his wife; you hit him on a raw note.' He chided.

Don stood against the wall of the pub under a small canopy, it was tipping down with rain, and he held his head in his hands.

I can't help that, everyone knows about his wife! 'He retorted rather unkindly.

George could see Don's face was full of fury and his eyes were blazing.

'But what did he mean about Gisela?'

'You shouldn't take too much notice of Len.' George said as he stood in front of him hoping this comment would take the heat out of the situation.

'People in villages can be very cruel.' He continued. 'Especially when it was so obvious his wife wasn't innocent whilst he was away. That is why he reacted like he did.' George put a hand on Don's shoulder.

'You forget he has a child to prove his wife's infidelity!'

'Yes that's as maybe, but what about my wife—what about Gisela.' Don said steadying himself against the wall as just for a moment his head spun a result of drinking on an empty stomach; then he gave a deep sigh and pulled himself together.

George felt drips of rain fall down his back and moved closer under the canopy thinking deeply before he replied.

'Well Don. 'He looked the other man in the eye.

'Look at it this way, you have only Len's word for what was said about Gisela; the whole village knew what happened with his wife, I honestly have not heard anyone mention about your good lady.' He tried a smile, but was met with a scowl from the other man.

'My wife told me that the Americans welcomed the villagers to their camp, there were children's' parties and things, it could have been misconstrued by Len; he probably doesn't know the facts!'

'Perhaps that is so.' Don snapped.

'But there is no smoke without fire! I am not having my wife talked about around the village, and myself being made a laughing stock.' Don looked down and George could see he was fighting to get control of his emotions.

'Len might be the forgiving type, but I am not!' Don spat the words out.

George didn't know what to say.

'Think it over before you say anything at home. 'He suggested lamely.

Don's face was still dark with rage as he lifted his eyes to meet George's once again.

'I had better be going home.' He said.

George was now very concerned; he had got to know Don well when they had been confined together in Egypt and he remembered well his explosive temper which he often took out on someone. George himself had sometimes been on the receiving end of this, tonight with the mood he was in, would take it out on his wife?

He stood in front of Don blocking his path as the other man tried to make a move.

'Look' He said his former military companion as he tried to reason with him.

'Just watch what you say, you were not perfect when you were away and fortunately only you and I know about that! What would happen if that information got out? You only have Len's word for the fact that your wife was up at the camp; mistakes have been made.' George was pleading now.

'Please don't go home and do something you might regret.'

Don shrugged his shoulders unable in his blind fury to reply, staring at his companion he threw his jacket over his shoulder pushed George out of the way and walked off down the road in the direction of his house.

George watched him go a sinking feeling in his heart hoping that Don wouldn't take this evening's announcements out in his wife. He turned on his heel opening up the door of the pub to reunite himself with his pint and Len, deciding to himself Don was one of the most unreasonable people he had ever met, if he hadn't caught a milady for being unfaithful to his wife he wouldn't be in the position he was in now and yet he couldn't accept perhaps his wife had seen another man which could have had an entirely innocent explanation during his long years away. It was double standards but George could hardly tell Don that!

Gisela glanced at the clock, Don was late, and she guessed he had stopped off at the pub on the way home then she glanced out of the window at the rain which seemed to have come on suddenly that wouldn't put him in a good mood she thought, he hated getting wet.

She looked at the brown envelope which was propped up against one of the Worcester dogs that graced each end of the mantle shelf. It arrived this morning after Don left for work and she was sure it was the letter whose non arrival Don had worried over for weeks now, it was very official looking with Don's name typed on the front so it had to be important.

Perhaps the letter would be the answer to Don's dreams; she had been treading on eggshells for weeks round him, he had been so moody and downcast since his return home, yet for her and the children she knew the letter might have a certain foreboding.

Hugo came in stamping his feet on the coconut matting by the door after removing his shoes outside, he'd been down to the brooks with Mickey when the rain came on and his hair was now plastered on his head with rivulets running down his face. The boys liked to fish in the many small streams than crisscrossed the brooks on this flat land at the foot of the downs, in the spring there was frog spawn, then newts followed by sticklebacks, and minnows all of which were fun to catch keeping the two boys busy for hours.

'Sorry I'm late mum.' Hugo apologized as he looked at the clock.

'Never mind I expect you were enjoying yourself, best get those muddy socks off though.' Gisela admonished her son noting the wet footprints across the flagstone floor she'd polished that morning with 'cardinal red' polish.

'Then you'd better get upstairs dry your hair and read, your father will probably be in soon, he is late so he has probably gone to the pub, so it won't do for you to be down here will it?'

Hugo needed no second bidding, he tore off his socks depositing them into the dirty linen bin, then taking a biscuit from the tin on the side and a small glass of milk from the churn he balancing them in one hand as he made his way up the narrow staircase of the cottage to the attic room he occupied at the top of the cottage.

Gisela sighed as she watched him go; these couple of months since Don had been home permanently had been the most difficult in her life. Not only was he terribly moody because of the work he had to do, but he took it out on the children especially Hugo.

Gisela confided in Peggy about this problem;

'Well.' Her neighbour had commented.

'I have heard quite a few men have found the transition from their lives in the services to Civvies Street very difficult indeed especially where children are involved.' Peggy said.

'Remember up to this time you have had complete control, Don has made just brief visits home over the years; now he is home all the time he is flexing his authority over the family.' She smiled sympathetically.

'It is a difficult situation for you to be in.'

Peggy didn't add that she thought it especially difficult for Gisela with her children entering the difficult teenage years but her heart went out to her neighbour, because she knew there were other difficulties with their marriage, and this problem was just adding to it.

Gisela heard the crunch of footsteps on the gravel outside of the cottage, then the sound of Dons feet scraping the iron outside the back door. Steeling herself she looked into his countenance as he came through the door, her heart sank to her boots his face looked like thunder.

Although her heart was pounding she waited quietly whilst he removed his jacket and washed his hands in the kitchen sink; experience had taught her to say nothing when Don was in this sort of mood.

She quietly attended to the meal she had prepared for him which had been on a saucepan with a saucepan lid covering it for at least an hour.

Aware of Don's temper her first thought was that perhaps the letter would cheer him up so she reached up taking it from the mantle shelf and put alongside the knife and fork she'd laid out previously on the table.

Don sat down at the table putting his head in his hands staring at the vacant space in front of him, whilst Gisela busied herself putting his meal in front of him.

The envelope remained beside his knife; if he'd seen it he certainly didn't mention it as he silently tucked into his food.

As he finished he pushed his plate across the table and looked up into her eyes, alarm gripped as she saw there something she hadn't seen for a long time, not really since the terrible time they had before she'd returned to Austria just before the war.

To waylay what she could only think was a confrontation ahead she picked up the envelope he seemed to be ignoring.

'This came for you today. She said putting it into his hand.

'It looks official the one you have been expecting perhaps?'

Looking down he ripped the envelope open pulling out the sheet of paper and quickly read the contents.

To Gisela's relief a different expression came over her husband's face, and she was grateful that at least this must be the news Don had been waiting for!

It seemed whatever had been troubling him before he came through the door had suddenly vanished, although he didn't say anything his expression completely changed and he sat silently looking at the table cloth.

Gisela was used to Don's silences, at times he treated her as though she was an imbecile; she had come to realize that a lot of English men treated their wives in this way as though they had no brain and didn't even need a proper education; she though perhaps that is why Don was so hard on Hugo and expected a lot of him the girls in his book would just grow up to be obedient housewives and mothers.

The war had changed things, girls were more outgoing now and Don would find that out especially as the girls were now in their teens.

Don looked his wife in the eye.

'The letter was the news I was expecting.' He said, and Gisela was relieved to see a smile now played at the corner of his mouth.

'And it appears that they have given me the job because I am a family man. 'The smile didn't reach his eyes and she could see that there was still something that he was not pleased about and her heart sank as he continued.

'We shall be moving into a prefabricated home they have allocated us, one of the first they have built on this estate in one of the suburbs of London, where I shall be working.' He paused for a moment and his eyes grew dark and narrow, she knew immediately whatever was bothering him was about to be revealed.

'I was in the pub tonight and Len suggested you went up to the camp when the Americans were here; the whole village knows the reputation his wife had for entertaining those men!' His cheeks coloured up as he spoke and Gisela could see he was far from pleased about this information.

'Perhaps you can tell me whether or not it what I heard tonight is true.'

For a moment Gisela didn't know what to say, her liaison with Kirk had been entirely innocent and every time he'd been here at her home Peggy had been here with them. Unlike Rose whose house was in the middle of the council estate where comings and goings were observed by many people, their cottages were down this lane which was set a bit apart from the main road that ran through the village, she was sure only she and Peggy knew about Kirk's visits.

'I did go up to the camp.' Gisela said her voice faltering as she added.

'The Americans were very good, giving parties and goodies to the children, most of the families went up for the treats that were on offer for everyone.' She looked down not wanting to meet his eyes, he observed this at once.

'As long as the treat enjoyed wasn't a relationship with my wife!' Don retorted sarcastically.

'Nothing improper took place.' Gisela said truthfully, turning her reddening cheeks towards the sink where she began washing up Don's plate.

Don got swiftly up from the table and grasped her arm rather tightly.

'You are quite sure?' He looked her in the eye his jaw set firm. 'It seems to me you are hiding something!'

'No I am not! I can assure you of that, please let go of my arm you are hurting me.' Her voice was firm although she trembled inside afraid of her husband in this mood.

He let go of her arm, and she ruefully rubbed the red mark he'd left.

Don was silent for a while, his eyes not leaving her; she could feel them boring into her back as she finished the chores.

'I shall have to take your word for it!' He said finally as he walked away from the table to relax in the sitting room.

She glanced in at him a few moments later he had taken a cigarette out of a packet in his pocket and lit up which appeared to relax him a bit.

'Thank goodness that letter arrived today.' She told herself silently; she could never mention that Kirk had been to this cottage, and fortunately she had Peggy for back up should that ever came out, but knowing Don's temper she just had to hope the truth was never revealed.

CHAPTER FIFTEEN

Late May 1947

Mr. Morishstein his spectacles perched on the end of his large nose was carefully cutting out dark grey suiting to a pattern he'd arranged on a long table.

Sylvia glanced over at her employer then she waited patiently whilst he snipped through the last piece of the material knowing to talk to him when he was thus engaged could result in a mistake in the cutting which would ruin a whole piece of material.

Finally he raised his right hand, with the scissors poised in midair a triumphant look came into his face as he turned to find Sylvia's face turned expectantly towards his.

'I have finished that seam you asked me to unpick. 'She explained.

'What would you like me to do now?' She said expectantly.

He glanced over his tortoiseshell glasses at a clock high on the wall above them then he stroked his short goatee beard thoughtfully before rubbing his back which was aching from being in the same position over the bench for such a considerable time.

'It is five twenty, and you have done a good days work so you can leave now, it will save you rushing for the bus.' He gave Sylvia a smile that lit up the corners of the eyes that stared out from his thin face.

'Thank you.' Sylvia kept the reply brief, she knew from experience saying anything more would be lost on him as her employer had already lowered the scissors and was again snipping away at the material.

She mused how he managed to keep the wide sleeves of his black tunic out of the way of the large scissors in his hand as she made her way to the coat stand to put on her outdoor clothes.

He was a wiry man and the skull cap he wore on the back of his head with an almost defiant air he had refused to remove throughout the war years so there was no mistaking Jewish his roots.

Sylvia had great admiration for him, proud to show anyone of his heritage, not that you could mistake it with his surname, style of dress and large nose.

Mr. Morishstein commanded a lot of respect locally, people came to do business because not only was he was good at his work, he was also honest and respectful; when people locally discussed the persecution of the Jews in Nazi Germany there had been a great deal of sympathy for him especially when it became common knowledge he'd lost quite a few of close relatives in the concentration camps.

Sylvia at first found it a bit difficult to discuss her relationship with Karl at work especially when the terrible atrocities in the concentration camps were published and spoken of; even though the war had been over for nearly two years fresh things were still coming to light. When she did tell Mr. Morishstein about it she found her employer was a man who bore no grudges.

He just said.

'There are good and bad in all people.' Sylvia sincerely wished her father felt the same!

She looked at her reflection now sideways in a tall slim mirror by the coat stand as she prepared to leave the premises, flicking her long hair down her back she took her jacket from the hook and swung it over her shoulders, it was a cream boxy affair with a dark red collar that came just above her narrow waist it went well with her pencil slim skirt, that finished half way down her calf.

Taking a second look into the mirror to see that her appearance looked alright, she took her powder compact and lipstick from her bag to refresh her makeup before pulling the door handle towards her, the sound of the small bell that rang when it was opened made its presence felt she raised her hand in a swift salute to her employer, he waved the scissors in her direction as a parting gesture.

Closing the shop door quickly behind her she sauntered down the side street where the tailors shop was situated into the high street, there was a stiff breeze blowing off the sea which funneled down into this road so she drew her coat more firmly around her shoulders to keep out the cooling evening air.

As she wasn't in a hurry she paused for a moment to observe the hats that were on display at the shop on the corner; pleased to see an extremely pretty one in cream with a red rose gracing its side which had been admired by her for some time hadn't yet been sold.

People didn't seem to wear hats so much now she thought to herself, people of her mother's generation still did, in fact most of the people she knew of that age never went out without a hat on their heads and it had only been since 1942 that the church of England had abolished the ruling forcing all women to wear hats in church perhaps she reasoned that had something to do with the clothing rationing?

She glanced at the clock in the middle of the square, it was not quite five thirty she had time to kill, just time to pop into Woolworths before they closed to pick up a few Kirby grips for her hair, she sped past the few coach built prams still deposited at the end of the shop by the mothers finishing their shopping, to the haberdashery counter.

Tonight she was in no rush for her bus as she was staying in town to meet Karl, and they were going to the pictures together; they had met at a few of the dances at the village hall since the spring, but this was the first time they had actually been to the cinema together alone.

Coming out of Woolworths with her purchase she glanced again at the clock. Karl would only just be finishing work, then he would have go back to his accommodation, wash and change before getting the bus into town to meet her at around six thirty; she smiled to herself her heart racing she couldn't wait to see him!

Sylvia had felt nervous about the prospect all day, which is why she had to unpick that seam at work that she had stitched badly.

They had to make the best of the time that was available; soon it would be the busy time on the farm with haymaking into the harvest. With many men still on active duty and with double summertime sometimes it was necessary to work on the farm until eleven o clock at night, so Karl would be expected to work long late hours and that meant she would hardly ever see him.

Sylvia continued along the high street until she came to the door of Lyons teashop which was situated opposite the seafront and the bus depot.

Going up to the counter to order a cup of tea and a sandwich she saw to her delight one of their pink buns covered in tiny white sugar lumps had yet to be sold, any sweet was a treat with the rationing especially on sugar, so she ordered this also, then she settled down by the window to watch the world go by.

From this seat in the café she had a good view of the seafront.

It was nice to see the foreshore clear now of the landmines and rolls of barbed wire that had been there for so long, there were very few people about to enjoy the promenade and the glorious summer weather that had followed the exceptionally cold winter, most of them were on the opposite side of the road in the bus queue that snaked around the corner

Usually at this time she was there too, jostling to get on the bus with the rest of the crowds and workers that appeared as the shops closed their doors about five thirty.

She smiled as two large gulls fought over a tasty morsel of fish presuming they had gleaned from one of the boats tied up on the pebbles that met the tarmac on the promenade. The fishermen had long since packed up, and were probably at home resting before setting sail later to fish through the night.

Sylvia gave a deep sigh as her conscience was pricked her again as it had done all day; against her better nature had told her mother a white lie saying she was off to the pictures with Janet after work, this weighted heavily on her as it went against everything that she believed in.

Actually it wasn't her mother that was against her relationship with Karl it was her dad, but Sylvia didn't want to put her mother in the position to lie to her own husband had the question arisen as to where she was this evening.

She wished that her parents were more like Janet's who welcomed Heinz into their home, with no animosity even though he had been a German Officer in the third Reich, whereas Karl was just a conscript!

Heinz and Janet had become close since their encounter at the village hop in the early spring, as he was due to return home soon he spent every moment he could with Janet.

Sylvia then reasoned to herself would she like a dad like Janet's who spent much of his spare time in the public house, her dad was a good man! If only he realize that Karl was a good man too and his nationality had nothing to do with what sort of a person he was!

A tap on her shoulder broke off her thought pattern and she turned to see Bridget Finch's dark brown eyes gazing at her, in one hand she was clasping several bags and a cup of tea was precariously in the other one.

'Err—Hello.' Sylvia got quickly to her feet pulled out a chair from the opposite side of her table, and took the cup from Bridget's hand as Bridget collapsed gratefully into it.

'I didn't expect to see you in the town. I have just been to collect some things for when I return to school.' Bridget said breathlessly adding.

'I am home on my Whitsun break. And I have just missed the bus!' She smiled.

'Mother usually picks me up but she is busy at one of her committee meetings with the vicar and Miss Baker this afternoon.' Bridget said by way of explanation

'There is twenty minutes to wait for the next bus so I thought a cup of tea would be nice!'

Bridget flexed her long legs under the table then slipped off her shoes.

'Ah that's better, my feet are really aching! That's the problem with fashionable shoes, but I love them they are so much better than the flats I have to wear at school.'

'Yes what price we pay for glamour.' Sylvia said sympathetically although her mind was in a quandary, her mother was due at Jean Finch's tomorrow it was more than possible that she would see Bridget there, how was she going to explain that she should have been with Janet?

'Did you miss the bus?' Bridget enquired.

'No I am off to the pictures.' Sylvia said quietly.

'That's a shame you could have given me a hand with all these parcels.' Bridget said with an impish grin.

'I shouldn't worry, there is bound to be someone on the bus from the village who will help.'

Sylvia could feel her cheeks burning; somehow she had to get out of this!

'Are you meeting Janet?' Bridget asked knowing the two of them spent a lot of time together.

'Actually—No.' Sylvia confessed

'I am meeting Karl.' She looked uncomfortable and swallowed hard

'Oh!' Bridget put the cup half way to her lips down on the table with a small bump.

'Oh!' She said again. 'I see.'

Taking in the slightly worried look on Sylvia's face; Bridget's quick mind caught the drift.

'Your mum thinks your meeting Janet?' She said slowly.

'Well yes.' Sylvia admitted.

Bridget picked up her cup again and taking a long swig she gazed at Sylvia over the rim.

'So it's best I don't tell your mother I have seen you this evening?' She gave an impish grin.

'Do you mind?' Sylvia's tone was most apologetic, yet her eyes had a pleading quality about them.

'I will probably see your mother tomorrow, and if I don't mention that I have seen you tonight, I don't have to lie do I.' Bridget said glancing down at her watch.

'Well—that's if you don't mind.' Sylvia felt relief flow through her veins.

'Mum's the word.' Bridget looked again out of the window.

'By the look of that queue I had better go and join it or I won't get on the next bus will I and I don't want to be here all night.'

Sylvia followed her gaze, the queue for their village bus had begun to snake round the corner out of sight Sylvia noted that Janet was there; her job at the Home and Colonial store meant she couldn't leave on the dot of five thirty when the shop closed, the girls there were expected to clean up before they left the premises and quite often Janet caught a different bus home to Sylvia.

'I think you are right!' Sylvia agreed with Bridget secretly glad now she'd had this conversation with Bridget as the latter could have mentioned in passing to her mother tomorrow she'd seen Janet on the bus home tonight.

Bridget swiftly got to her feet, gathered her bags together and makes her way swiftly to the door.

'Enjoy your evening.' She put her finger on closed lips.

'Mums the word!' Was her parting shot as she went through the café door.

Sylvia watched her go, very elegant in her dark green cape her long hair flowing behind her as she struggled with her bags; how Sylvia wished she had an uncomplicated life like her!

The bus now in the distance was getting ever nearer when a short while later she stood at the stop waiting for Karl; excitement burning deep within her as it always did when in expectation of seeing him.

Then suddenly the bus was here, she could see Karl through the window glass noting the way his hair curled over his forehead and the shape of his face as he stood ready to alight. He almost flew down the step to get off the vehicle, his blue eyes finding hers making her heart flip.

Taking her small hand into his he kept it wrapped up as they walked round to the cinema to join a queue for the film behind a board that stated 'House Full.'

They had to wait some twenty minutes before they got to the front, and the commissionaire announced that two one shilling seats were now available.

Sylvia paid for the tickets at the kiosk; Karl received very little money and this was a grouch of the PoW's who often did more than a full day's work either on the land or on other projects such as building and road works with little recognition at all.

Inside the confines of the cinema they followed the torch of the usherette as she saw them to their seats which mercifully were on the end of a row so they didn't have to clamber past anyone else; it also meant Karl's long legs could have a bit more room with the aisle seat.

It was warm in the cinema so Karl helped Sylvia off with her jacket, the seating pricked at her back through her thin blouse so she moved closer to him.

The secondary film had started so she tried to concentrate on this but she was conscious of his presence and kept looking sideways at the strong contours of his face. Karl looked down and took her small hand in his own large one, tired from her days work she rested her head against his shoulder; he smelt of the outdoors and fresh air; once or twice she nodded off waking with a start from one of these naps to find his arm firmly encased around the back of her neck; which he quickly removed when the lights went up for the interval.

Karl went to fetch them tubs of ice cream which they ate with relish as they listening to the organ playing.

His eyes misted over as he looked into hers.

'It reminds me of home.' He said.

She squeezed his hand to show she knew how this emotion affected him,

When the lights went down once more she found herself looking into his face as once again he rested his arm along the back of her chair.

The Pathe news had him sitting upright in his seat and she felt him stiffen as it referred to the Russians and their power over East Germany; observing the set of his jaw she once again pressed her hand into his squeezing his large one as the news continued realizing how hard it was for him to see his homeland displayed like this.

The main film was called 'The Constant Heart.' A wartime drama about English prisoners of war, it seemed to be a favorite subject of film makers recently.

She took sideways glances at Karl wondering how he felt about the films subject seeing as he was in a similar position in reverse, although the prisoners represented in the film were not free to move about like Karl was!

Sylvia knew Karl's understanding of English was still limited yet he seemed to take in the part Michael Redgrave was portraying without any difficulty.

She felt warm comfortable and safe; his strong features and square chin stood out in the semi darkness, springy fair curls hugged his head and side burns, his seven o'clock shadow rubbed against her cheek as he bent to kiss her lightly on the forehead when he realized her eyes were upon him, he lightly traced the shape of her face with his fingers in the darkness, and she longed to feel those same warm lips on hers.

After the film they waited at a fish and chip shop to be served, and then they companionably dipped their fingers into a shared bag of chips liberally dosed in vinegar and salt which Karl insisted on paying for.

'I have come to like these.' He whispered in her ear.

'I am glad' Sylvia replied, adding

'They are quite an English institution.'

He smiled, 'Would you believe that is something I was told, when I first came to England after being interned in America.'

'And you like them?' She smiled up at him and he lightly kissed her lips relishing the salt and vinegary taste.

'I like you better! You taste good.' He teased kissing her again as she smiled up into his face.

They wiped their fingers on the newspaper that covered the greaseproof paper the chips had been wrapped in before disposing of it in a nearby bin.

Then they went to the bus stop together.

Sylvia aware that her father would be at the other end to meet her, dare not let take them take the bus home together, so they had to part company here and Karl would get the next bus back to their village which left half an hour later.

It tore at his heart strings to stand in the shadows and watch her board and then take a seat on the bus, her shiny black hair framing her face she smiled down at him through the window.

It was in his opinion ludicrous that they had to take separate bus journeys home; all he wanted to do was take care of her, why did her father have this attitude?

The bus suddenly sprang into life and he watched as her palms pressed against the glass in a last salute, the bus jolted forward belching out smoke from its rear, then she was gone.

Karl stood under the light of a street lamp analyzing his feelings for quite some time.

That he loved her there was no doubt and he knew that was never going to change, he wanted so much to be able to love her openly as Heinz was able to do with Janet, and for them to be married but would that happen?

She had been sixteen just a few weeks ago; so marriage was now possible but he also knew the age to marry here without consent was twenty one for her and that almost five years away!

It seemed a life time, yet so sure he was of their love he knew he would wait if it took that amount of time, and he was sure she would also!

CHAPTER SIXTEEN

June 1947

'Are you going to Janet's today?' Karl said as he glanced at Heinz when they came out of the camp washroom together.

Karl was envious of the relationship his companion had with Janet's family, they had made him so welcome at their home. He and Sylvia they had to make do with meeting outside the cinema or in a café and he knew Sylvie hated this as much as he did; she had tried many times to make her father see reason over the situation and failed miserably.

'Yes! I am seeing her later, but I have other news.' There was twinkle in Heinz eyes and Karl could hear the excitement in his companion's voice.

'Well are you going to tell me what it is?' Karl asked curiously, he could see that the change had affected Heinz's whole body; it accentuated in the smile that had previously played around his mouth and which now lit up his whole face.

'I have just received a date to be repatriated, I am going home, probably sometime at the end of August!'

'Well that is good news!' Karl playfully slapped his companion on the back.

'The camp commander told me just an hour ago.' Heinz face fell a bit although the smile didn't fade a small frown knotted his brow.

'Well it would be good news but there is just one thing—Janet.'

There was a second of complete silence, as Karl digested this news, then he looked across again at his friend.

'What will you do about that?' He enquired.

'I don't really know.' Karl could see the pain in Heinz eyes as he confessed.

'It will be hard to leave her.' His eyes once so hard, were soft and thoughtful.

'To be honest I never realized you could love another human so much; and I shall not forget her!' He sighed.

'But I am needed at home, my father wrote they are in a bad situation, things are really very grim there.'

Karl touched his arm sympathetically.

'It seems the same for everyone. You remember Hans who was with us and came from my area of Germany?'

'Yes, he went home some weeks ago.' Heinz admitted.

'I received a letter from him yesterday. 'Karl patted his pocket.

'If you think things are bad in your part of Germany read this! From what he says, it is far worse where my home is.' Karl took a folded envelope from his pocket taking out one single sheet of paper from the rest of the letter he handed it to Heinz.

'As you know Hans didn't return to his home town, he knew it was now under the control of the Russians, his fiancée got out to the American sector and he returned there; he has sent me this letter he has received from relatives now under Russian authority.' Karl pointed to a section of the handwritten page.

'Look the Authorities have even blackened out part of the letter, where they try to describe the conditions.'

Heinz looked at the sheets of paper in front of him observing the whole sentences which had been scored through.

'I see what you mean.' He stood and read the letter through again.

'If you really look you can make out some of the sentences scored through and it is dreadful!' Karl said trying to control his voice through a threatening lump in his throat.

'I know it is very hard for you who come from what is now the Russian sector. I have to admit I am glad to be going back to the region where I live and not to rule by that lot!' Heinz face serious now as he spoke extended an arm to his friend.

'You can't know how much I wish that too.' Karl said.

'But that isn't to be. I have just got to make the best of what I have; and of course I have Sylvia!' A smile came over his face at the very thought of her.

'There is no way I could leave her now; she is all I have to cling onto.' No one could doubt the conviction in Karl's voice.

For a moment Heinz looked a trifle worried; was Karl clinging onto Sylvia because he had no one and nothing else?

Immediately he put such beliefs from his mind, he had seen the love that shone out of both of their eyes when they were together, he knew it was a rich genuine love; he chided himself that he could have such thoughts.

'I am going to the beach later, the girls are going to be there, I have to give Janet my news then; do you want to come?' Heinz said hoping to make amends for his uncharitable thinking.

'Yes that would be nice.' Karl's face beamed at the thought of seeing Sylvia, although it ranked a bit inside that Heinz should know where the girls were and he didn't; he supposed it had been discussed when Heinz had been with Janet last evening, if only this could be the same for Sylvia and himself!

Sylvia and her friend Janet picked their way carefully over the stony beach and settled their belongings just above the flotsam left by the high water mark, in a nest of towels they donned their bathing suits, then stretching the towels on the stones they settled down to enjoy the sunshine.

Many people were enjoying what the seaside had to offer today, appreciating the sun after the bitterly cold winter that had just passed; it was only early in June but the weather had been hot and summery for the past few weeks making the beach an attractive place.

It was rare for Janet to get a Saturday afternoon free; she worked in the 'Home and Colonial' shop in town and usually had Wednesday afternoons as a half day, this week they had been stocktaking on Wednesday afternoon so Janet had today free as a special dispensation and it was she who had suggested this visit to the beach knowing Sylvia didn't work on Saturday afternoons.

As the tide stopped washing the stones and began to recede Mickey and Hugo who had come with the girls got into their bathing trunks, got to their feet and then took off to enjoy the pleasures of the water.

Until comparatively recently most of this beach had been 'no go' area; now the seashore had been cleared of the landmines, barbed wire, and huge concrete anti-tank blocks that had graced the area for many years, some had been systematically buried under the wide green swath that fronted the beach area, and some were deposited on open ground at the back of a local park.

A lot of this work had been done by the PoW's so that people could once more enjoy the delights of the seaside.

'Be careful in the sun.' Peggy had warned her daughter when Sylvia had made her intentions for the day known over breakfast. Realizing how much more flesh girls these days revealed than when she was young; Peggy wanted to spare Sylvia the pain of the sunburn she herself had suffered years ago even though it was only on her arms!

'Don't fuss mum!' Her daughter had retorted going on to point out she had a darker skin than her mother, inherited from her father which meant she didn't burn so easily.

When Mickey had heard of Sylvia's plans for the afternoon, he'd cajoled his sister to include him and Hugo on the visit to the beach.

'We won't be a problem.' He promised giving her an endearing smile.

'Well you can come.' She said thinking back to how she and Janet had enjoyed the delights of the seaside as quite small children before the war with their mothers sitting on deck chairs watching them.

'Be careful not to go out of your depth when you go in the sea.' She told him aware he couldn't swim, this was not really surprising not only had his very young days been spent in London far away from days out at the seaside, but until recently the beach had been a barricaded as a strictly 'no go' area,

Fortunately both Sylvia and Janet had learnt to swim before the war and continued the practice at the local baths in town once in a while.

The two girls were enjoying a bit of sunbathing when Sylvia turned her head to find Mickey standing by her side picking up an old tin bucket they had brought along with them, it had been Sylvia's before the war, she and Janet had used it to make sandcastles with the ancient spade Mickey now held in his hand.

'Hugo and I are going to see what is in there' He announced pointing to the dark green rock pools covered with slimy green seaweed that the receding tide had now left behind.

'Hugo says they are full of small crabs and tiny fish.' He was jumping up and down with excitement.

Sylvia smiled; such simple things made this little lad happy

'See you put anything you find back, and watch you don't fall, that weed is very slippery.' Sylvia told him, going on to remind him that sea creatures didn't live out of the water.

She leant on her elbows to watch him go leaping over the stones to join Hugo; those were the same stones the two girls had gingerly trod on in their bare feet a short time ago and it seemed all the sharp ones dug into their feet, Sylvia marveling to herself at the resilience of his youth.

Janet sat up and hugged her knees. 'Well it's nice to see them enjoying themselves.' She said quietly looking down at her feet, then she gave a very heavy sigh.

Sylvia ever the observant one sensed something was wrong.

'Is everything alright?' She enquired.

Janet sat in silence looking straight ahead; Sylvia could see her lips were quivering.

'For heaven's sake Janet, you've got me concerned, what is wrong?'

'Can you keep a secret?' Janet asked looking up straight into Sylvia's eyes, a worried look knotting her brow.

'Well you have been keeping secrets for me when I have told my mother I was with you when in actual fact I was with Karl.' Sylvia looked away as she felt her cheeks go hot, she hated deception and even discussing it with Janet like this had a bad effect on her conscience.

Feeling Janet's eyes on her she looked up again into a very worried pair of bright blue eyes.

'Well I am pregnant! A defiant look came over her friends face.

'There I have said it! She said.

There was a long silence as Sylvia digested this news. Then a look of absolute horror came on Sylvia's face; this was not the news she had been expecting!

'Err, are you absolutely sure?' The words came out in a stutter.

'I am absolutely sure.' Janet's eyes began to fill with tears.

'It only happened the once.' She told her friend. 'We just got carried away.'

'I see!' Sylvia nodded her head in disbelief, she didn't really see how Heinz could have put Janet in that position; she was positive Karl would never do that however strong their feelings were, she knew like her, he had principles, despite the fact they had to lie to go to the pictures together.

Sylvia had realized some time ago that Janet's parents hadn't the strictness of her own. Janet had told her that Heinz was on occasions allowed up to her bedroom, something her mother Peggy would never allow.

'It was so that we could get away from the younger ones down stairs.' Had been Janet's explanation when they had discussed it.

Sylvia could hear her mother's words echoing now in her ears if she knew of the situation.

'That was asking for trouble.' How right Peggy's words were!

For it looked as though trouble is what Janet had got!

Gaining her composure Sylvia asked.

'Have you told Heinz?'

'No not yet.' Sylvia could see uncertainty standing out in Janet's eyes.

'I must admit I am very scared.' She looked fearful and her voice wobbled.

'He is expecting to hear any time now that his repatriation papers are through, and he will be going home.'

'Hum, yes that will be a difficult situation.' Sylvia's voice echoed her concern but really she didn't know what to say! Panic rose inside for her friend; she knew how judgmental people were especially in the village where they lived where everyone knew so much about everyone else, there had been so many instances of that during the war years, but in a way people understood the urgency of life then, they were not going to take a lenient attitude now that peace had returned.

The two girls were so absorbed in their conversation that Sylvia was startled as she suddenly looked up to see Heinz and Karl walking across the stones in their direction.

Both men slipped down beside them one on each side.

'I am really surprised to see you!' Sylvia stuttered as she gazed mesmerized into Karl's blue eyes her cheeks burning as she became conscious of the fact he was taking in her figure displayed in a bathing suit, she quickly pulled the towel which she had been sitting on from under her and put it round her shoulders suddenly embarrassed.

'Heinz seemed to know where you would be.' Karl nodded towards the other couple sitting alongside.

'Oh I see.' An unusual stab of jealously hit Sylvia.

Janet had mentioned earlier to Sylvia that Heinz had been round at her house the previous evening; presumably she had told him then that they were going to the beach this afternoon, she envied Janet that she was to be able to be open about her relationship with Heinz, taking him home without anyone making comments about who he was or what nationality.

'You look hot. 'Karl commented noting Sylvia's burning cheeks.

'Can I get you an Ice cream?' He nodded towards a vendor on a bicycle with a large tub in front who was on the narrow path that ran alongside the beach green.

'Yes that would be nice!' Both girls agreed as the two men got to their feet and made their way over to the ice cream seller.

Sylvia wondered if Karl was being kind as she was sure he could tell she was embarrassed at showing off so much of her body in her swimming costume, quickly whilst their backs were turned getting the ice cream she struggled in the towels to get herself dressed before they came back.

Although Mickey and Hugo had been out of earshot, they soon realized who had arrived and ran over when the two men came back each with a handful of cones filled with the white ice cream that Karl had insisted on paying for.

Sylvia clothed now in a pretty summer dress which came comfortably well below her knees took her portion from his fingers, noting he'd brought enough for the boys also so he must have noticed them playing on the rock pools.

The six of them sat on the stones and ate the delicacies in silence, enjoying the treat.

The boys soon polished off their cones and wiped their sticky mouths and fingers on their swimming trunks before taking off again back to the delights of the rock pools.

Karl got to his feet and gazed out to the wide stretch of sand with the sea now well out in the distance.

'Do you fancy a walk out there?' He said directing his conversation to Sylvia.

'Do you want to come?' Karl asked the other two as he took her hand to help her to her feet.

Heinz now lay on his back on the hot stones, his fingers entwined in Janet's

'No we are quite content to sit here.' Came the rather lazy reply

'I think he has something to say to Janet.' Karl said slowly as they carefully walked barefoot over the stones

'Yes I think she has news for him also.' Sylvia looked rather grim.

'And it is probably something he doesn't want to hear!'

Karl looked puzzled; Sylvia decided not to enlarge on the conversation deciding it wasn't her place to do that!

'Let's go over there.' She said changing the subject and pointing to a groyne on the far side of their stretch of beach.

She clung to him for support over the rough areas of stones until they came to the flatter sand stretching out to the sea in front of them it seemed to go on for miles where the tide had left it behind.

The warmth of Karl's large hand sent a rush of adrenaline through Sylvia, looking up into his tanned open smiling face with the bluest of blue eyes she suddenly felt weak at the knees.

'Race you across the sands.' She said suddenly as she pulled her eyes away from his face, aware of the churning of her heart, she hoped the exercise would take her mind off the thoughts now spinning through her brain.

They ran across the wet sand the tide had left behind; then they sat quietly just above the water line on the pebbles their backs against a groyne fighting to get their breath back after the exertion, the quiet hush of the waves soothing to them both. In quiet contemplation, contentedly observing the horizon and the boats in the distance making their way up the English Channel they sat for some considerable time in silence, very content and at peace with each other

Karl ended the silence when he drew a small grey envelope from his trouser pocket.

'I have this letter from Hans.' He said softly.

'You remember Hans?' She nodded in recognition.

'Yes he spent Christmas day with us didn't he?'

'That is the same one. He returned home several weeks ago, this is the letter he has written to me.' Sylvia took in the unusually serious expression on Karl's face.

'He originally came from the Russian sector near to my family home, Hans fiancée got out to the American sector before the border closed, and he has been able to join her there.' Karl explained.

He promised to see if any of his relatives still in the Russian sector could find any trace of them of my family. 'Karl's bottom lip quivered a bit and Sylvia stretched out and touched his knee, her heart full with compassion, he'd spoken so often about his parents and sister she felt she almost knew them, it was obvious by the way Karl spoke about them they had been very close.

Karl took a sheet of thin paper from the envelope carefully unfolding it.

'See here. Look!' He pointed to areas in the letter that had been blacked out.

Sylvia took the one page sheet from his hand noticing that although it was on German and she couldn't read it, certain words and phrases were marked over in dark ink so that they were illegible.

'Why would they do that?' She asked looking mystified.

A frown knotted between Karl's brow and his usually soft and cheerful features became firmly set as he continued the conversation.

'Han's says my homeland is almost a police state, my father always feared the Russians more than any other thing!' His voice trailed off sadly.

'Some of the other men at the camp who have received mail from the Russian sector said their letters have been decimated in this way also!' He looked down at the sheet in his hand.

'I will read to you what I can.' He began to translate.

'You think things are bad where you are with the rationing, they are ten times worse here.' Karl's voice faltered as he tried to come to grips with his broken English and his emotions.

'The family home was badly bombed—We live five of us in one room. I can't say too much it is forbidden.' Karl held the letter up to the light.

'I can just make out the last bit through the black—they are telling Hans not to come back!'

Karl sat for a few moments a faraway look in his eyes, the paper in his hands squashed firmly between his fingers which were visibly shaking.

Sylvia gently took his hand in hers, stroking it softly.

'It will be alright you can make a new home here now.' She told him.

'Leibe.' His English failed him as he took her into his arms and cuddled her close.

'You have made my life bearable again!' Tears spilled down his cheeks which he quickly brushed away with the back of his hand.

Sylvia folded herself into his arms finding it impossible not to return the look in his eyes, and they sat rocking each other, sure in their love.

A bit later he picked a piece of sea grass growing from the groyne beside him and dangled it above her nose making her sneeze as she lifted her hand to push it away he grasped her wrist; the look in his eyes was now open and she could see the desire there, he teased her again with the grass holding it above her lips.

'Sylvia Leibe.' He whispered in her ear his English words failing him again in the emotion of the moment.

She melted under her gaze knowing at that moment no matter what anyone said or did they would never be parted.

'Now you are sixteen could you think of marrying me?' His English again faltered in emotion

She swallowed back the feeling that threatened to engulf her before she replied breathlessly.

'Yes, that is what I want.' Tears stung her eyelids, as she added, 'If only it was possible.'

'You mean your father will object?'

'Yes I know he will.'

Karl lowered his eyes

'Will he ever agree?' He said slowly

'I can't see that happening—its 5 years till I am of legal age, that is twenty one.'

'I would gladly wait until then, my dearest heart.' She put her hand in his when he said that.

'I am not going anywhere.' He smiled down at her.

'Not back to your parents and sister if they are found?' She asked.

'Look I want to make things clear, it is never going to be easy for me to go back to my homeland as I told you my old home is now in the Russian Sector and that isn't—how do you say it? Good news!'

'But.' His voice was serious now, and Sylvia could see the pain standing out in his eyes as he continued.

I couldn't go back to any part of Germany and leave you, my heart wouldn't let me.—.' Words failed him for a moment as he put his hand on his heart.

'What I feel in—here it is for keeps, even if it takes five years; I will wait—.'

Sylvia sat up suddenly.

'It won't take that long, I won't let it.' Determination filled her voice as she continued.

'I will appeal to my mother; I am quite sure she will see sense and help me get round Dad.'

Sylvia didn't add about her parent's history and their long engagement. But it was one argument she was sure would win her mother's approval, and she was going to make sure that it did!

Karl looked over to the clock on the green above them and Sylvia's eyes followed his.

'Good heavens is that the time.' She exclaimed as she got to her feet.

'We had better get back Janet and Heinz will wonder where we are!' She said.

'And I can see the boys waving to us.' She pointed to them in the distance.

Karl looked at her sideways as she held her hand out to pull him up from the pebbles.

'I meant every word I have said today.' He said holding her hand tightly.

'Yes I know you do; so do I.' Her brown eyes were shining with real sincerity.

'I think Heinz will have been glad of the time to speak alone with Janet.' Karl remarked as they walked back along the sands.

'Yes I think they will have had a lot to say to each other.' Sylvia agreed.

Janet had watched Sylvia and Karl walk away with some trepidation, she turned to the man now resting on the pebbles by her side and sudden lump rose in her throat; how was she going to tell him her news, she felt sick to her stomach.

She leant up on one elbow and looked into his eyes, he seemed different somehow she could sense an air of excitement about him.

He took her hand.

'I have news.' He was obviously excited as his English became more broken and muddled.

'Do you really.' Janet felt uncomfortable, what was coming next?

'At last, I have the date.' Janet's heart sank to her boots; instinctively she knew what was coming next and this was news she didn't want to hear

'My repatriation notice has come through! I am going home!' There he had said it!

For a long moment she sat in stunned silence this couldn't have come at a worse time; he saw dismay in her eyes and the joy that had been in his expression began to fade.

He cupped her face in his hands he knew how he would miss her, and realized suddenly that she was going to miss him!

'I shall not forget you!' She could see the sincerity in his eyes and the smile that played at the corner of his mouth, for a moment she wondered if it would still stay there when she told him her news.

'Once I am settled you can come to me; that is one thing that is certain.' He stroked her face hoping that this would soften the blow of their parting.

'It may take some time though; our country is in a terrible state, worse than here I am told.'

Tears filled Janet's eyes and spilled down her cheeks, her voice now filled with fear.

'You can't leave me.' The blue eyes met the brown ones and held their gaze.

'You can't leave me now' she repeated real fear in her voice.

'I am pregnant with your child.'

For a long moment Heinz looked puzzled, Janet wondered if he understood what she had just said as she knew his knowledge of English was limited.

'Pregnant?' He repeated her words, looking rather stunned.

'Yes.' She patted her stomach panic rising in her throat as she did so; did he with his limited knowledge of their language understand?

'I am going to have your child!' She patted her stomach again.

The colour drained from Heinz face, it turned almost grey and for just a moment a hard look came into his eyes, it was a look she had seen sometimes when she first knew him, and it frightened her.

He turned his gaze away unable to meet hers, looking over the sands in front of them and there was a long silence.

Panic rose in Janet's throat, had he understood what she said and more important what would he do now?

Heinz found his voice, but in shock it was the German language that issued forth from his mouth.

'O mein Gott!!'

Janet sat in utter silence; was that all he could say. Didn't he understand the seriousness of the situation?

Tears welled up in her eyes and streamed down her cheeks as his eyes turned back to hers.

'I don't know what to say.' His English always very hesitant almost failed him at this emotional moment he looked down at the pebbles beneath his feet almost wishing he could bury himself beneath them.

Janet now felt fearful of her future began to feel guilty about what had happened and the fact that she had to tell him; yet it was his responsibility also, even though he had the date through for his repatriation home, surely he wouldn't leave her now!

Suddenly he turned his face back to hers, she could see in his eyes he'd come to a decision.

'I will be there for you!' His English failed him again at that point and he searched his brain for the words.

'We will be married.' He got the words out at last, but she could tell his heart wasn't in it, she clung onto the fact he had said he would be here for her, yet inside she felt cold, unhappy, and unloved and her shoulders shook with great sobs.

His arm slid round her shoulder and he held her close, she could feel the warmth of his arms yet she shivered with cold, fear still lay heavily within her, her mind in a whirl, she felt things were far from settled as she relaxed against his body and they lay in silence as the shock of these two sets of news washed over them.

They were still sitting there when the crunch on the stones announced the arrival of the other couple, with the two young boys in tow, so further conversation was impossible.

Sylvia looked across at her friend, it was obvious that Janet had been crying; both Karl and Sylvia knew half the story for her distress and it wasn't discussed as the Janet got to her feet and quietly gathered her belongings together ready to go home.

Sylvia had promised Mickey and Hugo a cold drink at a small kiosk adjacent to the beach.

'Do you want to join us?' She asked Janet and the two men.

'No I think I will go home.' Janet said and Heinz allotted to go with her.

They watched the two of them go across the stones as Sylvia gathered the boys belongings up together with her own, it was obvious that Janet had told Heinz, Sylvia could see that clearly from a haunted look that was now pinned to his face.

So the four of them remaining made their way over to a refreshment kiosk adjacent to the beach.

Donkeys had appeared on the sand and Sylvia pressed two pence each into Mickey and Hugo's hand so they could have a ride. The two of them sat for a while nursing cups of tea whilst they watched the boys, laughing together as they took their turns, reasoning that the donkeys must have notice the difference between Mickey's slight frame and Hugo's solid form.

Later Sylvia left Karl to go back to his accommodation and she took the boys home.

It was quite late when Heinz finally came back to his quarters; Karl was lounging in his bed half asleep when he heard Heinz shuffling about and putting his jacket in the small cupboard by his bed space.

Karl raised himself on one elbow and looked over in his companion's direction.

'Well how did Janet take the news?' He asked expecting his buddy to enthusiastically turn his face to his.

When Heinz looked staring into his eyes, Karl could see at once something was very wrong.

'I really don't know what to do.' Heinz spoke in German which was usual when the PoW's were alone in their accommodation.

'Did Sylvia say anything to you about Janet?' He asked Karl.

He looked mystified.

'No she just said you had important things to discuss. But I knew that! You told me about your repatriation date this morning didn't you?' Karl looked thoughtful.

'But thinking about it, that couldn't have been the problem could it, because you only told Janet about it after we left, didn't you.' 'Karl stroked his chin.

'So was there something else?' He finished.

Unshed tears stood out in Heinz eyes.

'Yes.' He said. 'There was certainly something else; Janet is going to have my child.'

For long moment Karl was speechless; the shock of this announcement showing in his face.

'What will you do now?' He stammered out at last.

'What can I do?' Heinz's face was wreathed in pain.

'I can't leave Janet to carry this burden, yet I am needed back home!' He almost spat out the words revealing the ache in his heart.

'What can I do?'

Karl could not believe the almost broken man in front of him was once the hard hearted, stony faced German officer he once knew.

'I really don't know!' Karl stammered out, he really couldn't think of anything else to say. He wouldn't have known what to do in the same position yet these words sounded so inadequate.

'What did you tell Janet you would do?' He inquired.

Heinz was sitting on his bed his head in his hands he didn't look up as he said.

'I said I would be there for her. What else could I say?'

Karl rose quickly and put his arm around Heinz shoulder.

'Well then you will have to be; there is a way out of this situation and you will have to find it!' Karl's voice took a positive note that he hoped would make Heinz think.

'Only you can decide; but I will tell you this; Janet has made a big difference to your life, anyone who knows you has noticed what a better person you have become, and it is largely down to her.'

Suddenly the lights were cut, so Karl could no longer see Heinz face.

'Well I suppose I'd better prepare for bed!' Heinz began to grope about in the darkness.

'I hadn't realized it was this late.' His eyes became accustomed to the darkness and he began to take his clothes off to put in his locker.

'Well it isn't really that late; it's just the rationing with the electric isn't it!' Karl remarked as Heinz threw himself onto his bed.

The conversation about the pros and cons of the situation went on for some time in the darkness as they continued to talk together. Sleep eluding them both; far too much was on their minds.

CHAPTER SEVENTEEN

On very hot sultry day Peggy rode her bicycle up to Sid's shop to collect the families' rations.

The breeze created by her exertions didn't stop the perspiration running down her face and she mopped it away before she twisted the pedals round the kerb and made her way into the store.

Sid looked up from his task as she approached.

'It is always nice to see a cheerful smile.' He told her adding.

'I have just got a new supply of butter; shall I cut your ration off?'

'Yes please do!' Peggy said looking round the shop to see what other wares Sid had to offer.

'Butter is the one thing I miss with the rationing.' She commented.

'I really hate being frugal with it. I really don't like margarine except for cooking!'

'Me too!' Sid's face beamed as he negotiated the large slab of butter onto a marble slab in front of him.

'You can't beat a fresh slice of bread with a nice bit of butter on it; the other stuff just isn't the same.'

Peggy watched closely as he cut from the large block, thinking how soft it was in this hot weather even though Sid was cutting it on piece of marble.

'It must be very difficult to keep things cool in these conditions.' She observed.

'Yes! Fortunately with the rationing it doesn't stay here very long.' He touched the marble slab in front of him.

'This helps!' Sid carefully wrapped the butter in greaseproof paper before weighing it on his scales.

'Yes I imagine it does, this has been an exceptionally hot summer so far and it is not quite July!'

'Yes I have heard the farmers are already saying they need rain.' He pushed the butter over towards Peggy.

'There are some bananas in that box behind you; do you want to take some for the family?' Sid pointed to a large light wooden box on the floor.

'Oh, thanks Sid, it's nice to have those again, Mickey had forgotten what they looked like until you produced some a few weeks ago.' Peggy picked up a small bunch of five and put them on the counter next to her other wares.

'That will be one each.' She said appreciatively.

'There is extra sugar for jam making this month also, I suppose you will take yours now.' Sid slid it across to her as he spoke.

'Please could you tell your lad we need a new accumulator this Friday? 'Peggy asked as she put the goods into a cloth bag, ready to transfer to the basket on her bike when she went outside.

'Yes of course I will.'

'We don't use the wireless much this time of the year; this time is has been weeks since it was changed.' Peggy said, adding by way of explanation.

'Everyone is too busy with haymaking!'

'Yes it's a busy time.' Sid's reply was brief; he was engrossed in wiping down the marble shelf.

Their conversation was suddenly interrupted by a small child bursting through the open door of the shop, followed by a red faced woman, frustration written all over her face.

The little lad's feet clattered across the wooden floor as he raced towards the counter. Peggy moved quickly across the floor grabbing the child just in time to stop a pyramid of custard packets carefully arranged by Sid from crashing to the floor.

'That was close!' Peggy said with feeling as she handed the child back to his mother Rose, she turned to Sid getting money out of her purse to pay for her wares.

'Thank you.' said Rose trying to bring the wriggling figure now firmly in her grasp under control.

Noting how tired and drained the other woman looked Peggy took her change from the shopkeeper then reached down and took the lad firmly by the hand.

'He can come outside with me whilst you finish your shopping.' She told Rose leaving Sid to serve the new customer.

Peggy managed to strap the little lad after much protest onto the seat attached to the front of the pram, the resulting shriek of protest disturbed the baby asleep at the other end so when Rose emerged from the shop with a laden basket, Peggy was busy rocking the pram to and fro in an effort to keep the two occupants quiet.

Rose took the Pram handle from Peggy's grasp and she reached for her bicycle; the two of them began to walking down the road together.

Rose gave Peggy a sideways glance.

'I suppose Sylvia has told you the news.' She said.

Peggy looked mystified.

'By the look on your face you have obviously not heard.' Rose looked rather sheepish as she continued.

'Well it isn't something that can be kept a secret for long; Janet is going to have that German fellow's baby!'

For a moment Peggy was rooted to the spot in complete shock not absolutely sure she had heard right!

'I am so sorry.' Rose was apologetic when she saw the look of astonishment on Peggy's face

'I thought your Sylvia would have told you!'

'You mean to say your Janet is pregnant!' Peggy could hardly get the words out.

Rose lowered her eyes as she continued with the conversation.

'Yes she is! Heinz has promised to stand by her. But I must admit neither her father nor I are happy about the situation.'

Gaining her composure, Peggy grasped the handlebars of her bike her knuckles standing out white as she continued her walk alongside the pram.

'I don't suppose you are!' She said quietly.

'I don't know how we shall cope.' Rose continued appearing not to notice Peggy's disquiet

'I suppose we shall have to make room at our house!' Rose had a catch in her voice and she sighed deeply.

'We haven't enough room as it is with all the little ones. We are overcrowded now.' Rose said quietly. 'And the housing situation being what is they are not likely to get anywhere else to live round here.'

Peggy swallowed hard unusually at a loss for words, she just didn't know what to say.

'Yes it is very difficult for you.' She said realizing at once this reply was entirely inadequate; she then looked down at her watch.

'Is that the time!'

'I have to get back; Harry is due in for his dinner at twelve thirty.' She put her leg over bar of the bike quickly bade Rose a swift goodbye and set off for home, glad she was able to use this excuse to leave; her mind was in an absolute whirl.

'Hi mum.' Sylvia burst through the door and put her bag on the table.

'What's for tea?'

Peggy coming through from the sitting room where she had been winding some skeins of wool went immediately to the kitchen range to get her daughters meal out that she had previously prepared.

It was customary in their house to have their main meal at mid-day, usually Harry, Ned and Peggy were present at this time; Mickey took 5 pence to school a day for his main meal there and Peggy plated up a meal to be heated up in the evening when Sylvia, who took sandwiches to work arrived home.

'It's quiet today where is everyone?' Sylvia asked as she sat at the kitchen table where a knife and fork had been laid out for her.

'Ned and your father are busy with a cow in calf; and Mickey has gone next door for tea with Hugo.' Peggy explained as she set the meal on front of her daughter.

Peggy got on quietly with some chores whilst Sylvia ate her meal pleased that for once she had her daughter to herself, with the family always around it was difficult to have time to talk, and with today's news she felt it was essential that they spoke, there were questions Peggy wanted answers to.

A mothers intuition had told her something about her daughter was different of late, it had been worrying Peggy for a while; sometimes she almost seemed to glow; other times there was a furtive in her eyes that Peggy had never seen before.

Sylvia was very grown up for a girl just sixteen, the war had this effect on this generation whereas just six years ago a girl would never go out alone in the evenings, now it was acceptable to go to dances in the local town; Harry insisted his daughter was on the ten o'clock bus home, and he would always be there to meet it!

'That was delicious mum.' Sylvia arranged her knife and fork across her now empty plate and pushed her chair slightly away from the table.

'Glad you enjoyed it.' Peggy said softly taking a seat at the opposite side of the table to her daughter.

Sylvia looked up from the table straight into her mother's eyes; she could see immediately something troubling there.

'I saw Janet's mother in the shop today.' Peggy gave her daughter a sideways glance and Sylvia felt her spirits fall; she knew that Janet's predicament would have been discussed by the two of them.

'Janet's mother told you the news then?' Sylvia said slowly.

A worried frown knitted Peggy's brows.

'Yes and I must admit I am very shocked, and I might add surprised you hadn't mentioned it!'

Sylvia took a deep breath and her eyes misted over slightly before she replied; she knew she had to handle this very carefully.

'Well as it happens I only knew myself the other Saturday when we went to the beach together; and it was a shock to me also!'

'I know what you are thinking mum, and yes before you ask I do see Karl when I am with Janet, but not at her house; Heinz goes to Janet's house most evenings after we have been out whereas you well know Karl and I have nowhere like that to go!'

Then with a new determination in her voice, Sylvia looked her mother straight in the eye.

'And I don't approve of Janet's parents attitude with regard to the couple, they are far too lax and the lack of restrictions in that house are far from good; you and Dad would never allow it.'

A glimmer of a smile came into the corners of Sylvia's mouth as she noted her mother's reaction to these words.

'And I am glad you and dad are like that!' Sylvia's face became serious again.

'But mum, Dad's attitude is too far the other way! You have met Karl; you even said at Christmas you liked him, well nothing has changed, he is still the same person!' She looked pleadingly at her mother and said. 'Would help if I could invite Karl round for Sunday tea?'

Peggy caught her breath, she had been expecting this, but now the question had been raised she felt an odd feeling of foreboding, yet she could sense the determination in her daughter's voice. Personally she liked what she saw of Karl, when he had been at their house at Christmas he seemed to fit in very well with most of the family; it was obvious that both Ned and Mickey liked him.

But there was the question of Sylvia's father.

Taking in the thoughtful look in her mother's eyes, Sylvia continued with the conversation.

'I know there is a problem with dad, he has to realize the war is over and we have to move on' Sylvia's face had a quiet defiance about it.

'You can't judge people by their nationality, there are good and bad English people, as well as German1'

Peggy was quiet for a few moments choosing her words carefully she could see a look of sadness in her daughter's eyes that were so like her fathers.

There was no assurance in her voice as she said. 'Yes I know you have a point, but I am concerned. Especially now with the news about Janet.'

'Mum I have tried to be up front about Karl, but Dad has forced me to become secretive, and really I don't like that!' The eyes changed to an appealing look as Sylvia raised them to her mother and gritted her teeth.

'I love him and I won't change my mind ever.' The words were spoken with real feeling.

'Yes I understand that, but will you still love him in a year's time? You could prove your love by being loyal for that year, and showing your father you are serious about this relationship.' Peggy extended her hands across the table taking her daughters into her own.

'It seems a long time, but a year will soon pass, this way you can prove to your father you are serious about Karl and you can put some things by for your future home.'

Tears welled up in the young girls face, as she rounded on her mother.

'I haven't the patience you showed when you were courting dad, I wouldn't have wasted all those years you did before you married because of his family.'

A faraway look clouded Peggy's vision.

'I must admit it wasn't easy. But the situation here is completely different; I am only asking you to wait a year!'

Sylvia had a new resolve in her voice as she spoke again.

'Yes I know you are; but Dad won't change his mind even after a year, you know he won't, once he makes up his mind; that's that! Her eyes flashed with annoyance.

'Your long courtship is proof of what Dad is like.'

Her eyes blazed with determination as she continued.

'This situation is completely different; there is something here we are forgetting. You and dad had family all around you, Karl has no one and isn't even sure that his family are still alive, the Red Cross has tried to trace them, but haven't yet had success, it is very difficult as they are now in the Russian sector of Germany.' She paused to catch her breath.

'And no mum, before you say it, it isn't because I feel sorry for his situation, and that he is alone.'

The brown eyes looked straight into her mothers.

'I know Karl will wait for me but I am not prepared to let him do this, and you know he has principles Mum, we could force Dad's hand by me getting pregnant couldn't we like Janet and Heinz!' She paused, waiting for her mother's reaction.

Peggy stared at her daughter in horror and disbelief

'I can't believe what you have just said Sylvie?' The shock in her eyes changed the whole expression of her face.

The look on her mother's normal placid features alarmed Sylvia, but she pressed on.

'That is not Karl's way; he was brought up to wait for marriage before indulging in that sort of thing.' Sylvia's cheeks were pink with embarrassment as she defended her boyfriend it was rare for mother and daughter to discuss intimate things.

Peggy lowered her eyes, suddenly feeling proud of the way she and Harry had brought up this daughter of theirs with obvious principles, people had changed during the war years, and being promiscuous seemed more acceptable.

Yet her heart felt heavy in her chest realizing nothing would help the trouble that lay ahead with Harry when he heard his daughter's news; she hated confrontations but could see that was what lay ahead!

'I don't think asking Karl for tea would make any difference to your Dad.' She told Sylvia, this statement making Peggy feel utterly dejected; she had always welcomed all the friends of the young ones under her roof and she knew that it wasn't right to deny this privilege to her only daughter; she also knew if she opposed this romance it could push the young couple together more

After a few minutes reflection, Peggy said resignation in her voice.

'But I think Karl should come, it's good to plan early, and it will give me the rest of the week to work on your dad.' She added with a smile she didn't feel.

'I will talk to him ahead of Sunday.' She said her heart heavy in her chest at the prospect.

'Thanks Mum, I am sure Dad will like Karl when he gets to know him better.'

Peggy looking at the glow in her daughters face, wishing she could match her enthusiasm, she faced a tough week ahead trying to bring Harry round to see that it was a good thing to meet Karl on a friendly basis it was almost an impossibility, but for her daughters sake she had to try.

She knew that Harry's bark was often worse than his bite, if he was put in the picture early enough, he'd accept the inevitable when it came; he would have to or risk being at odds with his own daughter which she was sure he wouldn't want!

She decided she would broach the subject with Harry when they were alone, which was more often than not when they were in bed at night; she only hoped he wouldn't get too cross about the whole affair and lose his temper, a great deal of tact would be needed she knew.

Come in and sit down Peggy invited Karl when Sylvia brought him over their threshold the next Sunday afternoon.

'Thank you.' Karl replied in his broken English, giving her a beaming smile.

Peggy busied herself making tea whilst the young ones made themselves comfortable on the Rexene settee in the small sitting room.

As she took the tea tray through, Peggy noted Karl's arm loosely about Sylvia's shoulders.

'Do you take Sugar and Milk?' She asked as she stirred the pot.

'Both please.' Karl looked over to her giving her another smile. Peggy could understand the attraction of her daughter to this tall, broad shouldered fair haired attractive young man, who if he had been of a different nationality her husband would have made very welcome.

Harry was mercifully missing, he and Ned were busy with the afternoon milking; they would be in later for tea; Mickey was busy upstairs occupied with an old Meccano set that one of Harry's younger brothers had let him have, so at the moment it was just the three of them here.

As Peggy had suspected Harry had been very angry when she had broached the subject of Karl coming to tea several days ago.

She reminded him that he had made the young German soldier welcome at Christmas

'That was different.' Harry snapped.

'We did that for the vicar, not to encourage our daughter's romance with one of them.'

Since that confrontation, Peggy had worked hard on Harry to make him see reason but she still wasn't sure how well she had succeeded!

The conversation between the three of them was a bit stilted as they sipped their tea, Karl still found English a bit difficult, he tried hard to make Peggy understand his position and how his parents were situated.

When it was time for the two women got up to prepare the afternoon tea table Karl was left alone staring into space in the small sitting room. He felt very apprehensive hoping he would be able to make Sylvia's parents see how much he loved their daughter and wanted just to make her happy.

His heart sank a little when he heard the back door open and Harry and Ned enter, he listened to them washing their hands in the kitchen sink before the sound of scraping chairs meant they were now sat down at the table ready for tea.

'Tea is ready.' Sylvia called through and Karl got to his feet; the butterflies in his stomach making him feel slightly sick as he prepared to face the family and Sylvia's father.

Fortunately Ned and Mickey kept the conversation cheerful over tea; the two boys always had plenty of banter between them and included the rest of the family in their jolly discussions so there were no long embarrassing silences. After everyone helped clear the table and wash up, they retired to the sitting room to play cards and a few board games, it seemed the visit was a success but Sylvia could see from the cautious look her father threw in Karl's direction when he thought no one was observing him he was far from happy about the situation

Karl later took his leave to make his journey back to his accommodation once more alone.

CHAPTER EIGHTEEN

August 1947

The noise from Don and Gisela's cottage echoed through Peggy's home as their house was cleared of its contents.

It had been necessary because of the narrow winding staircase in the cottage to remove the small sash cord windows from upstairs so that the larger furniture could be removed, eventually the iron frame of the double bed and the oak wardrobes were deposited into the van after much huffing and puffing by the removal men together with the rest of the families goods and possessions.

Don had left a week ago to commence his new job, and to set up everything for the family at their new abode leaving Gisela to arrange everything this end.

Farmer Philips made it clear it was essential to have the cottage vacant for a new worker to move in almost as soon as Don left and demanded to have the property vacated almost immediately.

The farmer had a grievance; Don was leaving his employment soon after returning from the services after he had let the family stay in his accommodation during the war. The farmer argued that he couldn't offer employment to another family without the accommodation being available to house them.

Although Gisela complained bitterly that she would have liked more time to get organized and she thought the Farmer very inconsiderate he was adamant about the situation and gave them one week to leave.

Part of the problem was Gisela was very apprehensive about moving on; although lately Peggy thought she had observed a change in her attitude when they shared an afternoon cup of tea just before the move.

'It is what is called a new town.' Peggy couldn't mistake the enthusiasm that suddenly seemed to be in Gisela's voice as her cheeks began to glow when anticipating her future.

'Don tells me these prefabricated houses have everything in them, electricity of course, and a proper bathroom and toilet, good facilities especially for doing the washing!' Gisela excitedly told her soon to be ex neighbour.

'Don has promised I shall have a refrigerator, he did say that some of the houses have them built in, and I shall have vacuum cleaner as soon as they become available.' Gisela paused to catch her breath.

'Don says that will be very soon. 'She finished finally.

'I am so glad!' Peggy showed she was impressed with a smile, never one to be envious of others she was really pleased that Gisela's attitude had changed from negative to a positive one.

'The only thing I wish is that I could take my neighbours with me!' Gisela's voice dropped as she brushed away a tear.

'You will make new ones, and they will probably be nearer your own age with all those new houses.' Peggy said brusquely, as she fought to control the lump rising in her own throat.

Peggy too hated change; you could never be quite sure what new neighbours would be like; and she'd shared so much with Gisela!

'No one will be as kind and understanding as you have been.' A tear brushed down Gisela's cheek, which she swiftly scuffed away with the back of her hand and a worried look crossed her face as her enthusiasm began to wane.

'Nonsense you mustn't think like that! Things can only get better it's a new start for all of you.' Peggy hoped her optimistic tone would steer Gisela back to more positive things.

She didn't mention to the younger woman she had heard quite a few times in the last few weeks arguments between the Gisela and her husband through the walls of their cottages, the walls were not thin, voices had been raised, and from what she'd heard the quarrels were not just about the coming move, both Don and Gisela were fiery people who lifted their voices in temper, and she'd heard Kurt's name mentioned once or twice when the voices were raised.

Don had spoken to Peggy about Gisela's relationship with Kurt, and she had truthfully been able to reply that whenever Kurt had visited Gisela she had been present; fortunately Don took her word for this and Gisela's trips to the camp were not mentioned.

'Thank you for that; Don doesn't get on too badly with the girls, its Hugo that worries me the most.'

'No better?' Peggy sighed; the two of them had this conversation some weeks ago when Gisela had confided in Peggy that Don found the relationship with his son difficult.

'Not any better!' Gisela repeated Peggy's words.

'You may find things different when you get to the new place and the children begin their new schools.' Peggy hoped she sounded more positive than she felt.

'I do not hold out much hope!' Was Gisela's sad reply.

'Many men have found it difficult to build up a relationship with their children after being away so long during the war.' Peggy took Gisela's hand.

'Their formative years have been shaped by you on your own.' Peggy didn't add what was on her mind that for most of the children's lives their father had been absent.

'You have done a good job!' She declared.

Gisela looked downcast as she continued.

'The biggest problem is that Don was a very clever child, and his son just doesn't take after him, so Don is very hard on the lad and he resents it.'

Peggy tried not to look bleak; she knew from Mickey that Hugo who was the same age as her evacuee could scarcely write or read.

'I think Hugo will miss Mickey most of all, they do so much together.' Gisela went on.

Peggy looked thoughtful.

'Well they would have to part company in September wouldn't they? Even if Hugo was here they would be going to different schools.' She pointed out.

'I suppose so.' Gisela still sounded doubtful, the information that Mickey an evacuee from the back street of London had passed his eleven plus when his own son failed his hadn't rested well with Don, this had caused more tension between father and son; Gisela was stuck in the middle of the resulting rows.

'The girls are not happy about the move either; Sonja is in her last year at school, she will be fourteen in just a few months and leaving, a new school for just this little time is hard.' Gisela said drawing the conversation away from her son.

Peggy wished her neighbour would be more positive, she knew many families would give their eye teeth to be in Gisela's position, in the cities many families lived in one room, which was why this job of Don's preparing and using his skills for prefabricated homes for these families was such an essential one.

She felt her patience slipping away with Gisela and tried not to make it show in her voice.

'Yes that I can understand your worries, but look on the positive side you are going to a new town and just think of the job prospects Sonja will have in a year's time when she begins to look for work!'

'Yes I suppose you have a point.' Gisela said grudgingly, adding it would serve Helga well also as she was only two years younger than her sister.

'There you are then.' Was Peggy's passing shot as Gisela got up to leave.

The noise from next door ceased and Peggy heard the heavy doors of the removal van close with a small bang.

Gisela appeared at the back door of Peggy's cottage, wiping a weary hand over her forehead.

'Everything is packed and loaded now.' She announced and the men are just off, so all I have to do is wait for a taxi to take us to the station.

They watched from the kitchen window as the furniture van chugged into life, the men climbing aboard and the van took off bouncing up and down as it negotiated all the ruts in the rough gravel road that led to their cottages.

A worried frown passed over Gisela's forehead.

'I hope nothing will be broken.' She said.

Peggy smiled recalling the last few days when all their spare time had been used packing china and precious things in newspaper.

'Everything has been packed very well as you know!' She assured her neighbour.

The crunch of tires sounded outside announcing the arrival of Gisela's transport to the railway station.

'It looks as though your taxi is here.' Peggy got up and went to the door, whilst Gisela rounded up her family who were sitting disconcertedly on the garden wall talking with Ned and Mickey.

Together Gisela and the two girls piled into the back seat of the cab with Hugo taking the front seat, with the smell of fumes belching out of the back the taxi negotiated the road; Peggy and the boys waved until it was out of sight.

As soon as they left, Peggy began to clear the table to make some scones; she'd just got the ingredients into the mixing bowl on the table and added the liquid when a tap came to the back door.

'Come in.' Peggy called out not looking up from stirring the contents of the bowl with a wooden spoon.

When she did she was astonished to see Winnie Baker standing there in her long black coat and button boots.

'I thought your boys would like these.' Winnie took a small pile of picture post magazines from the depths of the voluminous bag she carried in one hand; holding them out to Peggy who deciding they smelt rather musty wrinkled her nose and put them on the other end of the kitchen table away from her scones.

'Jean told me some time ago you lad is very bright and likes to browse through these and they are good to use in his homework.' Winnie was rather gracious in her approach, which was unlike her usual self.

Peggy sniffed and for a few moments was lost for words, this visit was unprecedented; Winnie never came here, the only time Peggy normally saw Winnie was at the reading room when they had both been delegated to do some work for the community.

'Yes indeed he is.' Peggy hoped Winnie wouldn't notice the slight tremor in her voice.

'Jean passes some of them on from time to time.' Winnie said giving Peggy a rare smile which revealed teeth that obviously needed filling.

'Can I take your coat?' Peggy asked suddenly remembering Winnie was a guest, she began to rack her brain as to what was the real motive behind this visit, she knew Winnie well enough to know that she never did anything without a reason.

'Thank you.' Her visitor removed it to reveal a long printed dress beneath that could have come out of the 1920's

Peggy hung Winnie's coat on a peg behind the kitchen door; then she pointed to the kitchen chair at the other end of the table.

'I hope you don't mind sitting there. 'She said. 'Whilst I finish this task, then I will make us a pot of tea.' Peggy swiftly poured some flour from a sifter over a small area of the wooden table she had cleared for the purpose, before turning out the mixture from the bowl and kneading it with the heel of her hand while Winnie watched her.

Cutting and shaping the scones she quickly put some milk on the top before putting them on a tin tray that she previously greased and floured transferring them in the oven, before turning to see Winnie had placed her ample form on the proffered chair ready to be waited on!

Pouring the hot water into the tea pot, Peggy glanced over to her visitor, surprised to see just a glint of sudden tears spring into Winnie's eyes.

Peggy brought the teapot to the table, and poured out a cup for them both, passing one to her guest, 'Would you like to take it through to the sitting room?' She asked.

'No I am alright here and you can keep an eye on your baking.' There was a tremor in Winnie's voice.

'Is there a problem I can help with?' Peggy asked with more kindness than she actually felt, it was well known that Winnie was the type of person who only cared about herself.

Winnie squirmed in her chair obviously reluctant to talk, Peggy waited silently for the other woman to open up to her.

At last the words came out almost in a whisper, as though Winnie didn't want to confide in Peggy at all.

'I don't know which way to turn,—my money is running out.' The phrase was spoken so softly that Peggy had to bend her head towards her visitor to hear it.

For a moment Peggy wasn't sure he had heard right, yet she could see from the look in her eyes Winnie was absolutely serious.

This news didn't come as a surprise to Peggy; many people who lived on the interest of their savings had been hard hit by the austere war years and were now finding life very difficult. She had often wondered how Winnie had managed with no apparent income except what her parents had left her many years previously.

Winnie's voice took on a pleading tone.

'Please could you help me I have no one else to turn too?'

With sudden hindsight Peggy realized this was true; Winnie was too proud to admit to anyone in the village she had financial difficulties it would mean losing face, and as Jean's confidant and friend she would lose her social standing, equally the same applied to the vicar.

Peggy sat quietly at a loss for the moment to see how she could do anything; Winnie kept her eyes downcast as she continued the conversation.

'You are very friendly with the Pemberton's.'

Peggy smiled. 'Well I wouldn't call it friendly; I am really only their char lady.'

Winnie raised her eyes meeting Peggy's, they were full of uncertainly and pain, Peggy's sympathetic nature was at once aroused, realizing that Winnie must have had to swallow a great deal of pride to come here especially to someone like herself who she had considered beneath her!

'You are able to talk to them.' She said.

'Yes they are very approachable, Mrs. Pemberton is especially kind.' Peggy agreed.

'Well could I call on you good nature to ask them something for me?' Winnie's eyes stood out like black buttons in her face, and Peggy could see a glimmer of hope there.

'Could you ask whether they have any positions vacant in their shop?'

Peggy's shock at these words showed in her face she couldn't imagine Winnie working behind a counter!

But her visitor's next remark made it clear that wasn't what Winnie had in mind!

'I thought I could perhaps work in the counting house, I used to do that when my parents owned it.' Winnie squared up her shoulders.

Then no one needs know that I am working there as I wouldn't be on show would I?'

It was on the tip of Peggy's tongue to ask why Winnie didn't approach Mrs. Pemberton herself, but she decided to listen to what else Winnie had to say first.

'I thought you could ask them just as a general enquiry, just say someone you know with experience was looking for a post like that, there is no need to mention at first that it is me!' Winnie said sheepishly

Suddenly all became clear, Winnie wanted Peggy to approach the Pemberton's so that she didn't lose face if there was no possibility of the position she wanted at the shop not being available.

Thinking quickly for an answer; Peggy stroked her chin for a few minutes before she spoke, an idea that might be a solution to the problem came into her mind.

'There might be a better answer to your financial problems.' She said.

The black button eyes suddenly looked up, and Winnies face swiftly took on a very different look as Peggy continued.

'You have a lot of space in your house and grounds; why not let some of it out? You have those two small lodges at the front, someone would be glad to make a home out of those.'

Knowing the government had requisitioned all empty houses from July 1945, Peggy had been very surprised that Winnie had been allowed to let the lodges remain empty, in fact Harry had said as much just a few days ago, adding the reason they had been overlooked was probably because they were not in a very good state of repair, besides here in a country village a lot of the houses were tied to farm jobs and most city dwellers wouldn't want to move to country districts.

Winnie's eyes looked straight into Peggy's over the rim of the teacup she had just held up to her mouth and a look of relief came over her features.

'Well that is a good idea. 'She said almost triumphantly. 'I knew you were the right person to advise me.'

Peggy couldn't help a small smile; she knew very well the only reason she was consulted because Winnie didn't have to ask anyone else and lose face, although she had to admit to herself it pleased her to see she had hit the right note with the spinster.

Winnie's face was alight now with expectation as Peggy continued talking about her idea.

'You could tell people you felt the need to help with the present dire housing situation, no one actually needs to know that you are doing it for the money do they?' She suggested.

The look on Winnie's face as she said this was phenomenal, her smile now reached her eyes making her face look almost young for once.

'Oh thank you so much Peggy I knew you would have the answer!'

'And you could ask Bill if he could put right any small structural repairs when he does your garden. He does that sort of work for the Finches, and the Vicar.' Peggy suggested.

'Yes I could ask him!' Winnie sniffed.

'Of course I'd have to insist he kept it to himself though, I don't want people knowing my business.'

Peggy smiled, Bill wasn't the type to keep anything to himself, so the whole village would be bound to know in a short period of time what Winnie was up too and Winnie would have to use his services, there was no one else available with a lot of men still away on active service.

'But it is more than just a few structural defects; a thorough clean right through is needed also' Winnie's tone changed and she looked appealingly in Peggy's direction.

'Well I am sure I could help you out there.' The words were out of Peggy's mouth almost before she thought about it.

'Yes well I expect I can afford to use your services.' Winnie's voice once again took on its usual superior air, and Peggy wished she hadn't offered so readily.

Peggy quietly swallowing down the indignation at Winnie's attitude, she knew from experience if she protested now Winnie would turn more belligerent about the situation, and Peggy didn't want an argument with her.

'You could always let out a few rooms in the main house if you think repairs to the lodges are too costly.' She suggested.

This remark brought a frown to Winnie's face, and was most indignant in her reply.

'Hum—Well I will have to see about that! I don't think I would like people trampling through my home! The lodges are different though, they can be turned into habitable places I am sure.' The glow now in her cheeks showed she was full of enthusiasm for this aspect of Peggy's suggestion.

'You are such a good friend.' She added as Peggy turned away to take the scones out of the oven.

'You won't mention this conversation to anyone will you?' Winnie clasped the table as she pulled herself up from her seat ready to leave.

'No I won't break a confidence.' Peggy said knowing Winnie would do anything not to lose face with the likes of Jean Finch and others in the village although she was still quite sure it would be common knowledge if Bill was asked to do any work for her visitor, knowing Winnie she would be very cagy about what she told him!

Getting a brown paper bag from the kitchen drawer, Peggy wrapped up two scones and passed them to Winnie who was struggling to put on her coat.

'Here have these for your tea,'

'Thank you they will go nicely with a bit of jam.' Winnie said appreciatively as she picked up her bag and turned to leave via the back door.

Peggy watched her go as she made her way down their lane to the village then on to the main road to where her house was situated; Peggy hadn't a lot of time for people who tried to put on airs and graces, yet she felt sad that this woman was too proud to admit that things were difficult for her just so that she didn't lose face with the people who thought they were the elite of the village.

Peggy decided she would have a word with Rose later, maybe one of the lodges would make a first home for Janet and her young man, it would be ideal as they were more than capable of doing the place up inside and turning into a home, so one of Winnie's lodges could perhaps be put to good use!

CHAPTER NINETEEN

Middle of August 1947

Sylvia finished putting a few pins in the hem edge of the cream dress now clinging to Janet's slender form.

'I will just put a few stitches in. It won't take a mo,' with lightening fingers Sylvia passed a sewing needle and thread through the material before standing back to admire her work.

'I must admit that looks good.' She said thinking to herself that no one would ever guess Janet was almost three months pregnant with that flat stomach!

'It's just the right length.' Janet remarked.

'Yes it is.' Sylvia agreed.

Janet looked at her reflection in the mirror and saw with satisfaction the soft shoulders, hand span waist and full billowing skirt Sylvia had carefully crafted to the 'New look' that was now in every fashionable paper.

She passed Sylvia a small chaplet of waxed orange blossom lying on the chair and her friend with deft fingers attached it with a few stitches to a small veil lying alongside before putting it on the top of Janet's long blonde hair.

'That finishes it off nicely; you look really lovely.' Sylvia declared.

'Yes she does.' A sudden announcement from the doorway made both girls turn to see Janet's mother standing there.

'There was a smugness in Rose's voice as she remarked.

'Just as well I never got rid of my wedding outfit; somehow it just stayed in a box up in the loft, I'd forgotten it was there!' Her eyes were glistening with unshed tears.

'I never thought it would be worn by my own daughter.' Rose quickly brushed away a tear that escaped and sniffed.

'At least not yet awhile, although I did think it might come later' she adding before turning appreciatively to Sylvia.

'You have certainly turned it into a very fashionable dress.'

Janet looked away; she didn't want these comments from her mother; she hadn't wanted to wear her mother's wedding dress, she would have preferred to be married in the suit she had seen in a shop in town and had saved her clothing coupons for.

'Never mind, it will look nice when I finish altering it.' Sylvia had told her friend when they discussed it together, you can use those coupons for some nice items for your trousseau, and there are some nice embroidered items of underwear in the shops now.

Sylvia proposed the dress was altered to calf length and not sweeping the floor as this seemed more suitable for the occasion as the setting was to be the registrar's office in town.

'At least she doesn't look pregnant.' Rose said rather thoughtlessly looking her daughter up and down

'I did say to Janet, she could have got married in church; the vicar would never know she is pregnant.'

'But I would mother!' Janet said crossly.

They had had this argument with Rose just a few weeks previously when Janet's mother had suggested they approach the vicar about the marriage.

'Well you have to have the banns on three separate Sundays for starters; which would delay things somewhat.' Had been Janet's argument.

'Well you could apply for a special license.' Her mother retorted adding.

'Then you could be married straight away, it was done a lot during the war!' Rose wasn't going to give up the on the argument easily, she had the opinion that the prestige of a white wedding in the church could do something for her social standing locally, especially as people had memories of her behavior during the war.

'Heinz is returning to Germany soon after the wedding! And you also might be in Germany by the time the baby is born. If people ask then I can always say the child was premature.' Rose had said confidently.

'Maybe that is so, but I couldn't stand there in front of the vicar and the village to make my vows, knowing I was pregnant,' There was an edge to Janet's voice as she continued.

'Anyway Heinz will be in Germany for quite a while before he is able to send for me! It is possible the child will born here and everyone will know the truth then wont they!' Janet voice was resolute as she said.

'I will have to live here, just think what a field day people would have at my expense if I got married in church, when six months later a baby turns up! I don't like this circumstances, but I don't have many options do I?'

'Well you got yourself into it.' Rose retorted her voice rising with annoyance.

'Let's not bicker over it.' Sylvia said quietly. 'What is done can't be undone, and our arguing about the situation isn't going to help is it?'

Janet glanced gratefully in Sylvia's direction as she said this.

She had been very upset and it had caused her much heartache when Heinz said he was still going to return to Germany after their marriage when his repatriation papers were finalized.

'I have a responsibility to my family.' He said simply.

Janet could feel the anger rising in her throat as she said.

'You have a responsibility to me also. Perhaps I don't matter that much, obviously less than your family out there!' A sob in her voice denoted tears were not far away.

Heinz still found English difficult and fought to get the right words out to explain.

'Yes you do matter, of course you do.' He touched her cheek as the tears spilled over.

'We shall be married as soon as possible, but it is sense that I return to Germany.'

'Why?' Janet demanded.

'Look at it this way please will you?' Heinz voice full of emotion struggled over the words.

'Here I am a farmhand, money in this position will always be tight, but in my own country as things start to sort out, there will obviously a lot of building work to do.' He looked straight into her eyes, and she could see the sincerity there as he continued with the conversation.

'Before I joined up I was skilled in building, I can make a good life for us there and help my family; my parents are elderly and I am their only son! I owe them something!'

'If that is the case why can't I come back with you now?' Janet beseeched him.

Heinz face grew serious.

'My family were bombed, they are living five to a room at the moment, it wouldn't be fair to take you there, with a baby soon to be born. You have your family here and they will take care of you until I am able to provide properly for you in Germany.' His deep brown eyes begged her to understand.

'I will send money as soon as I am settled.' He took her into his arms and kissed the top of her head.

Full of emotion he faltered over the English words.

'You are the world to me.' He stammered.

'I have to do this, it is the way forward for us both, eventually we shall all benefit.' She could see the look in his eyes and knew he was sincere.

'Will it be alright?' The doubt was still in her voice.

'Yes it will I promise!' He smiled and through the hurt she knew she had to trust and accept how things were going to be!

The rattle of teacups woke Sylvia; opening her eyes to see Rose bending over a bedside cabinet in the twin bedded room.

'It's going to be a lovely day.' Rose said as she drew the thin curtains over the small casement window letting the sunshine into the room; she was already fully dressed in what she would be wearing for the wedding with an enveloping overall covering all but the edge of her dress, a toddler clinging to her skirts she looked as tired and drawn as ever.

'Just as well your mother is doing the reception, or I don't know how I would manage.' She told Sylvia.

'I'll come up later and see if you want breakfast.' Rose turned on her heel and made a hasty retreat from the room, closing the door quietly behind her.

Sylvia pulled herself up by her elbow and glanced at the other bed, Janet was still comatose, and not wanting to disturb her she quietly took the cup and saucer and sipped the hot liquid, listened to the unaccustomed noise from downstairs, she heard Janet's father cough and the creaking of floorboards as he made his way to the bathroom.

Janet's eyes suddenly opened and she looked directly at the ceiling, before turning her face to her friend than she raised herself up to reach for her tea.

'I must say I am glad you were able to spend the night here, it would have been a bit of a rush this morning if you had to make your way over.' She said.

As soon as the two girls had gulped down their tea, Sylvia got to work fixing Janet's hair; time was of the essence as the taxi was booked for ten fifteen to take them to the register office in town in time for the wedding at eleven o'clock.

Sylvia had spent quite a bit of time last night winding Janet's hair in pipe cleaners, the resulting blonde ringlets Sylvia caught at the nape of her neck shaping tendrils of hair around Janet's face; it took some considerable time getting it just right before Sylvia was completely satisfied with the result.

Janet glancing in a mirror on her small dressing table commented appreciatively.

'Thanks Sylvie that looks really nice.'

Rose came in again and the two girls elected to forgo the breakfast offered by her previously.

'I couldn't face it.' Janet said the nerves in her stomach getting the better of her.

'.Neither could I.' Sylvia admitted.

Rose did appear sometime later with some toast which had a smear of margarine on it and Sylvia advised Janet to try and force some down.

'You don't want your stomach rumbling during the ceremony, or you feeling faint.' She said, hoping the joke would make Janet feel better.

Sylvia was just carefully pulling Janet's dress over her head trying not to disturb the work she'd done on her hair when the sound of Peggy arriving to organize the small reception later ensued from downstairs.

Sylvia glanced at the clock it was already nine thirty and she knew her mother would have her work cut out to get everything prepared for when they got back from the register office.

Originally Rose wanted a big occasion in the 'Reading Room' Janet's father Len had stepped in putting his foot down over this, he said that for the amount of people that would be present it wouldn't have be worth it, adding that it wouldn't be very popular amongst their friends and acquaintance that their daughter was marrying a German so soon after the end of the war, people would talk Len said.

Rose thought Len was looking at the fact that money spent on food could be spent on ale which was closer to his heart and she said so.

They'd had a spat about that.

'With the rationing there wouldn't be much food available any way.' Len said in defense of his actions.

'There will be enough for your ale though.' Rose retorted.

'Ale is rationed like everything else! So that is not an argument!' He said digging his heels in a final confrontation.

A lump rose in her mother's throat when Janet appeared in her wedding finery at the top of the stairs just before the taxi was due to arrive, the dress altered by Sylvia was now calf length and the hem just washed each step as she descended into the living room.

Sylvia put a small bouquet of sweet peas tied up with ribbon into the brides hand; her mother had brought them with her in her basket that morning.

'There.' She said. 'That completes the picture; my dad picked them fresh from the garden today.'

Janet buried her head in the lovely pastel shades of white, pale pink and mauve flowers.

'They smell lovely. I must remember to thank him for them.' Janet said appreciatively.

It was a small group that later piled into a taxi to town; Len had objected to this expense but here Rose had won the day insisting that the taxi was essential.

'Do you expect the bride to ride on a bus in her wedding dress?' She asked Len.

'If you had let Janet have her way and let her wear a suit instead of that dress. A bus would have sufficed' Len retorted.

'Any ways you know the situation with the petrol rationing don't you!' He snapped.

Rose quietly had a word with Bill who besides doing gardens, used his car as a taxi for the village when he could get a supply of petrol; he agreed to help out and a small fee was arranged.

Just Janet and her parents with Sylvia and two of Janet's older brothers squeezed in the vehicle. Peggy had elected to look after the younger ones whilst she prepared the small reception.

Rose was confident all would be in place on their return, poor Peggy was already beginning to wonder how she was going to manage to get everything ready with these little ones clinging to her skirts and poking their fingers into everything.

'I know you will manage. 'Rose perky hat on her head hitting the door frame as she squeezed her slight frame inside the taxi said as a parting shot.

Karl scarcely recognized the well-dressed man that exited from the washroom that morning in front of him, the borrowed brown soft tweed suit replacing the uniform worn by the PoW's, fitted him perfectly.

The PoW's were issued with a suit to go back home but this was only given at embarkation, never before. Fortunately Janet's father had recently acquired a demob suit on his dismissal from the army so the spare that he'd had for his own wedding in the 30's which now no longer fitted him due to his fondness for a pint of ale was available for Heinz.

A white shirt gleamed against Heinz's shallow completion and almost jet black hair, this also was a borrowed item, a somber brown tie and shining brown shoes completed the assemble; a vast improvement from the normal black boots that were standard issue and wore constantly by men at the camp.

Karl with the help of Sylvia managed to be suitably attired courtesy of Ned, who loaned him the suit Sylvia had altered for him from the tailors a short time ago, Karl slightly broader than the younger man filled it better.

When the two men had approached Harry for the day off; he made it clear to Karl he would have to make up the time lost at a time suitable to him! Karl thought Harry was being more than a little unreasonable, but he'd come to expect this attitude from that quarter.

Heinz didn't have the same problem, he was soon to return home anyway so his labour wasn't going to be available for much longer, and it would have looked very heartless of Harry not to grant him time off for his wedding day.

The two men left the Nissan huts together for the short walk to the bus stop for their journey into town. Before they left there had been much affectionate back slapping from the other men not yet repatriated who had come to offer best wishes and some banter when they left early for their work; there was no chance of any of them being able to get time of to support their former panzer officer on his wedding day!

Waiting at the bus stop there were curious looks and whisperings from the villagers waiting for the bus; they were accustomed to see the PoW's amongst the general population but they were usually dressed in their uniforms on weekdays when they were hard at work in the community.

Not a lot of people in the village knew that Janet was getting married, Rose didn't want to provoke the prejudice that still existed towards the PoW's in some quarters especially those who had lost loved ones during the conflict, and it was it wasn't common knowledge her daughter was pregnant. She knew as soon as it got out about the wedding and the fact that it was in the registry office people would put two and two together especially when Janet's condition began to show.

Rose shrugged her shoulders when this was pointed out to her.

'Oh well, when they are running us down they are leaving someone else alone.' She had snapped.

The bus was crowded when it arrived so it was standing room only into town some twenty minutes away, most of the passengers from the village talked amongst themselves about the two unusually dressed men, Karl and Heinz conversed in their own language quietly together so neither side really took in what others were saying.

Alighting at the bus station, Karl noted his friends white face and shaky hands so he suggested a quick cup of tea before they headed into the direction of the town hall where the registry office was situated.

'Pity we couldn't have something stronger.' Karl remarked, as Heinz slopped the hot liquid into his saucer, his companion nodded in agreement.

The tea seemed to steady Heinz nerves, and they headed up the town hall steps just as the taxi drew up with Janet and her family.

Immediately he saw his bride to be the love shone right out of Heinz face, as Janet alighted from the taxi he took her arm firmly in his for the short walk up a stone staircase to the registrar's office.

Len in his pinstriped demob suit drew back for a moment whilst everyone else went through the wooden door just ahead, drawing a cigarette from a packet in his pocket he lit it and took a long draw on the small white stick before quickly extinguishing it when Rose appeared in the doorframe and remonstrated with a few sharp words, then she took a firm hold on his arm and almost pulled him inside.

Less than fifteen minutes later that they all emerged, a new bright band of gold glistening in the sunshine on Janet's third finger; her brothers quickly disposed of a small box of confetti they themselves had cut up from coloured paper, throwing it over the couple and a lot of it over themselves.

A few photographs were taken on the steps, with an ancient camera that belonged to Sylvia's father, and then the boys piled into Bill's car for the journey back home together with the bride and groom and Janet's parents.

Karl and Sylvia stood on the pavement to wave them goodbye before going hand in hand the short distance down the road to the bus station.

Sylvia gave her companion a sideways glance, she hardly recognized the man at her side dressed in his borrowed suit, he looked so handsome, his usually unruly hair slicked down with a touch of grease made his forehead seem wider.

For some unknown reason she felt strangely shy.

'That will be us soon.' Karl said softly.

She gazed up into his blue eyes.

'I wish—.' A lump in her throat stopped her saying anything further.

'He bent down and fleetingly touched her lips with his, a defiant note in his voice as he said.

'It will be.'

Tears sprang into her eyes, and she fished in her handbag for a handkerchief, only to find Karl putting one into her hand.

'Don't cry leibe; It will come right!' He hugged her close his English failed him in this emotional moment.

'I wish I could be as sure.' She said as they turned the corner to see their bus already on the stand belching smoke as it revved up its engine ready to leave.

'We will have to run.' She said, and he held her hand very firmly as her high heels bit into the pavement.

Puffing and panting they collapsed on a seat just as the bus took off; laughing together which lightened the mood they slid into each other on the wooden slatted seats.

Having paid the conductor, they sat quietly slithering together when the bus negotiated corners on the bendy road back to the village, Karl liked this it meant he could feel the closeness of her in her thin summer dress as she rolled against him, he wanted badly to kiss her but knew he couldn't in this public place so he teased her and they laughed together.

They were still laughing at some shared joke when they arrived at Janet's house, where the reception was already in full swing; a small knot of people had assembled there mostly close friends and family.

Karl looked with admiration at the buffet Peggy had prepared; small bridge rolls stuffed with egg and cress, and sausage rolls Peggy made with her own mixture of meat inside, little meat really mostly flavored breadcrumbs and herbs, and there were several varieties of homemade cakes and biscuits.

Karl's eyes were then drawn to the three tiered cake in the centre of the table; he looked at it incredulously.

'How did your mother manage to make that with the rationing?' He questioned.

Sylvia tapped the side of her nose.

'Wait and see.' She told him with a secret smile.

Karl's face was a picture when about half an hour later the bride and groom were called on to cut the cake and a cardboard apparition was removed to reveal a small fruit cake underneath that wasn't even iced.

'I would never have believed that wasn't the real thing.' He whispered quietly to Sylvia.

'My dad made it for his niece when she got married at the beginning of the war!' Sylvia explained.

'It has been used several times locally since sugar has been rationed.'

After the cake was cut, Janet and Sylvia went upstairs so that Janet could change into her 'Going away' outfit, a tweedy green suit that she would have preferred to wear for her wedding.

Although it had been a quick arrangement Sylvia had managed to sew her friend some pretty lingerie made out of parachute silk that Jean Finch had passed on to her in the final days of the war, and Janet had managed to get some embroidered nightdresses (embroidery on underwear had been banned since April 1942, and only recently allowed again) Sylvia now packed all of it lovingly into a small suitcase stroking the soft cloth with her hands, she knew the couple were not going far, only to their new abode which was to be the lodge at Winnie Bakers, but reasoned it was their wedding night and it was good to have some pretty things.

When Peggy had first suggested the lodge to them the suggestion was greeted at first with some dismay.

'You know how nosy Winnie is.' Janet had said with rather superior attitudes that made Peggy rather cross as it hadn't been the easiest thing to get Winnie to agree to let them have the tenancy at all.

'And anyway the place hasn't been lived in for years.' Janet added.

The only other option open to the couple was a small room in her mother's already overcrowded house so they decided there was no other option but to take up Winnie's offer.

Janet insisted Winnie wasn't told the truth about her condition as they scraped together to pay the rent six weeks in advance to give Janet a bit of security.

Heinz always careful with money had managed to save a little from the small amount the PoW's received for their work after their lodging money was taken out. He was aware that he had a sizable amount of money on deposit in a bank in Germany, but didn't say too much about it reasoning it was probably now worth very little with the economic situation being what it was there.

During the past couple of weeks Karl, Sylvia, Janet and Heinz spent all their little spare time doing up the lodge, distempering the walls cream and pink and scrubbing the floors, it came up quite presentable, with new linoleum on the floor and several bits of furniture they managed to acquire it now had quite a homely look about it.

Janet decided she would keep her job at the 'Home and Colonial' and tell no one about her pregnancy as she would have immediately been asked to leave; it was against the firm's policy to employ pregnant women. She knew she would have to work to support herself until Heinz got a job back in Germany; hoping that would be before her pregnancy became too obvious; pre-war she wouldn't have been able to work once she was a married woman but hostilities had changed all that.

Now the two of them stood together to say their goodbyes to the family before walking the short journey to the lodge, Rose with tears in her eyes kissed her daughter goodbye.

Although they were only going down further into the village and she could see her daughter every day for the time being she knew that a bigger separation wasn't that far away.

Sylvia and Karl stayed behind to help Rose clear away as Peggy had already left to see to her family's tea.

Later on the two of them walked together to the gate of Sylvia's house and Karl continuing down the lane to the Nissan huts alone.

CHAPTER TWENTY

'I'm taking some tea up to the harvest field; do you want to come?' Peggy asked her daughter the weekend following the wedding.

'Yes that would be lovely!' Sylvia said quickly slipping on her sandals.

She tried not to sound to enthusiastic but inside her heart slipped a beat as it would be a chance to see Karl who Harry had kept very busy in the past week after taking time to attend the wedding.

When mother and daughter left the house some twenty minutes later Peggy was grasping a large basket so Sylvia quickly took the other side to distribute the weight as they walked companionably together.

'The men are at Stammers Mead today.' Peggy announced as they made their way across the village to this site which was at the very low slopes of the downs where the last of the wheat harvest was being gathered.

Harvest was an especially tiring time; the introduction of 'double summertime' during the war meant that it didn't get dusk until ten thirty at night and this meant that the men worked in the fields until very late, some of the men then had to be up in the morning to milk the cows at about five thirty.

As the two of them walked along they could see the dust rising from the machinery as it scythed through the corn long before they reached the lane that ran adjacent to Stammers Mead.

This was on the far circle of the Phillips farm before the downs began to rise above and the last place the soil was good so it could be ploughed before the top soil became too thin and mostly chalk.

This present summer had been a long hot one and the chalk showed through the soil more than usual and in many more places. In a normal summer there was enough grass here for the sheep to clip at the edge of this field, this year everywhere was brown and wasted and only couch grass showed through in small green patches; this was no use at all to sheep so they had been relegated to pastures further down the hill.

As soon as they entered the field Sylvia was kept busy looking down to avoid the spiky cut edges of the corn which pierced through her cotton socks and sandaled feet making them quite sore, she tried to walk on the rough ground at the very edge of the field to avoid it, so it was sometime before she looked and saw Janet who waved them over she was busy unpacking the picnic she'd brought for her and Heinz on the softer grass by the hedge.

Sylvia slipped down beside her, whilst Peggy unfurled a table cloth, setting it out alongside them before depositing the food she'd brought in the basket onto it.

Sylvia looked over in the direction of the men and her heart fluttered when she recognized Karl with Heinz alongside handling fork loads of straw on the top of the Rick being built ready to use for the animals in the winter months.

It was quite a feast Peggy was now laying out on a gingham table cloth, she had as usual excelled herself with delicious egg and tomato sandwiches together with sausage rolls, a seed cake and bottles of cold tea, water and Peggy's homemade squash.

Harry had seen their arrival, and now looking up from the machinery he was operating he gave the men the signal to stop. Everyone then all wandered up the field to join the ladies after washing their hands under a tap at the end of the field and Peggy produced a small towel from her basket for them to dry their hands.

Karl slid down on the grass beside Ned and Harry together with several other men from the camp who were working on the harvest; he looked over to Sylvia and gave her a shy smile.

The PoW's were given no extra food when they worked late but Peggy always made provision for the ones working on the farm although this bit into her families rations.

Fortunately their hens were good layers, and tomatoes came from the ones Harry grew in the garden, bread had come off rationing just that July which made life easier and she was now able to be generous with this also.

All was quiet as the men bit hungrily into the picnic then they settled back to enjoy a well-earned short rest before continuing their work.

After eating Karl made his way over to Sylvia with the last of his tea in a mug, he took her hand and then the two of them walked away from the main group to just a little further up the hill where they could look down at the village below. Harry's eyes narrowed as he watched them go, but decided not to say anything after Peggy shot him a warning glance.

The view below was particularly good from Karl and Sylvia's vantage point; everywhere they looked was a sea of colour, mostly shades of green, with brown dotted here and there due mostly to the lack of rain.

Sunshine flashed off the many greenhouses where tomatoes and salad stuffs grew; the area was famous for this and it made up a great deal of the produce from Farmer Phillips farm, the smell of cut corn hung on the air, a musty smell together with the dust raised by the harvesting and made worse this year by the dry summer caught Sylvia in the throat making her cough.

Karl passed her his cup of cold tea, which he hadn't quite finished.

'That's better.' She said as the liquid hit the right spot.

'It is a beautiful place here.' Karl observed.

'Even if my home wasn't in the Russian sector of Germany and everything was alright, I could still live here very happily.' He said quietly.

'But you know I am very surprised that the Luftwaffe didn't bomb the greenhouses as the sun makes them shine so brightly!'

'Well mostly the raids were at night, and concentrated on the big cities, which was fortunate for us, I might not be here if it wasn't so!' Sylvia replied.

His face took a more serious tone.

'Yes, I agree with that, after all if it wasn't for the war, I should never have met you!' She squeezed his fingers and looked into his face just as a frown appeared on his brow.

'Something wrong?' She asked.

'Not really, it's just that most of the men at the camp have now got their repatriation times. We have been told that quite soon the camp will be closed and it will mean that I will have to find lodgings quite soon if I want to stay here.'

'Do you want to stay?' She asked quietly noting the edge in his voice as he said.

'There is no way I would do what Heinz is about to do and leave you, but Heinz position is very different to mine and I understand it, he will make good money as Germany rebuilds, and will be able to provide better for Janet there.'

'Yes I suppose that is so.' Sylvia sounded rather doubtful, and Karl went on to explain.

'Heinz was trained in the building industry before he joined up; you forget he is quite a few years older than me! I joined up straight from the Hitler youth so to my regret got no qualifications.' He sighed.

'But I repeat I would find it very hard to leave you whatever the circumstances.'

Sylvia looked thoughtful, not really knowing what to say, she knew what she would like to happen!

Karl turned her face to his and his blue eyes looked straight into her rich brown ones, she could see the love and sincerity there as he put her thoughts into words.

'I would be so happy if we could get married, and have a home here together.' He touched his finger with his lips and put it on hers; her heart swelled and ached with the same love that shone so honestly through his eyes.

Wrapped up in each other they didn't hear the approach of Janet and Heinz who had walked down the narrow path at the side of the field hand in hand and now dropped to the ground stretching themselves out alongside the other couple

Sylvia could clearly see the fear of the unknown that shadowed Janet's eyes, Heinz was due to go back to Germany in just two days and she wondered how she would feel if the same circumstances applied to her!

If Heinz wasn't able to get Janet to Germany before the child was born and there was a possibility this wouldn't happen, how was Janet going to manage alone? Once Janet finished work there would be no money at all and it would soon become apparent all that she was pregnant! If the money for the rent of the lodge wasn't paid Winnie Baker wouldn't wait, Janet would be homeless and how was she going manage with food and other things she would need for the baby, it was a serious question!

Heinz had promised that money would be sent as soon as he was settled; he said he had savings in Germany, but it was doubtful whether the bank was still operational. It was all so doubtful and up in the air.

'You will keep an eye out for Janet when I go.' Heinz said suddenly, his worried face turning in their direction but looking directly at Sylvia.

'Yes we will do what we can. You know we will!' She said with more conviction than she felt.

Heinz english had come on in leaps and bounds since the spring, thanks to his close association with Janet, and he now could be better understood.

'Yes I know you will.' Heinz's smile didn't reach his eyes.

'But it is a worry! I am sure it will all work out, my father said the building trade is starting to build up in the town where they are and my skills will be needed' Heinz voice had a more positive note to it.

Sylvia suddenly felt optimistic about the future.

'Do you think we shall be sitting here in ten years' time, looking back and saying how well things have gone?' She said with a giggle.

'With a couple of children each!' Karl and Sylvia said in unison, this made the girls collapse in laughter lightened the situation somewhat, Heinz who still had a frown between his brows didn't see any amusement in it at all, but then he didn't really understand the English humour.

'Great minds think alike.' Sylvia observed when she gained her composure.

A puzzled look knotted Karl's wide brow.

'I don't think I will ever understand your little British sayings.' He observed.

'Well as long as you understand the important things.' Sylvia replied as she followed Janet's gaze down to the workforce further down the field that were moving back to the hayrick.

'Looks as though you are required back at work,' She said rather sadly.

The four of them looked in the direction of the Rick that was half finished. Ned was already standing on the top waiting to pile up more straw and the rest of the laborers were beginning the task of getting the machinery going once again.

Heinz and Karl rose quickly to their feet ready to join the others aware recriminations could set in if they didn't return to the task, even though Heinz was returning home in just a couple of days, a full day's work was still required of him!

The two girls sat for a few minutes in quiet reflection as they watched the back of the two men make their way down the narrow path to the Rick.

'I really don't know how I am going to manage after Monday.' Janet said sadly opening the conversation, Sylvia could see dread in her eyes.

'I haven't said a lot to Heinz because it would spoil this brief time we have together, but already one or two people have made comments about me at work.' A worried frown appeared in her forehead.

'What sort of comments? You certainly don't look pregnant' Sylvia said softly.

'Well the morning sickness has been getting me down, and that isn't easy when you are working in a food shop!' Janet declared before adding.

'The girls there are not very kind and I know they talk about me, although they know I am married, they also know that Heinz is a German PoW and that's enough to set their tongues wagging.' She sighed.

'I wish I could walk away from it right now, and go back to Germany with Heinz and take our chances there. I have suggested it quite a few times, but he won't hear of it!' Tears stood out in her eyes, she quickly scrubbed them away with the back of her hand.

Sylvia put her arm round her friend.

'It will come right, I will be there for you and so will Karl.' She said with more conviction than she felt, Sylvia didn't know how they were going to be able to help; they had very little money and enough problems of their own already trying to convince her parents they were serious about each other, but she wasn't the type to let a friend down.

The two girls got to their feet and then wandered down the field together joining Sylvia's mother who had just finished putting all the things back into the basket ready for the journey home.

Nothing further was said about the conversation the two girls had previously as the three of them walked down the lane together, in the village they parted company to go back to their homes.

Janet cut a sad figure as she made her way to the dark entrance to the lodge at the edge of Winnie's house. Peggy turned to her daughter as they watched Janet go.

'I feel really sorry for that girl; she really doesn't know what she is up against. Just married this should be the happiest time of her life and just look at her!' She gave a sideways glance in Sylvia's direction. 'I must admit, I am glad that isn't you!'

Sylvia remained silent, she was glad also she wasn't in Janet's position, glad too that she knew Karl wouldn't put her in that situation, the way they were going was the right way, even though it was going to be an uphill struggle to make her parents see that!

It was at the harvest festival two Sundays later that the Reverent Hounsome shaking hands with his parishioners as they left the church, leaned forward to Karl and pressed his hand into his

'Could you wait for me in the vestry before you go off; I have some news for you.' He said.

Karl went back into the church, just as Sylvia and other members of the choir were hanging up their long vestments and adorning their outside clothes.

Sylvia looked at him enquiringly as he came up to her. Now the busy harvest time was over he was free on Sundays and today he was invited to have lunch with Sylvia's family.

Harry had objected when Peggy had first suggested it, but she pointed out that if they didn't make Karl welcome at their house it would only drive the couple to meet in secret and ultimately push them closer together; privately Peggy liked Karl and had no problems with his nationality, she only hoped perhaps Harry would see the good in him in time, although she still had reservations about Sylvia settling down with one man at only sixteen.

'The vicar says he has some news for me so you go on because I know you like to help your mum with the lunch, I shouldn't be long.' Karl told Sylvia.

'That sounds ominous.' A smile lit up her face as it always did when she saw him. Although her voice was serious as she said.

'Well I hope it is some good news!'

Karl touched her lightly on the shoulder, and she felt the warmth of his hand through the thin summer coat she was wearing and the now familiar longing that this always brought went through her being.

'Are you sure you don't want me to wait with you?' She said looking into his blue eyes.

'No you go on; I will try and be there by twelve thirty; I know your mother likes to be punctual with lunch, but I am not sure how long I will be.' He answered giving her a quick hug before releasing her.

'Seeing you have nearly an hour, it should be long enough.' She said in a teasing way.

'I'll see you back at our house then.' Smiling she turned on her heels, and her footsteps echoed round the stone walls as she made her way to the wooden door that led to the porch and outside, he watched her go, her trim figure and shapely legs reminded him how lucky he had been to find her.

The church was now empty and for a moment Karl stood and admired the fruit flowers and vegetables arranged around the font and in front of the altar to celebrate the harvest festival, the air was filled with the smell of the chrysanthemums, it wasn't a smell Karl particularly liked it reminded him of funerals, and this always made him melancholy with thoughts of Wilhelm and ultimately of his family back in Germany, they could well no longer be alive.

Reminiscing to himself he recalled that this time last year the PoW's were coming to church under an escort how things had changed, now the remaining men still here were completely free to come and go as they pleased, and soon the PoW camp would be closed for good.

For the first time in a long time Karl actually felt he belonged somewhere, thanks to Sylvia and to a degree her family, the exception being her father!

Karl turned suddenly as he heard a voice boom from behind.

'Are you having dinner at our house?' Harry descended the three small steps from the organ in front of him; Karl was taken by surprise he thought Harry had already left with the rest of the family.

Kart had noticed a change in Harry recently he seemed more approachable especially now work on the farm wasn't so hectic, the younger man had been invited to Sunday dinner with the family most weeks. He hoped this was a good omen but with Harry's temperament you could never be sure.

'Yes Sylvia has invited me, and of course your wife!' Karl said almost apologetically as he realized he'd missed the hostess out.

'I am just waiting for the vicar; he said he has something to tell me.' He told the older man by way of explanation.

'Otherwise I would have walked down the hill with Sylvia.' He finished.

'Well let's hope the vicar has some good news for you!' Harry gave a rare smile suddenly thinking perhaps there was news of Karl's family; he knew the vicar had been implicated in trying to get information for Karl about them.

A smile lit up Harry's face at this thought, if that news did come through Karl would possibly return home! Now that would be good news and probably knock on the head Karl's relationship with his daughter! But in reality Harry knew it was highly likely that the Reverent Hounsome wanted to talk to Karl about something going on at the camp, it was generally acknowledged that the vicar valued Karl's opinion about certain matters to do with the PoW's

'Don't be late, Peggy likes the meal on the table for twelve thirty sharp' Was Harry's parting shot as his heels clipped along the stone flagged aisle and he made his way out of the large oak front door of the church.

Just then vicar came rushing in, calling out to Karl as he came to where the young man was standing.

'Sorry to keep you.' The Reverent was breathless and could hardly get the words out.

'The Misses Marshall had some parish news to speak about, and it is almost impossible to get away from them without appearing rude.' The vicar almost flopped down in a pew and signaled for Karl to join him patting the seat beside him, the vicar took out a large white handkerchief from his beneath his vestment and mopped his brow before returning it to its place, and then with a smile he turned to Karl.

'I didn't want you to have to wait for the news I have.' Karl could hear the buzz of excitement in the other man's voice as he slid his trouser bottom into the wooden pew alongside the vicar.

'The Red Cross rang me rather late yesterday evening with some news about your family; and I thought you would want to know about it as soon as possible.'

For just a moment Karl didn't think he had quite heard what the Reverent had said; the room spun slightly, the news wasn't a bit what he was expecting and the complete shock showed in his face.

The vicar took up the look and paused for a moment before looking Karl straight in the eye.

'Did you understand what I said? 'The vicar was mystified; he knew Karl was fluent in English so he hadn't addressed him in German like he would have most of the other PoW's

'Yes—Of course Yes!' That was all the words that would come out of Karl's mouth, he felt elation rise within him, yet fear also wanting desperately to hear what the Reverent Hounsome had to say but something seemed to be holding him back; suppose the news was bad was the thought that immediately went through his mind.

'The Red Cross has traced your people; the farm where they lived has been taken over by the Russian authorities, your mother and sister are at present living in one room just outside of Dresden.' The vicar looked serious and took Karl's hand in his.

'But it isn't all good news; sadly your father has died.'

For a long moment the shock of what he had just heard stunned Karl's brain, he tried to talk, but the words wouldn't come out, white as a sheet he looked down and put his head in his hands.

The vicar used to dealing with such situations put his arm round Karl's shoulders.

'Sit quietly for a few moments.' He advised kindly.

'It is a lot for you to take in.'

'The Red Cross is forwarding the address so you can get in touch and there is more information, which they have promised to forward to me as soon as they have it.'

Karl sat in silence for a few moments fighting his emotions; the Vicar still with his arm around the other man's shoulders was silent letting the information he had just imparted sink in.

Finally Karl looked up; with unshed tears in his eyes he took his pocket watch out and glanced at the time.

'I'd better go, Sylvia's mother has lunch at 12 30.' He said the words seemed to be coming from a long way off.

'Knowing Peggy she won't mind if you are late, especially when you share this news with them all.' The vicar said holding out his hand.

'Nevertheless I don't want to keep them waiting!' Karl got shakily to his feet looking about him as though in a daze and began to walk slowly away.

'You sure you will be alright.' Concern etched the Vicar's voice as he called after the receding figure.

'Yes I am sure.' Karl picked up his feet and almost rushed out of the door; he had to get away and think his own thoughts and put this news in its rightful prospective.

Karl never recalled walking out of the church or any of the walk back to Sylvia's house, he just knew he had to see her, she was his anchor, and his whole world never was his need of her so urgent.

Sylvia knew immediately when Karl walked through the back door that something was very wrong, he seemed in a daze with a mixture of joy and sadness etched into his face.

'You have had some news about your family.' She said knowing instinctively that was what was.

She stood behind him and helped him off with his coat then steered him towards a chair at the kitchen table already laid up for dinner he seemed in a trance.

Peggy turned from the kitchen range where she was giving the last basting to the roast meat for dinner, she took one look at Karl's pale face and it was immediately obvious to her he'd had a shock, she quickly made and poured out a cup of hot sweet tea which she put it into his hands.

'Drink that down.' She ordered then turning to her daughter she said.

'Don't ask him any questions, he will tell you when he feels a bit better.'

Over the meal Karl told them his news and all of the family Harry included rallied round him. The banter Ned, Mickey and Karl usually made with everyone over the meal was sadly absent as they let Karl recall what the Reverent Hounsome had told him, and let him speak about his family.

Afterwards when the washing was done they all sat together in the small sitting room and Harry brought up the subject of Karl's family again, looking at Karl out of the corner of his eye, he said.

'It must be so nice to know that your mother and sister are alive.'

'Yes, it is a great relief, as I said over dinner I don't have any details about their situation yet, the Red Cross is going to send particulars through as soon as possible.'

'Well at least you have somewhere to go back to now.' Harry said quietly.

Karl didn't really know how to reply to that, he knew Harry's words had undertones, and his thoughts were obviously on the fact that Karl would now be returning to his family, which had implications on his relationship with Sylvia.

But Harry's remarks had made Sylvia very cross she like her father had a quick temper, she had watched her father closely since dinner time when Karl's position had become clear and noticed her father's attitude had completely changed, she could see where his thoughts were lying; Karl would return to Germany and hopefully completely forget all about her!

She knew this would suit her father, he'd always been against their union; well if that's what he thought he was very wrong, she was sure their love was strong enough not going to change and Karl would not be returning back to his homeland whatever else happened.

She decided there and then it was best to get the situation out into the open straight away.

'Karl won't be going back dad.' Sylvia's eyes flashed defiantly as she faced her father.

'You don't realize how bad things are in his part of Germany.'

Her father's face was now turning a shade of puce.

'I don't think you can make decisions for Karl, it might be easier for him to stay here than to return home!' Harry's voice raised an octave as he replied.

'Please don't get angry.' Karl's quiet voice cut through.

'I want the best for your daughter, and I do want us to get married, I love her too much to return home and leave her here.' He said simply.

Sylvia was really angry now.

'How could you bring this up, when Karl has just heard that his father has died.' She snapped.

Harry was adamant, his voice sharp and his eyes cold as he looked straight at the two of them and said forcefully.

'It's best to get things straight into the open, nothing will happen between the two of you until Sylvia is of age, that is twenty one, and it is no use you thinking otherwise!'

Sylvia looked across at her mother who had raised her eyes from the jumper she was knitting.

'Why don't you and Karl take a walk?' Peggy suggested she knew it was no use arguing with Harry when he was in this mood, and to continue the argument would only antagonize him and his daughter more, she also realized it wasn't kind to antagonize Karl after he'd had such devastating news.

Sylvia rose from her seat and took Karl's hand, snatching her coat and his from a hook on the back door, she swiftly put it hers over shoulders then the two of them quietly went out of the back door hand in hand.

Harry settled down in his armchair; but Peggy got up and went into the kitchen to prepare some scones for tea, torn inside between her husband and her daughter she felt she had to do something to keep her thoughts straight, deep down inside she knew this wasn't going away confrontations lay ahead between the two of them and she was stuck in the middle!

It was late when Sylvia returned alone; Karl had left her at the door to make his way back to the camp as he had an early start the next day on the milking rota.

Sylvia's heart sank to her boots as she was greeted with an ominous silence from both of her parents as they raised their eyes to hers, she saw her father's features were set like concrete.

Seeing the downcast look in his daughters face her father immediately set about the defensive of his stand against her.

'It's no use looking at me like that Sylvia I am not going to give in to you!'

Sylvia rounded on him,

'It's because of his nationality!'

'No it isn't just that Sylvia you are only sixteen, and it is too young to marry!'

'So you would rather I wait until I was over thirty like you and waste all those precious years.' She retorted.

Her father ignored that remark and continued.

'You have a good life, and much to look forward too, I don't want you to do something you will regret.' A smile played at the corner of his mouth, making Sylvia feel more cross because she could see that it was false.

'The only regret I will have is not fighting for Karl; it isn't going to change Dad, he will wait till I am twenty one if he has to, but I am not prepared to wait that long,' Her eyes so like her fathers flashed defiantly, she hadn't quite so quick a temper as him, but could make her point when roused, her face was red now and her cheeks burnt.

'You are not going to take away four years of my life!'

'You have no choice! That is my last word on the subject!' Her father turned his face now puce with fury into his newspaper.

'That's what you think.' Sylvia turned on her heel and made her way out of the room; she knew it was no use arguing with Harry when he was in this mood, but there had to be a way out of this and she was deter med to find it.

Peggy sighed from her armchair at the other side of the fire place, she would talk to Harry about the situation later when he'd calmed down, but from the set of his jaw she knew it would be almost impossible to change his mind, it niggled at her, it reminded her of the years of loneliness she had suffered when Harry had refused to get married and put his family first. She could see her daughter and Karl had something special she realized also that a year seemed an awful long time when you were young but knowing her daughter she was aware Sylvia was unlikely to change her mind however long it took!

CHAPTER TWENTY ONE

Sylvia was still feeling exasperated the next day, and she mulled over in her mind the events of yesterday as she left the cottage for work, so engrossed she was that she failed to hear the bus approaching her stop to take her to town. Fortunately there were other people waiting as it screeched to a halt and she ran down the lane just in time to climb aboard. Taking a seat near the front she gave the exact fare of 6d the price of the return fare to town to the conductor standing at her elbow ready to issue her ticket.

The bus sped along to the final village stop brakes screeching once again as it pulled up where a collection of people waited expectantly for its arrival.

Glancing out of the window and watching people board Sylvia was surprised to see Bridget in the queue she thought her friend returned to her boarding school a few of weeks ago.

Bridget's face was wreathed in smiles she slid into the seat beside Sylvia.

The bus, one manufactured during the war had wooden slatted seats instead of upholstered ones, so as the bus started off the two girls had to hang on tight to avoid slipping on the surface and banging into each other which caused a smile between them.

Sylvia turned to her companion.

'You're early today.' She said opening up the conversation. 'And I am surprised to see you; I thought you'd returned to school.'

Bridget sounded apologetic as she replied.

'Yes, I should have returned for the autumn term which is to be my last before I leave in the spring for Switzerland. 'Then a serious look took over her face.

'My dad has to go into East Grinstead hospital for another operation in the next few days; Mum doesn't show it to others but privately she does get into a bit of a state when these things come round, so I decided she needed my support during this time.' Bridget said by way of explanation.

'And surprisingly she didn't object to my being off school, so she must really be worried at the moment!'

Sylvia didn't voice her surprise at this revelation; but Bridget was quick to pick up on the look she gave.

'Yes I know that isn't the way Mum comes over, she does give the impression she can cope with anything! To be fair she can cope with most things; she is just a bit vulnerable over my Dad, even though she doesn't show it!' Bridget said quickly adding.

'Dad has been very brave, but then so has mum. They had a very different life before the air crash.' She added quietly.

'Yes my mum told me about it, she talks a lot to your dad when up at your house.' Sylvia said.

'My Dad has a lot of time for Peggy; although nearly blind he is a shrewd man and recognizes genuine people.'

Sylvia gave a satisfied smile as Bridget said this; it was nice for someone to compliment her mother, who she knew did sterling work in the village with little recognition.

'Your Dad is a very courageous man. 'Sylvia said with real feeling in her voice, continuing.

'All the pilots that saved us during the battle of Britain are we all owe them all a great deal!'

Sylvia could hear the sadness in Bridget's voice as she spoke.

'Yes we do and so many of them have been badly injured, I have met many of the brave men, some of them with worse injuries than my dad, the sight is the worse problem with him, it does restrict him so! The rest he can put up with. 'Bridget was quiet for a long moment then she said.

'This isn't generally known and he certainly wouldn't tell anyone this, but he was ok when he bailed out of the plane when it crashed landed, he had just a broken arm.' A tear glistened at the corner of her eye and she fished a handkerchief out of her handbag to blow her nose.

'He went back to save a colleague and the two of them were caught in the flames that suddenly burst out, they were both horrifically disfigured by flash burns, do you know even his eyelids were burnt!' She blew her nose again.

'He hasn't been able to see properly since, the last time he really saw me I was nine, and he doesn't have a clue what I look like now.' Bridget scrubbed away tears that now threatened full flow.

'I find that the hardest thing of all!'

Sylvia looked at her companion swallowing hard on a tearful lump in her own throat before replying.

'Yes I can understand your feelings there.'

She was silent as the bus conductor who was now at Bridget's elbow disturbed their conversation, Bridget fished in her purse for the fare.

Sylvia was grateful the conductor had come along at that point, so that she didn't have to say any more, she wasn't sure she could keep the tears that threatened in check when she thought about Bridget's father, so she glanced out of the window.

The bus had now left behind the houses of the village open fields and meadows were on either side of the road and would remain so on the journey until they reached the edge of the town.

Two figures in the distance working on the cloches arranged in rows in the fields caught her eye, she couldn't see their faces as they were bent low over their task, she was sure one of the figures was Ned, the other one could be Karl who often worked with their evacuee.

Bridget having paid the conductor followed her friends gaze.

Glad she could now change the focus to something other than her father's demise; Bridget put a hand on Sylvia's knee, and pointed to the figures in the distance.

'Do you think one of them is Karl?' She asked.

'Yes I think it might be; one of them looks like Ned and Karl often gets to work alongside him.'

Bridget smiled 'You like him a lot. Don't you?'

'I didn't think you knew that?' There was no mistaking the surprise in Sylvia's voice.

Bridget smiled at her friend's naivety;

'I have seen you together at the village hop and on other occasions remember!' She said quietly not adding it was obvious they thought a great deal of each other it showed in their faces!

Bridget looked thoughtful for a moment then she spoke again.

'I suppose Karl like a lot of these men will soon return home, I hear the repatriation of them is going ahead apace now.'

211

Sylvia looked down at her lap so that Bridget wouldn't see her eyes and read anything into her expression.

'Yes. Heinz has recently returned Karl though comes from the part of Germany now in the control of the Russians.' She lowered her voice. 'He doesn't want to go back!'

'If I am honest I have already heard that quite a few of the men are in that position. I must say that with the situation there you can't really blame them!'

Bridget replied before glancing at her companion again and hesitating a little before she spoke.

'Please don't take the wrong way what I am about to say will you?'

'Err—no!' Sylvia looked up to see Bridget staring straight at her; she was very forthright like her mother and spoke her mind.

'I have read in the newspapers recently that some of these men want to marry local girls to make their stay here more comfortable.'

Sylvia felt her hackles rise, then a fury started to make itself felt from the depths of her being; her first thought was why Bridget who she viewed as a good friend would say things like this in fact how dare she say things like this!

Then another thought went through her mind; was this people really thought? Or had her mother put this in Bridget's mind? Her mother had the opportunity when she was at work and it would be a subject that she would find more than a little difficult to discuss with her daughter as it would appear she was being unjust; also it was bound to cause a rift between the two of them, knowing Sylvia would defend Karl.

'Has my mother said anything to you about this?' Sylvia asked softly outwardly giving no sign of the turmoil now going on within her.

'Why do you say that?' Bridget looked a bit put out, and then she stroked her chin thoughtfully before giving her reply.

'Well I have to admit you mother did say she was worried about the situation with Karl.' She hesitated before adding.

'But that has nothing to do with this! Please don't be annoyed for me asking that question, you know me always go in feet first!' She paused looking sideways at her companion giving her a wry smile.

'I do have your best interests at heart no matter what your mother says or for that matter thinks.' Bridget said, adding,

'I don't want to give offence who am I to tell you what to do? I just wanted to make sure you know the facts.' Bridget patted Sylvia's hand.

Sylvia eyes flashed 'Yes I do know those things, but unless you are in my position you can't have any idea what I feel about it.' She then added.

'And yes I do love Karl, maybe I am young, but I do know my own mind.' Sylvia struggling to keep her feelings in check surprised herself with the intensity of her reply.

'Perhaps that it what your mother is most concerned about, you are so young to think of tying yourself down! I don't think that I could commit myself to someone and I am a year older than you.' Bridget said defensively.

Sylvia was indignant and it showed in her voice.

'If you don't mind me saying so, my life is very different from yours, I left school at fourteen and have been in full time employment ever since.'

'Yes I know that is true!' Bridget quietly replying. 'I have been sheltered from so many things; I don't even know what it is like to work!'

Sylvia nodded in agreement, she could feel her temper cooling off a bit, this wasn't Bridget's fault, she had led a sheltered life, and hadn't any idea what life was like for people like Sylvia, but to her credit at least she was interested in how other people lived, which was more than could be said for many in the village, like the Cookson's for example.

'And I shall spend at least another eighteen months education if my dad has his way.' Bridget continued.

'My parents think this is all for the best because this is the way they were brought up, but life is so different now; I sometimes wish they understood that. With the world in the state it is in, I feel I should do something more useful than a finishing school in Switzerland!' Her voice took on a wistful tone.

'But I couldn't let them down, it's expected of me!' She finished the words with a small sigh.

Sylvia felt her spirits lift a bit at Bridget's words; she always thought Bridget was happy with her privileged life.

'I can see your situation isn't what I thought, I suppose we all wish for things we cannot have and we all have to consider other people's feelings, but I also believe you have to stick up for things you know are right, don't you?' Sylvia had real feeling in her voice.

Bridget nodded in reply as Sylvia continued.

'The most important thing is that I trust Karl, I know he is honest; it is true that in his case he won't be returning to his homeland even though it seems the Red Cross has located his family after all this time!' Sylvia hesitated for a moment catching her breath.

'They are in the Russian sector of Germany.' Sadness echoed her words.

'You know from the news how badly these people treat the population there, and it is far worse than what is reported, Karl has had a letter from his friend Hans. He says the conditions are terrible quite a lot of the letter he sent was censured and blanked out; he advised Karl not to return.' Sylvia took a deep breath.

'It seems that Karl's mother and sister are still alive, yet it would be foolish for him to go back, he has a much better future here and the government has said that these men can stay.' A tear stood out in the corner of Sylvia's eye.

'But can you think for a moment how lonely Karl feels? He is in a strange country that was recently at war with his, and he has no one here at all. And it isn't that I feel sorry for him either in case you were thinking that, I will wait until I am twenty one to marry him if I have to. I am convinced neither of us is going to change,' Sylvia's face and cheeks were ablaze as she defended him finishing with these words.

'Karl has said he will wait until I am twenty one if he has too.'

Bridget waited a moment digesting Sylvia's outburst before replying.

'Well I'm glad and relieved to hear you say that! It wasn't easy for me to be so open with you! I felt I had to bring it to your attention before someone else did. It is much easier to talk to some one of your own age than an older person who will lecture you.'

'Yes it is.' Sylvia agreed giving Bridget beaming smile, if by chance her mother was behind the conspiracy she knew Bridget would give a good impression when she reported back, that was the nature of the girl.

'I will marry Karl no matter how long it takes no one is going to stop me!' Sylvia determinately as her thought went back to her last night's confrontation with her father.

'No matter how long it takes, I won't change my mind, I have even thought about eloping to Scotland.' She finished.

Bridget's looked taken back by this news and her eyes widened.

'You wouldn't would you!' There was an edge to her voice.

Sylvia smiled at her friend's reaction

'The trouble is we couldn't afford to or to spend the time there required before we could marry. I believe the residential qualifications are three weeks before you can marry.' Sylvia exclaimed.

'That is a long time!' Bridget said thoughtfully.

'Yes there are so many questions about that!' Sylvia said.

'For instance where could we stay if we did go? A boarding house would be expensive and we have no money!' Sylvia sighed before adding.

'So that would also be out of the question wouldn't it?'

Bridget looked admiringly at Sylvia before her face took on a more thoughtful expression it was a few moments before she spoke again, her next remark stunning Sylvia.

'Have you ever considered asking the court for their permission for your marriage?' She asked.

Sylvia gave Bridget a puzzled look.

'What do you mean?' The looks in her face a mixture of curiosity and surprise.

Bridget smiled and with a triumphal note to her voice she said.

'Well it is possible to apply to the court if consent to a marriage isn't given.'

'Is it? I didn't know that.'

Bridget's smile now exploded all over her face.

'Look.' She said. 'I will have a word with my dad and see what he says, he knows quite a few on the bench, I won't mention that it is you I am enquiring for; it would put him in a difficult position if it came out to your mother when she is working!'

For a moment Sylvia was quiet, not knowing how to reply.

'You would do that for me? 'She stammered out.

'Yes, it would be a pleasure and indeed why not?' Bridget's voice had real feeling in it.

'You have made me see things in a different light.'

'I don't know what to say!' Sylvia's voice echoed her feelings.

'Well wait and see what I come up with!' Bridget said with a twinkle in her eye.

They sat for a long moment in silence watching the fields flash by the window of the bus both deep in thought.

Sylvia broke the silence, steering the conversation into safer waters.

'You mentioned your Dad a bit back; he is a very brave and kind man.'

'Yes he is! Bridget's face lit up when she spoke again about her father.

'So are so many of the others who were very badly injured in the war. We shall see them when we go to the hospital; there is a very famous surgeon Archie McIndoe there who has rebuilt so many of the faces damaged by fire and other things during the war.'

'Yes I have heard about him.' Sylvia acknowledged

'A lot of people don't realize how brave these men are.' Bridget's voice was serious now.

'Yet they are so cheerful; they have a club they call the guinea pig club, we have a drink with them whilst we are at the hospital, they are such a jolly crowd you would never believe how they have suffered, they never show it.' Bridget wiped away a tear that appeared at the corner of her eyes.

'It cuts me up every time we go, yet I wouldn't miss it for the world, it brings everyday problems down to size!' Sylvia looked away so that her friend wouldn't see the unshed tears in her own eyes, she'd heard so much about how badly injured some of these young men had been, especially those who had been in the Battle of Britain, and knew first hand from seeing Bridget's own father how badly damaged they were.

Glancing now out of the bus window, Sylvia observed houses were now flashing by the bus windows, so they were nearly at their destination.

Turning to her companion she said.

'You won't mention to my mother our conversation today will you?'

'No I promise that I won't, it will be our secret.' She patted Sylvia on the hand.

'But I will make enquiries about the court and let you know.'

The bus screeched to a stop at the terminus.

'Thank you so much you have given me hope! 'Sylvia affectionately squeezing her companions arm as she gathered her belongings together ready to alight.

'Hope all goes well with your Dad.' Was Sylvia's parting shot as she rushed off to her work, leaving Bridget to raid the shops!

CHAPTER TWENTY TWO

During the first week in October things came to a head for Janet; she collapsed at work and throughout the kafuffle that followed she had to admit to her employers that she was pregnant.

They were sympathetic, but company rules forbade pregnant women working; an exception had been made during the war years, now that there was peace and employment was more plentiful the company had returned to their pre-war conditions so they had no option but to dismiss Janet immediately.

Mr. Morishstein had just left for the bank and Sylvia was alone in the shop when the shop bell rang, quickly putting down her work she got to her feet to attend to the customer and looked straight into the tear stained eyes of Janet who fell on her shoulder and sobbed as though her heart would break before she poured out the events of the morning to her friend.

Fortunately the girl had gained her composure somewhat when some five minutes later Mr. Morishstein returned to the shop, seeing at once the girl talking to his employee was very distressed the kindly man looked at the clock and suggested that Sylvia take an early lunch to talk to her friend.

The two girls quickly made their way to Lyons tea shop; the smell of food wafting up as they entered made Janet feel a little faint so Sylvia took matters into her own hands insisting Janet sat down whilst she fetched tea and sandwiches from the counter for them both, then Sylvia insisted that they demolished the food before they spoke further.

'What will I do' Janet said as she drained her cup, despair ingrained her face, as she looked Sylvia in the eye.

'I can't go back to my mothers, they are already overcrowded!' The wail in her voice rose with anxiety,

'There is no way I shall be able to stay where I am, I can't afford the rent.' The tears flowed again.

'You know what a field day Winnie Baker will have at my expense if I don't pay on time, she will enjoy gossiping about that round the village!' Janet looked down at the table.

'She will have enough to gossip about when my condition becomes obvious also won't she! I wish I'd taken my chance and gone with Heinz it can't be any worse than this!'

Janet looked up again her eyes puffy from crying Sylvia was at a loss now as to what to say to comfort her friend, glancing round she observing the café was now filling up with the lunch time crowd and people beginning to look in their direction because it was so obvious Janet was upset; so she thought quickly how to get out of this situation.

'We can't really sort this out here can we?' Sylvia drained her cup and got to her feet gesturing to Janet to pick up her bag from the floor. The two girls walked out of the tea shop glad to be away from eyes and ears that were straining to know what was going on between the two girls.

They walked to a seat on the promenade, the wind blowing off the sea into their faces dried Janet's tears and put a bit of colour into her pinched cheeks, but her face remained a picture of misery.

Sylvia looked at her friend; she was at a loss to know what to say!

'At least let's look on the good side of things.' She advised hoping he voice sounded more hopeful than she felt.

'Remember Heinz insisted he paid the rent six weeks in advance before he left, so that is a plus and you have already received some money from him, I am sure when he knows the situation he won't let you down.' Janet looked down at her feet saying nothing.

Sylvia glanced at a clock on the pier head. Mr. Morishstein would be expecting her back at work shortly; turning to Janet she said.

'I have to go back to work, I suggest you make your way home and I will come over as soon as I have had my tea tonight we can talk together and see what can be done to sort things out' She suddenly smiled.

'You know I have an idea about what could be a solution, but it would take too long to sort out now, it could be the answer to the problem.'

Janet rose reluctantly as Sylvia got to her feet and picked up her handbag.

'Come on, I will come with you to the bus station.' She said linking her arm through Janet's as they walked along together.

The bus was already on the stand when they got to the terminus and Sylvia encouragingly put her arm round her friends shoulder.

'Go to your mums, at least then you won't be on your own.' She coaxed as Janet prepared to board the vehicle.

'I can't do that!' The tears formed in Janet's eyes once more.

'All I will get is I told you so from her!'

Well go home put your feet up, I'll come round tonight as promised and together and we will talk this through, there is a way out of this; we just have to find out what is the best thing to do.' She said encouragingly.

Giving her friend a slight push towards the waiting transport she watched as Janet sat herself in a window seat.

The driver started the engine and Sylvia saw the conductor was now at Janet's elbow, with a swift wave, she moved away quickly walking back to the tailor's shop to resume her duties, her mind in a whirl.

Seeing his employee once more settled back to her work, Mr. Morishstein left to get his lunch leaving her in charge of the shop.

Sylvia sat for a while looking at the fine stitching she had done that morning on a suit for one of their wealthier clients, the work she was doing required her complete concentration but the situation she'd just witnessed took her mind off her work and she still hadn't really pulled herself together when Mr. Morishstein arrived back some 45 minutes later.

She was pleased to see that her employer had another person with him as he let himself into the shop; her heart rose perhaps the distraction would mean he wouldn't notice that she had done very little in his absence.

Mr. Morishstein took the new arrival into his office at the back.

Sylvia worked quickly and had just finished the required task when Mr. Morishstein called out to her.

'Would you come in here Sylvia please?' Her feet echoed on the wooden floor boards as she scuttled across in her high heels at his bidding.

'This is Mr. Eve.' Her employer introduced the man now sitting opposite him.

'It is nice to meet you.' Sylvia looked into the pale blue eyes of a man who held out his hand to her and gave her a beaming smile as he shook her small proffered one in his.

His accent seemed strange; Sylvia wasn't sure exactly where the man came from, deciding it had a definite American twang about it.

'Mr. Eve has a proposition for us.' Mr. Morishstein said.

She looked puzzled; it was most unlike her employer to ask her opinion about anything to do with work, usually she just did whatever was asked of her.

Mr. Eve bent down to take something from a box Sylvia had seen him bring through the door when both the men had come back a short time ago.

She looked on in amazement as he set a small machine like object onto her boss's desk, clamping it firmly down on the edge of the table.

Mr. Morishstein thinks you will soon be able to master this Mr. Eve explained as he took in Sylvia's mystified look.

'It repairs Nylon stockings.' He said by way of explanation, and then he took a small packet from his pocket and withdrew a pair of sheer examples.

Putting one very carefully over a small mushroom type stand at the bottom of the machine, he plugged in the machine and proceeded to show them how to mend a ladder in the stockings. Sylvia watched enthralled, nylon stockings were a luxury, it was only since the Americans had been billeted here during the war that people in this country had become aware they even existed!

She had heard they were available on the 'black market' at a price well out of what Mr. Morishstein paid her; even silk stockings were a luxury!

Because of clothing rationing during the war most women only wore stockings for special occasions, young ones like herself often painted the back of their legs with gravy browning to make it look as though they had seamed stockings on, her mother Peggy had lisle ones that had been repeatedly darned.

'What do you think' Mr. Morishstein asked his young lady assistant.

She looked down at the examples that Mr. Eve laid out in front of her, she couldn't believe how sheer and fine they were, she was almost afraid to touch them.

'Do you think you could do it?'

'I would like to try' Sylvia said rather nervously; the enthusiasm she usually displayed over anything new seemed to be missing on this occasion as she sat down at the seat Mr. Eve had vacated and began to work on the small machine following his instructions.

At first she was afraid she would ruin the material that was almost like gossamer in fineness, soon she found that for all its fineness the nylon had strength and in just a little while Sylvia had neatly mended a very small pile of nylon stockings, to both the two men's satisfaction.

'Well if this will bring in as many customers as you say it will.' Mr. Morishstein said to the other man looking in Sylvia's direction.

'And this young lady agrees to operate it; I will give it a trial.'

Mr. Eve gave a beaming smile before he said.

'Well you will of course have only a few customers at first with the clothing rationing. But nylon stockings are available readily if you know where to find them!' He looked at Mr. Morishstein knowingly tapping the side of his nose.

'And I am told on good authority, that clothing coupons will be removed in the foreseeable future, then nylon stockings will be available and all the women will want them!' Mr. Eve's smile was convincing.

'You will also be first in the district with a machine to repair them, as they won't be cheap!'

It was a very satisfied Mr. Eve who left the shop some half an hour later, with a month's trial of the machine agreed upon.

Mr. Morishstein who had seen him off the premises turned to Sylvia who had resumed her work.

'You won't mind Mr. Eve's suggestion that you operate the machine sitting in the window space.' He asked.

'No as it faces north the sun isn't going to be a problem.' Sylvia replied with a smug grin, she would have done anything for the penny her employer had offered for every five pairs of nylons mended, this was to be over and above her weekly wages; the only problem was that at present not many people wore nylon stockings, they seemed only to be available to the wealthy who had a lot more money than the people she knew, but time would tell!

She glanced at the clock as her employer started to put his working implements away, she was surprised to see it was almost time to catch her bus; at least this afternoons activities had made the time past quickly by and taken her mind off the difficult evening that lay ahead with Janet.

Sylvia pushed her plate back as soon as she had finished her evening meal and looked at the clock.

Peggy followed her gaze.

'Going out?' Her mother asked as she took the plate from the table and put it in the washing up bowl before running a cotton mop swiftly over it.

'Yes I am going to see Janet; she came into the shop today and was a bit upset, so I said I would go round after tea.' Sylvia got to her feet, and glanced out of the window so that Peggy wouldn't see her face, her mother was good at reading expressions and converting them into conclusions, Sylvia didn't want her mother to have an inkling of what was on her mind until she had discussed it with Janet.

'I thought I'd go straight away before the dusk comes down.' She said as she reached for her coat on a hook on the back door.

'Could you drop Mickey off at 'The Sunbeams' on your way, it's at the Salvation Army Hall?' Peggy asked looking up.

'Yes of course, if he is ready now.' Buttoning up her coat Sylvia reached for her scarf.

'Better make sure you wrap up its quite chilly out.' She called to her brother.

'I did want to listen to Dick Barton on the radio.' Mickey protested from the depths of an armchair in the sitting room.

'You can always catch up with the omnibus on Saturday.' Peggy said in a voice Mickey knew best not to argue with.

'But I won't know what is happening, and everyone at school will, besides there is a good film on at the Odeon cinema club on Saturday morning when the omnibus is on.' Mickey pleaded.

'I am sure your friends will fill you in about what happens tonight, and it will give you something to talk about tomorrow!' Peggy insisted drying her hands on a tea cloth before taking his coat from a peg on the back door and holding it out to him for him to put his arms into as he reluctantly got up from the chair.

'Can you pick him up on the way back.' She asked her daughter adding. 'Your Dads gone down the pub for a pint and to pay his slate club tonight so I am not expecting him back till later' She paused a small smile twitching at the corner of her mouth.

'I suppose Karl will meet you at Janet's so he will walk you home won't he?'

'Yes he will mum!' Sylvia felt a certain elation buzz through her, just a few months ago her dad was picking her up from the local hop, now it was acceptable that Karl would walk her home, and it was alright to see Karl at Janet's!

That's what I called progress she thought, she was sure her mother had put a few words in to try and make her father see things her way a bit after the confrontation she'd had with her father a few weeks ago.

A few moments later Sylvia and Mickey were sloshing their way through the puddles now filling fast with autumn leaves in their small lane that led to the village although he'd seemed reluctant to go to 'Sunbeams' now he was out, Mickey was busily filling Sylvia in about what was accomplished there and how much he enjoyed it.

'They have a magic lantern show tonight.' He said.

'I'm sure you will have a good time.' Sylvia told him as she affectionately as she tousled Mickey's hair.

Leaving him at the entrance to the small Salvation Army hall situated in the middle of the village she continued on to her destination, she hadn't far to go it was nearly opposite to the opening that led to the lodges in front of Winnie Bakers house.

Out of the corner of her eye she had already observed Karl waiting in shadows just inside the entrance as they had previously arranged. The cigarette he was smoking lit up his face just enough for her to outline his rugged features, he kissed her lightly on the lips as soon as she approached making her senses tingle; then taking her small hand into his own he touched her fingertips.

'Your hands are cold.' He chided.

'I forgot my gloves.' She said by way of an excuse.

In the gathering darkness they quickly made their way up the narrow path to the lodge, glad this gave a certain amount of cover from prying eyes that lurked in the large house at the end of the drive.

Janet heard their footsteps on the path and opened the door quickly to welcome them, the yellow light encircling her shone forth in a welcome halo as she took their outdoor coats and hung them on a small hook at the back of the door.

The lodge was small, the front door opening directly into a miniscule hall which in turn led straight up the stairs to two bedrooms; a door to the left led into to a small kitchen, and from the kitchen a door led to an equally small living area into which Janet now ushered her guests.

In the few weeks before the wedding the four of them had spent a good deal of time here cleaning and scrubbing away fifteen years of in occupancy. The floorboards round the grey linoleum square in the middle were now stained a dark brown and a couple of rag rugs sat cozily in front of the fire; curtains now firmly drawn over the two small casement windows Sylvia had shortened from an older pair Peggy had sorted out.

Karl and Sylvia sat down on the small brown utility Rexene settee they had managed to get with a docket from the government, this together with a double bed for upstairs was the only furniture available to help the newly married people, the rest of the sparsely furnished rooms were provided by gifts from family and friends.

Sylvia smiled to herself as she thought back to the task of getting the double bed up the narrow staircase, even with the two fit young men it had been a struggle, the narrow staircase twisted round and round; somehow Karl and Heinz puffing and panting had managed to do it without knocking the fresh dark green paint that had barely set.

Janet retired to the kitchen to make them drinks whilst Sylvia quickly filled Karl in with the day's events, so that when Janet appeared with three steaming cups he was aware of the situation.

'You look more cheerful now.' Sylvia told her friend over the cup she held to her mouth before taking a sip.

'Yes! I was in shock when the 'Home and Colonial' dismissed me like that.' Janet admitted.

There was a softer look in Janet's eyes now although a worrying frown still knitted in her brow.

'I have been able to analyses the situation a bit this afternoon.' The frown deepened somewhat.

'It doesn't resolve the situation though'

Karl looked thoughtful, his next statement taking them both by surprise.

'Well you know that I have to move out of the accommodation I have at the camp quite soon, what if I moved into the spare room upstairs and pay for that?' He looked from one face in front of him to the other taking in Sylvia's shocked expression.

'No! That isn't a good idea!' Sylvia said rather sharply her face contorted.

'You and I would know that there would be nothing wrong, but can you imagine what Winnie Baker would say. She would have a field day!' Sylvia said with conviction.

Janet nodded in agreement.

Karl looked a bit put out. 'I don't care what people think!' There was an edge to his voice as he continued.

'You and I know there would be nothing wrong and that is all that counts, after all Janet is married to Heinz!'

'Yes but this is a small village and people misconstrue the truth.' You could hear the determination as Sylvia took a deep breath and continued.

'I have another plan.' Two pairs of eyes looked in her direction.

'What you think of this?' She paused.

'How about I move in here with Janet?' Continuing she said.

'With what I am earning and with the money Heinz sends we could manage until the time comes for Janet to join Heinz couldn't we.' Sylvia looked triumphant at her suggestion looking from one to the other.

There was complete silence.

Janet was the first to speak.

'You would do that for me!' Her voice was incredulous, and the worried frown so apparent before, rapidly disappeared as she took in the full force of Sylvia's words.

'Yes I would! Don't you think it would be the answer?' Sylvia said convincingly.

'Just give me a bit of time to sort things out at home and I will move in.' She glanced across at Karl who was now looking at his feet, a sure sign she knew that he wasn't wholly happy about this situation.

Karl looked up into Sylvia's eyes.

'What would be better is if we got married and both moved in here together.' He said simply.

Sylvia momentary looked very shocked, before a smile spread over her face as she took in the prospect of what he had just uttered.

'Yes that would be a very good idea, and then when Janet joins Heinz we could stay on here and make it our home.' Then a shadow came over her face.

'BUT, let's face it.' She added sadly.

'It won't happen; you know my father would never agree.'

'There has to be a way Sylvie.' Janet now much brighter joined in.

'It is such a good idea!'

'Yes, but you know the problem, I tell you it will not happen.' Sylvia's face was really downcast.

Karl looked from one to the other then addressed Sylvia.

'Couldn't we go and explain the situation to your parents?' Adding hopefully. 'You never know they might agree.'

'We could, but I can't see it making any difference.' Sylvia said really downcast now.

'But now we have somewhere to live, how can they object?' Karl insisted.

'My dad would without a doubt; my mother might be persuaded; but I have my doubts that she would go against my father; he can make life difficult you know what his temper is like!' Sylvia's voice was very quiet, as she added.

'You know how it was when we have faced him before.'

'But surely now you have somewhere to live, his attitude could be completely different.' Janet said.

Sylvia didn't reply she just looked at the clock.

'I have to pick Mickey up in a few minutes.' Suddenly glad to something to take her mind off the situation it was depressing enough without dwelling on something she could not change.

Karl got to his feet, and Janet fetched their coats from the hall.

'I'll be in touch in a day or so,' Sylvia told her friend as Karl held out her coat for her to put her arms in.

'You are not to worry, we will be able to sort this out in the way I suggested, and you will be alright.' Conviction showing in her voice.

'My father can't stop me moving in with you and we can combine our income and get by until you go out to Germany.'

'Yes I know that now, I can't thank you enough.' Janet squeezed her friends arm. 'You have taken a weight off my mind.'

Sylvia gave her a quiet smile, she wished with all her heart that moving in the lodge could mean that she could marry Karl, but knew this wouldn't happen, she did hope that perhaps her father might see that moving in with Janet showed her to be responsible and able to cope on her own. She decided to keep this thought to herself.

Karl and Sylvia went out into the darkness waving Janet goodbye as she stood in the doorway, bathed again in light from the lodge.

There was heaviness in Sylvia's heart as their footsteps crunched through the autumn leaves under foot, she knew a confrontation with her father was always a difficult thing to do, and she was tired after the eventful day at work and the problem with Janet. A run in with her father was the last thing she wanted now, but it had to be faced, and she reasoned perhaps they should face him with this plan and see what transpired.

The trees at this end of the pathway from the lodge were close together so that even the street lamps just ahead didn't penetrate through; Karl held her close, he could see in the dim light the tension in her face.

'Perhaps it would be better not to say anything about this tonight.' He said attentively.

'No, I suggest we do it as soon as we have picked Mickey up.' She said grasping Karl's hand tightly, if they didn't do it now it would just be put off, and would have to be faced tomorrow or the day after.

Her Dad was usually in a good mood after he'd enjoyed a rare evening out with a pint and his mates at the local so perhaps this could be a good time! Besides they should be back before he made an appearance and if they put the situation to Peggy they just might get her on their side; it was an unlikely as she was loyal to her husband but worth a shot.

'It will be alright leibre, you will see.' Karl whispered encouragingly; Sylvia wished she could feel as confident!

It was obvious Mickey had enjoyed his visit to the Salvation Army as he bounced down the road between the two of them; he liked Karl who always treated him like a little brother.

'Do you want a hot drink?' Sylvia called through to her mother when they came through the kitchen door, and she immediately put the kettle on the hot plate of the kitchen range ready for Mickey's cocoa that he always enjoyed as a bedtime drink.

As soon as it was ready Mickey went upstairs hot drink in one hand and carefully balancing a candle holder in the other.

'Be careful with that!' Peggy warned him, the gas lights in the cottage didn't extent to upstairs and she was always wary of the fact that candles could cause a serious fire.

Sylvia took three steaming cups through to the sitting room, depositing them down on the small occasional table.

Karl was now resting his long legs on the settee patted the space beside him indicating to Sylvia to sit down.

Seeing her mother had put down her knitting to consume the hot drink, Sylvia decided to bring up the subject of their marriage straight away.

'Mum we would like to ask you what you think.' Sylvia asked hoping that asking for an opinion from her mother would be better than just announcing any plans.

'You know that Karl has to move out of the camp quite soon?'

Peggy nodded in reply a sinking feeling in her stomach; she knew whatever was now forthcoming would mean a confrontation with Harry.

'We have been talking to Janet; she has that spare room at the lodge.' The words were hardly out when Peggy rounded on her daughter her reply unusually sharp.

'Karl can't go there! That would set people talking, and anyway I can't see Winnie agreeing to that!'

'I agree, Karl couldn't go there, but there are other options, we could get married and take over the lodge when Janet goes to Germany!' Her daughter retorted.

There was an ominous silence as Peggy digested this bit of news, then she turned and faced them both.

'You can ask your father but I can't see him agreeing to that!' Sylvia could detect sadness in her voice as she dropped her eyes to her lap.

'He will have to agree to it sooner or later.' Sylvia declared firmly.

'Have to agree to what?' Three pairs of eyes turned to the doorway.

Harry stood there he had come quietly in at the back door.

Sylvia's heart sank, she had hoped to get her mother on side or at least make a good case for them both before her father returned, it was difficult enough to have to be the spokesman because of Karl's limited knowledge of their language without having to take on both her parents.

But this was important!

She took a deep breath and continued.

'Agree to us getting married!' There she had said it, she could only hope her father had returned in the usual good mood he generally did after an evening of association with others and supping ale at the 'Gardeners Arms.'

Her father's expression changed in a second.

'No I won't!' He said fervently.

'You are too young for one thing and you don't have anywhere to live either.'

Sylvia's hackles began to rise.

'We do have somewhere to live.' She declared two red spots now in her cheeks.

'The lodge at Winnie Bakers, Janet will soon be going out to Heinz and we can take it over.'

'Sounds as if you have worked it all out behind my back!' Harry said sarcastically.

'Except for one thing! You are too young to marry and I won't be giving my consent.' Harry's face darkened, his eyes full of fury.

'And another thing Winnie Baker might not agree to have you come to live at the lodge, especially if I have a word with her to say I don't approve!' He brought his fist down on the small occasional table making the cups on it rattle.

Karl sat quietly, he hated confrontations and he had learnt during his association with Harry to be quiet when he was in this mood; it was useless to argue with him it got you nowhere.

Sylvia her hackles' rising was now in full flow.

'You won't stop us!' She declared rising from her seat, two bright red spots in her cheeks, she marched past her father.

'Come on Karl lets go for a walk.' She flounced into the kitchen, snatched her coat from its hook, and opened the back door with Karl following meekly behind they went out into the night.

'She'll get over it.' Harry remarked, sitting himself down in his armchair and taking his pipe from his pocket.

Peggy got to her feet to make Harry a night cap, she remained silent it was no use arguing with Harry when he was in this mood; much better to wait and appeal to his better nature when the heat had gone out of the situation.

She knew Sylvia was impulsive but she was also aware that her daughter knew her own mind and wasn't likely to change, the worry was this attitude of Harry's was pushing the young couple closer together.

Sylvia her cheeks hot with fury, walked hand in hand with Karl, down the lane that led to the village, tears coursing down her face in frustration, Karl bent down and gently wiped them away with a handkerchief from his pocket.

'It will be alright leibe' He said softly.

'I wish I had your confidence.' There was no conviction in her voice.

They walked hand in hand through the dimly lit village; in a dark spot they looked up at the stars shining through on this almost moonless night, it was cold.

'There will be a frost before dawn.' Karl remarked cuddling her close.

'I only hope my father doesn't cause any trouble for Janet with Winnie Baker.' Sylvia said suddenly.

'If he talks to her, she could decide that she doesn't want Janet in the lodge, and then where would she go?'

'I don't think your father would go that far, he only said what he did to make his point to you.' Karl replied.

'Well I hope you are right!'

Sylvia didn't want to go home, but there was work tomorrow and she reluctantly parted company with Karl at the corner of the lane almost outside their cottage and he continuing down to the camp.

Letting her in the back door she saw her mother sitting at the table.

'Dad's gone to bed; he has an early start tomorrow.' Peggy said quietly.

Sylvia kicked off her shoes, a defiant look on her face.

'It won't make any difference mum what he says, Karl and I will not be waiting until I am twenty one to marry, and we won't be doing what Janet did!' She spat the last words out.

'I have been told it is possible to apply to the court for permission, and I shall look into that!' She picked up her shoes and made her way towards the small door that led to the staircase.

'Goodnight mum.' She gave Peggy a smile.

Peggy sat at the table for some time after this deep in thought, it would be an uphill struggle but she knew she had to try and make Harry see sense or cause a rift between him and his daughter, and in her heart she wasn't prepared to see Sylvia go through the long lonely years she had waiting for Harry even if she had been a lot older than her daughter at the time.

It was clear to see these young people loved one another and she didn't think even if Sylvia was so young that was going to change, she wasn't that type of girl!

CHAPTER TWENTY THREE

November 1947

An autumn wind blew leaves along the pavement whipping up the short sharp shower of rain that was falling, it made Karl scurry for cover up a stone stairway where a small canopy overhung the entrance to a large impressive grey building just beyond.

Once there he clutched his stomach unable to stop the nervous churning inside, never had he felt so lonely and afraid.

He wished he had taken the advice of one of his fellow inmates back at the camp and eaten a hearty breakfast he had offered to prepare for him using precious rations; instead he had forced down a cup of tea and some dry toast.

He often had and in particularly recently wished his mother and sister could have been here to face this day with him, yet deep down inside he knew that even if he'd been back in his homeland nothing would stop the quest that lay before him, nothing in the entire world was as overpowering as his love for Sylvia.

He couldn't really believe this day had arrived, they had both been grateful to Sylvia's friend Bridget who had found out the details for them about applying to the court, if it wasn't for her he wouldn't have been standing here today.

Thoughts spun through his head, here in was in his former enemy's country applying to get permission to marry a British girl!

He was a prisoner of war;—Well actually when he thought about it he was an ex-prisoner of war, he could return home as many of his compatriots had; but for him it was different—he had Sylvia.

His face softened when he thought about her, he loved her with such intensity, she was all he wanted in in the world; he could not imagine life without her!

So much depended on the outcome in court today yet such was his love if it didn't go the way they wanted he knew he would wait until they could marry even if it was when she reached the age of consent over four years away when she was twenty one.

He sighed that seemed a lifetime away!

Two men dressed smartly in black suits pushed past him shaking their black umbrellas free of the rain right in front of him, they went on straight through the large brown door that lay just ahead, could these be the magistrates who would decide on his future with Sylvia he wondered? They looked just ordinary men, yet so much depended on their decision.

Sylvia had explained to him that everyone in the country was on a high about marriage owing to the fact that the Princess Elizabeth was to marry Phillip Mountbatten this month; Karl wasn't sure that was going to help their situation, Sylvia was convinced it might.

She had also hoped her mother would put in a good word with the magistrates to state she had no objections to the marriage even if her husband did!

Karl liked Harry he just didn't understand why he was so prejudiced towards his race; Sylvia had told her father on many occasions 'there are good and bad in all people' to no avail, she had gone on to explain to Karl why Harry felt the way he did, but Karl couldn't really understand why Harry couldn't take people on face value.

It had thrilled him when the Reverent Hounsome had insisted on sending a character reference to the court on his behalf, he owed a great deal to the kindness of the Reverent who had also had a word with Winnie Baker to get her to agree that they could share the tenancy of the lodge with Janet until she left and then take over the occupancy themselves. At first he felt guilty about approaching the vicar about this knowing Harry had threatened to stop Winnie agreeing to them having the lodge.

Sylvia had explained to him that Winnie would lean over backwards to please the vicar, so he got in before Harry could stir things up, although this weighed heavily on his conscience.

Karl scuffed his shoes against the stone steps, the rain had eased and the sun looked as though it might break through the clouds; to pass the time he looked at his reflection in the glass panel in the door in front of him, a blonde haired square face stared back, smoothing down the unruly curls that had sprung up on his head in the rain with the back of his hand he was quite annoyed when they refused to obey.

Would the magistrates notice that he didn't have a suit? Except for his working clothes these were all the clothes he possessed, the magistrates couldn't expect anything else could they?

These men would be aware he was an ex-prisoner of war who didn't even have a demob suit issued to the men leaving the services wouldn't they?

He pulled a Fair Isle pullover he wore under his jacket down over his brown cord trousers, then straightened his tie; as he adjusted his tweed jacket he tweaked the collar of his shirt into place on the outside of the lapel.

Looking at his reflection again he wondered would these people think him smart enough.

Ex-prisoner of war those words echoed through his brain again, he pulled himself up to his full six foot height.

Yes! Ex-prisoner of war that's what he was now and free, all he wanted was to be able to marry the girl he loved more than life itself, surely that wasn't too much to ask!

BUT how were these magistrates going view it?

Taking a watch from his pocket he glanced impatiently at it; it was five minutes past the hour, turning the watch over he looked at the back into its silvery depths, Mr. Morishstein, Sylvia's employer had given it to him explaining it had belonged to an uncle of his at the time this had touched Karl deeply.

Karl liked this man from the minute he'd been introduced to him when he met Sylvia from work.

There was no animosity in him although Karl had felt uncomfortable knowing how badly his race had treated the Jews, Sylvia had previously explained to him that Mr. Morishstein had lost quite a few of his relations in the concentration camps.

But at that first meeting Mr. Morishstein had held out his hand in greeting and treated Karl very well on every other occasion they had met since, with all the problems the Germans had caused the Jews you would think Sylvia's employer would feel animosity rather than her father!

Karl could feel the impatience building up inside him, surely Sylvia should be here soon!

He wished now he'd insisted she had taken the day off instead of arranging with her employer to take an early lunch break for the hearing, she gone on to explain when they talked it over they really couldn't afford for her to take a day's unpaid leave, she said if they obtained the courts permission to marry, she would need the precious leave she was entitled to for a honeymoon.

He smiled again to himself 'Honeymoon' he couldn't afford to take her away! Then his mind started working overtime, just a few days honeymooning with her fabulous no matter where it was spent!

He had to drag his thoughts away from this prospect; they had to get over the hurdle in front of them first before they could begin to think of the joys that could lie ahead.

Lost in thought he hadn't realized the watch was still in his hand, glancing impatiently at it again he sighed, she said she'd leave the tailors where she worked on the hour, the court was only ten minutes' walk away so she should be here with him by ten past, that was still a couple of minutes away.

He thought of her hurrying through the crowds in the centre of the town where the tailors were situated, he could see her slender figure rushing through the throng, her long black hair trailing from her shoulders, her usual high heels digging into the brick pavements, how she managed to walk on them he never knew, she insisted it made her five foot two closer to his six foot height.

Thoughts of the confrontation they had both had with Sylvia's father recently came back into his mind when he and Sylvia had stood before him and explained to him they intended to apply to the court for permission to marry; Harry had held his ground.

'Just because the country has gone mad with all this talk of the heir to the throne getting married, it doesn't mean to say you'll get permission.' He snapped his face almost purple with rage.

Later they brought the papers from the court to show him they were serious about their plans, he refused even to look at them, adding Karl only wanted to marry his daughter to stay in this country This made Karl usually a mild tempered man extremely cross, he had tried so often and failed to make Harry realize that he wanted to marry his daughter because he loved her and to imagine life without her was impossible.

The war had now been over for over two years, things had moved on, Harry it seemed had not!

Anyway he didn't have to return to Germany, the government here had made it clear that the German prisoners of war would be able to stay if they wanted, especially if their homes were now in the Russian sector of their homeland.

A drip from the canopy fell down onto his head pulling him back to the present, he didn't want to look at his watch again, so he strained his ears, no sound yet of her high heels clipping along the brick pavements. His face paled as a negative thought went through his mind, would she come?

She couldn't have had second thoughts could she?

His heart raced faster, he strained his ears yet again, he was sure he could hear the sound of her approach, the sound became closer it had to be her!

He left the shelter of the canopy to glance down the road.

'Yes, there she was a headscarf covering her head because of the rain, the navy blue gabardine raincoat clinging to her slight form was tied firmly in the middle with a belt, accentuating her slim waist.

The rain was coming down again faster now the rivets ran down his hair then down his back but he didn't care; grasping her hand firmly as she came up to him he planted a kiss on her lips.

Together they ascended the steps to the court house to face the magistrates and their future together.

Half an hour later the two of them literally bounced down the steps of the town hall clasping each other by the hand their faces beamed in the stiff breeze that had blown up taking away the rain that had been pouring down when they entered the building.

'I can't believe it.' Karl's face was wreathed in smiles as he clutched Sylvia's shoulder drawing her close.

'I can't believe they agreed to our marriage!'

Sylvia clung to his arm, she couldn't get her head round the fact that unexpected had happened.

They had gone in court today expecting a real battle with the magistrates only to find that Peggy had lodged a letter agreeing to their union, and although opposition was still apparent from her father, the magistrates took into account he hadn't been there to voice it, neither had he given any written word that he opposed the motion before them, in the absence of this the magistrate agreed to let the marriage go ahead.

Taken into account also was the Reverent Hounsome's good character reference, and the fact that the couple had found a place to live!

'I don't honestly believe my father thought we would take matters this far.' Sylvia said as a sinking feeling replaced the euphoria that had held her a few minutes previously, she wished that her father had given his blessing unconditionally without all this kafuffle, yet nothing was going to take away the joy of this day, she could marry this man who was at her side, and now it couldn't be stopped, she just dreaded the confrontation that was bound to come later when they faced Harry that night.

Sylvia glanced at the watch on her wrist.

'I have to go back to work.' The sudden urgency made her voice rise a bit.

'I have had just over my allotted hour.'

Karl looked despondent.

'It is a pity we both have to rush off.'

'Well we will need the time off later!' There was a mischievous look in Sylvia's eyes.

'And anyhow it will take my mind off the confrontation with my dad later wont it.' She sighed.

'We wouldn't have been able to say much before this evening would we? He will be at work this afternoon.' She glanced at Karl's face.

'And you have to work with him.' Karl's jaw hardened.

'Yes I know, and it will be difficult not to tell him about the events this morning!' Karl turned his head and looked towards the town hall clock just above them.

'I shall have to hurry the bus is due to go in minutes, I had better not offend your father by taking any more time than the hours I was allotted.'

'Did he ask where you were going?' She enquired.

'I only had to clear my absence with the warden at the camp, so he wouldn't have known.' Karl explained.

'He just knows what time I am due back at work.'

'Will you have time to put on your working things before you go back.' Sylvia asked.

'I have asked one of the other men to bring my working clothes to the shed so I can make a quick change.' Karl explained as he reached down and pulled her close kissing her lightly on the lips before holding her at arm's length for a moment and looking into her eyes, his face alight with a smile that seemed to stretch from ear to ear.

'Well we tried to show him the papers but he refused even to look at them!' Sylvia's spirits sank bit as she thought about this, it was going to be the hardest job of all to tell him they had defied him in this way, especially when her father discovered that Peggy had stood up for them by sending a letter to the court.

Hand in hand they now rushed down the road anxious to fulfill their work obligations, Karl to board a bus now waiting on the stand to take him back to the village, and Sylvia to make her way back to the tailors it was going to be easy to concentrate on her sewing this afternoon!

CHAPTER TWENTY FOUR

The rain started spitting again as soon as Sylvia got off the bus at her stop after work.

Making her way down the lane to their cottage, she let herself in the back gate and immediately noticed her mother's sheets blowing in the wind on the line. A frown crossed her forehead taking away some of the euphoric air that had surrounded her this afternoon after the court case had gone in their favor today. Her mother never left the washing out this late, by now it would all be ironed and put away to air.

Fear gripped her, something was obviously very wrong.

She let herself in through the back door to a silent kitchen, looking in the direction of the table she saw that it wasn't laid out, and the plates from dinner were piled high on the draining board, something Peggy never did; her mother had obviously left the house in a hurry.

She touched the kettle on the back of the range it was scarcely warm, reaching for the teapot under its cozy on the table she felt that too, it was almost cold a sure sign that it was some time ago that the tea had been made.

Panic rose in her throat and a shaky feeling came into her legs as she transferred the kettle to the hot plate, she would she decided feel better for a hot cup of tea.

Glancing up to the window she saw the rain had now begun again in earnest and was splashing down the panes onto the window sill.

'Drat.' She said to herself as she quickly took the laundry basket from under the kitchen sink and rushing into the garden to snatch the washing from the line before it was soaked through. It was only when she put it on the kitchen table she realized that her legs seemed to be folding up beneath her and she pulled a chair from under the table top and almost fell into it.

A noise from outside announced Mickey's arrival and he burst through the back door puffing as though he'd been running a race, the rain dripping from his cap.

Sylvia got to her feet taking a long look at the two bright spots in the young man's cheeks and his over bright eyes.

'What is wrong?' She demanded as she took the cap from his head and helped him off with his outdoor coat.

Mickey couldn't get his breath; so it was a couple of minutes before he spoke

'It's Dad.' Panic was etched into the young man's face, he struggled to speak.

'He's had an accident, Mum and Ned are with him at the hospital.' He said at last.

Sylvia looked down at the tablecloth; sudden tears burning at the back of her eyes, as long as she could remember her dad had never even taken one day off work for illness and now he was in hospital.

Looking up she now saw fear in Mickey's eyes, obviously upset over what had happened, it was as though his whole world had come crashing down about him.

He was the closest to a younger brother Sylvia was going to have and she drew him close putting her hand round his shoulder.

'Tell me what you know.' She said softly trying not to show the alarm now rising within herself.

'I came in from school to see an ambulance clanging down the lane, Mum and Ned were standing in the back doorway just about to rush off down the field. Ned said Dad had fallen through a glass cloche injuring is arm and head.'

'Then Ned told me to go to Gran's until you were due home, as they would be going to the hospital in the ambulance with Dad.'

Sylvia took a long look at Mickey's white face and thought quickly, giving the young lad something to do would take his mind of things she decided.

'Can you help me fold up the washing in the basket?' Sylvia pointed to where she'd put it on the table.

'It will save mum doing it when she gets back, wont it.'

She pulled out the sheets and Mickey took one end whilst she took the other and together they stretched them out across the kitchen folding sides to middle in neat piles.

They had just finished the task when the back door opened and Ned almost fell over the doorstep, followed by Peggy.

Seeing the white shocked face of her mother Sylvia immediately pushed a chair beneath Peggy's ample form and her mother fell into it.

Sylvia made the quickest pot of tea ever and put a cup of the steaming liquid well laced with sugar into her mother's hand which was visibly shaking.

Sylvia poured a cup out for Ned and herself, sipping the hot sweet liquid she looked over the rim of her cup at the two of them, almost afraid to ask what had made her mother who was always the one to cope so well in any crisis so disturbed.

It was Ned who broke the silence and Sylvia could hardly believe what she was hearing.

'If your Karl hadn't been on hand this afternoon, I doubt that Harry would have survived.' He said.

Then he went on to explain.

Harry had accidentally fallen through the glass on one of the cloches; the glass had splintered and severed a main artery and Karl who was nearby quickly put his hand over the pulsating artery.

'Get my tie out of pocket of my jacket in the shed.' He instructed Ned who flew to do his bidding.

Karl isolated the affected limb with a tourniquet to stem the blood flow with the tie whilst Ned following Karl's instructions raced off to get help.

Not an easy task as the nearest phone box was outside Sid's post office nearly a half of a mile away.

'Fortunately Karl had that tie in his pocket and he was able to use it straight away.' He paused.

'And the other thing was he knew what to do! I didn't have a clue!' Ned said with real feeling in his voice.

'The ambulance men said he could have bled to death with the time it took to get an ambulance to him, without a doubt Karl saved his life.' Ned had to look away so that the tears in his eyes were not visible.

It took Ned took a few moments to regain his composure before going on to explain why they had kept Harry in hospital.

'It wasn't the artery they are worried about.' He explained. 'Karl's action had stopped a massive loss of blood; Harry's blood pressure is very high and as he can't remember falling there is a cause for concern, there is also a possibility that he has broken his leg in the fall, the leg is so swollen the diagnosis will be made tomorrow when Harry had rested it a bit.'

Sylvia digesting this news felt slightly euphoric that if they hadn't gone to court that morning Karl wouldn't have had the tie in his pocket to stem the bleeding.

The elation quickly evaporated when she glanced across at her mother who was almost slumped in her chair nursing her drink; the fight seemed to have gone out of her and she was staring into space.

Sylvia got to her feet realizing for the first time in her life she would have to take charge of the situation.

Hoping she sounded more positive than she felt she came round the back of her mother's chair and put her arms around her mother's shoulders.

'Dad will be alright mum! We can all pull together until dad is better no matter what diagnosis the doctors make.'

It suddenly dawned on her why her mother was worried the tied cottage they lived in was attached to Farmer Phillips, and tenancy was subject to Harry working continuously on the farm, if his leg was broken it could be months before he could return to work.

'I realize what the problem is.' Sylvia stroked her mother's hair. 'We will talk over the pros and cons of the situation later, now it would be best for me to prepare something to eat, the boys are hungry.'

Instructing Mickey to lay the table and Ned to make up the kitchen range, Sylvia went to the larder and took out some fresh eggs and some cheese, with bread from the bread bin she set to work, after instructing Mickey to put some toast on a fork in front of the kitchen range, she made some passable scrambled eggs with cheese and toast and put in front of them all.

The boys suddenly realizing they were hungry wolfed it down.

'Try and eat something.' She said encouragingly to her mother who was just playing with the food on her plate.

The boys were just clearing away the table and helping Sylvia with the washing up, when a knock came at the back door, immediately they all knew it was Karl.

Ned flew across to open the door, and he entered the small kitchen.

Peggy looking up suddenly and at once came back to life, getting to her feet she took the teapot from the kitchen range.

'Fetch a cup.' She instructed Mickey indicting a seat at the table for Karl, she looked sideways at him smiling with real gratitude she said.

'I can't thank you enough for what you did today.'

'Anyone would have done the same!' Karl's reply was quiet, his face coloring up with the praise.

'Well they didn't and you did—Thankfully!' Peggy exclaimed as she poured tea from the pot for them all.

Ned sat down at the table and drank deeply into his cup before beckoning the others round; he suddenly seemed grown in stature as he took charge of the situation.

'We shall have to make some plans.' He said a new serious tone in his voice.

'You know the situation here; if Dad's leg is broken, he isn't going to come out of hospital and straight back to work is he? And the knock on the head won't help the situation.'

A worried frown creased into Sylvia's forehead.

'All I can say is Dad is in the best place at the moment.' She looked thoughtful.

Peggy's worried frown deepened, and a tear glistened in the corner of her eye as she spoke.

'That's the thing I am most afraid of that we could lose our home!'

'Yes we all know what the situation will probably be with regard to Mr. Phillips.' They all nodded in agreement.

'We have to make some plans then approach Mr. Phillips with them, after all we don't want to leave the cottage do we!' Ned said looking round at them all.

'We know that Harry is the main bread winner, and although I do as good a job as any man I receive just a lad's pay.' He said despondently.

'But surely Mr. Phillips will know that Dads accident happened whilst he was in his employment!' Karl said quietly.

'You might think that was so.' Peggy tone was sad.

'It doesn't always happen like that. I have known people to be forced out of their home even if an accident at work was the cause of the problem.'

'Why were Gisela and her family allowed to remain?' Exasperation showed in Ned's voice.

Peggy had a certain resignation in it as she replied.

'Well the farmer was pushed into that because of the war situation. Just think how it would have looked if he had to force a family out because of the bread winner being called up for the war effort, the government would have had something to say about that, not to mention how it would have looked locally.'

'It's a pity the government don't have something to say about the rights of people injured in the course of their work!' Ned retorted, before adding.

'Look mum, I am working for Farmer Phillips, surely that would make things right with him!'

Peggy's face dropped.

'With respect to you Ned, it isn't just the work, it's the money; Dad will not be paid if he doesn't work, although you work hard you don't get enough money to keep us going do you? A tear dropped down Peggy's face onto the table cloth.

'Although everyone knows you do a man's work!'

Ned looked thoughtful for a moment.

'Well if I stopped the money that goes to my mother!' He said fervently.

Sylvia looked up taking charge of the situation, and four pairs of eyes turned in her direction.

'There is no need for that and any way it will only cause trouble.' She paused for a moment before continuing.

'There is a better way. I know you are aware that Karl has to move out of the huts where he lives quite soon now. I haven't mentioned this before but I have already made tentative plans to move in with Janet to help out before the baby comes as she is no longer able to work. So Karl can have my room here.' The shocked look on her mother's face showed she didn't like this idea, and she gasped out the words.

'You mean Karl move in here?'

'Yes and I will live up at the lodge with Janet!'

Sylvia looked her mother in the eye, her voice appealing.

'Farmer Phillips should be happy, he will get his rent and he will have two workers living in his tied cottage to do his work wont he! Let's face it what can the farmer say?' She went on.

'The work would continue as it always has, it is always quieter on the farm in the winter and Dad hopefully will be fully recovered by the spring when it gets busy.' She finished with a triumphal note to her voice.

Peggy shook her head in disbelief, but Ned seeing this was a good solution to their problem quickly took over the conversation.

'It's a good plan Sylvie! If Harry comes home with a broken leg, he won't be able to deal with the stairs and other chores so we can all have to share in helping.' Ned turned to Peggy.

'With respect, he will be too heavy for you to manage won't he? And with Karl here it will make it so much easier.'

Peggy nodded resigned to the inevitable, even if it meant that her daughter would be living down the road.

'We haven't asked Karl what he thinks.' Sylvia said almost apologetically as she turned towards him.

'We are all taking it for granted that he doesn't mind if we put this plan into action!'

The four of them turned to the blonde headed man sitting at the table.

'Yes of course that will be alright.' Karl's smile lit up his eyes.

Sylvia felt so proud of him, without question he was going to help them out of an extremely difficult situation and that after saving the life of a man who hadn't been as kind to him as he should have been!

'So that's settled then.' Although her smile didn't reach her eyes it was obvious that a weight had been lifted off Peggy's shoulders as she spoke, Sylvia was aware though she still had reservations about the plan put before her. It was late when the family finally agreed on all the details and it was agreed that Karl would move in to Peggy's house the following weekend.

After a very eventful day, Sylvia saw Karl off the back doorstep as he made his way back to the camp. It wasn't until she was getting into bed that she realized their news from the court hadn't been mentioned.

CHAPTER TWENTY FIVE

With all disturbance of the next few weeks, Karl and Sylvia's news was pushed into the background and never got a mention, both of them realized with the effort of moving house and the problems with Harry this wasn't the time to pursue their own interests. As the days slipped by it seemed like their day in court hadn't actually happened.

When Sylvia though about it she was grateful it had taken place because otherwise Karl wouldn't have had the necktie in his pocket and this had saved her father's life, out in the fields it wouldn't have been easy to find something suitable to isolate an artery.

Harry's condition proved worrying and he was ordered by the doctor to stay at the hospital in town for the foreseeable future. His sudden collapse and loss of consciousness had to be investigated and the leg proved to be broken in two places so that was another problem.

'Thank goodness for the health service.' Peggy said with heartfelt gratitude; it had only been brought in by the labour government that year, no one in this household thought they would need its services so soon!

Previously the family had belonged to a 'Panel' for which a reasonable amount paid weekly ensured a doctor was available when needed, hospitals could prove expensive and relied on charity for the poorer people.

When they approached Farmer Phillips about the situation at the cottage, he was happy to accept the arrangements they had discussed; he already knew Karl to be a good worker, and in Harry's absence was grateful that he wouldn't have to take on more expensive staff to fill the gap that his best and most reliable worker left. Farmer Phillips offered no extra to the ex PoW pocketing the money he would normally have paid to Harry so he had an added bonus, this had been expected and the family was just grateful they still had a roof over their heads and they could manage.

At the weekend Karl moved his belongings into Peggy's and Sylvia moved her things over to the lodge, there the two girls pooled their resources, fortunately Heinz was good at regularly sending what money he could afford, so things ticked over nicely.

The actual time the two girls spent together was quite limited as Sylvia felt she had to support her mother. She tried to spend every other evening over at her mother's house, this also meant she could spend some time with Karl who found himself working longer hours to make up for the shortfall Harry's absence left. Sylvia found living with her friend hard going, she'd been brought up in a household where her mother kept a neat and tidy home which was always spotlessly clean, and Janet's ways were quite the reverse.

Rose, Janet's mother's house was always untidy and perhaps that was to be expected with the amount of children she had, but Sylvia did wonder if perhaps even when Rose only had one child she had always been this way, it was very irritating when on return from a hard day's work she found Janet's washing up still in the sink, the fire not cleared out ready for relighting, and the place looking as though it could do with a dust.

Janet was a hopeless cook and Sylvia missed her mother's nutritious meals because Janet had little idea how to go about preparing food or indeed how to budget even with the extra food rations she received for being pregnant, it seemed there was always very little in the cupboard and she had no idea how to 'make do' with what was available, it fell to Sylvia in the evenings to made a passable meal for them both in the limited she had after she arrived home from her work.

Sylvia told no one about this situation knowing that the present situation was temporary, but even making allowances for the fact Janet was in the last two months of her pregnancy Sylvia still felt very frustrated with her friend, especially as they ate at her mother's three times each week.

Peggy had been adamant that Sylvia had her evening meal with them on the evenings she spent at their house.

'I don't want you to be out of pocket.' Her daughter said.

'I can manage an evening meal!' Her mother insisted.

'I get the vegetables out of the garden and you know me I can stretch the meat ration out, and now I go to town most days to visit Dad I am able to get fish off the boats on the beach; at least that isn't rationed!'

'But you do have to pay for it.' Her daughter observed.

Sylvia saw the gratitude in her mother's eyes as she added

'I can manage now Karl is here!'

'Yes mum, if I become half as resourceful as you I shall do well!'

Peggy's cheeks burned as she accepted this praise from her daughter.

It wasn't long before Peggy invited Janet over on the evenings Sylvia came, feeling sorry for her because she was alone most of the day, soon Peggy said to come for her evening meal also.

Sylvia was glad of this as she never felt sure that Janet was getting nutritious food for the growing baby when she was not there, she insisted, so that this wouldn't be added burden Janet gave her mother a small amount from the extra food rations available from the government for expectant mothers.

Karl slipped easily into the family's routine and Peggy found it a great comfort to know that there were two men in the house that could be called on for help when needed.

Visiting times at the hospital were strict, one hour a day in the afternoons which didn't suit this families' busy schedule at all. Sylvia after a tussle with matron who said it upset the hospital routine managed to get to see her father for a short time every other day after work, her mother went on the bus in the afternoons opposite days to Sylvia. Ned because of work commitments could only manage weekends.

Children were forbidden on the wards so Mickey didn't get to see Harry at all during his hospital stay, although quite often now he was at high school he caught the same bus back to the village as Peggy, so was able to help her with any extra things she managed to bring back from town when she toured the shops before the time came for Harry's visit.

It was almost a month before Harry was told he could be discharged from hospital.

Bill's taxi was out of the question to bring him home, Harry wasn't able to bend his bad leg because of the nature of the break, so an ambulance was arranged to bring him home. Told by the hospital Harry's leg would have to remain in plaster for some considerable time to come; Karl and Ned between them brought his bed down to the sitting room so that he wouldn't have to manage the narrow curved staircase in the cottage at night.

The matron agreed after some negotiation he could come home on a Saturday afternoon so the family could all there to greet him.

He arrived on a cool late Autumn day white faced and much thinner than his former self.

'It's good to be home.' Were the first words he uttered after Ned and Karl carried him up the back doorstep, and took him straight into his armchair in the sitting room, soon the family were fussing around him, and Sylvia was delighted that he seemed to have lost his former animosity towards Karl.

Although it had been explained to Harry that Karl had saved his life; he had no recollection of the event, in fact the whole event and quite a considerable time previous to this seemed to have been wiped from his mind. This meant he had no recollection of the his argument with his daughter and her young man over their wedding plans and the subsequent court case.

Peggy also seemed to have wiped this from her mind because she made no mention of it either.

Janet heard regularly from Heinz, with no news forthcoming as to when she could join him in Germany as the weeks passed by it became increasingly obvious that this wouldn't be until after her confinement as both the midwife and doctor advised against the journey in the last six weeks of her pregnancy.

As the days progressed Janet got quite a few sly looks from the villagers as her stomach began to increase in size; particularly Winnie Baker.

Rose caught Winnie one day discussing her daughter's demise.

'I'd never have let her have that lodge if I had known the situation.' Winnie was heard to say.

Rose always sharp of tongue, was quick to point out to Winnie she was happy to take money for the privilege!

But Rose remained tight lipped when she was asked when the baby was due, hoping perhaps it would arrive late and silence the gossips.

But that was not what the baby had in mind when it decided to put in an appearance early in December some four weeks before the due date

Janet had been very weary for a few days, and Sylvia had begun to take her breakfast in bed before leaving for work in the morning so that she could relax before rising later.

On this particular day whilst she balancing the tray in her hands Sylvia pushed the door open with her foot; stopping short when she saw Janet was lying almost in a ball in the bed and giving out a loud groan.

'I think the baby's started.' Janet said through clenched teeth as she held on to the edge of the bed.

Sylvia quickly put the tray down on the bedside table spilling the tea into the saucer in the process; butterflies rising in her stomach she felt panic begin to rise deep within her.

'Shall I fetch your mother?' The words came out in a rush.

Janet pulled herself up on her elbows; as the pain spasm passed.

'Yes, that would be the best thing to do! 'Janet smiled weakly.

Concern edged Sylvia's voice as she said.

'I don't like leaving you like this!'

Janet smiled at the worried frown now on her friends face.

'I will be fine the pains are quite far apart, the midwife told me baby won't come until they are close together so tell mum not to rush, she has to get the children off to school.'

She shifted her position then sitting upright sipping her tea she looked as though nothing was happening at all.

'The district nurse told me the early stages take a long time, so there is no need to worry, I shall be alright.'

'Yes I suppose it does!' Sylvia voice didn't sound at all sure as she quickly made for the door leaving her friend finishing off what tea was left in the cup.

Scampering down the stairs Sylvia threw on her coat, picked up her bag and rushed down the lane to Rose's house.

Rose curlers falling over her forehead opened her door in her dressing gown, the rest of her hair encased in a brightly coloured turban remained invisible, and she was puffing heavily on a cigarette that was clamped firmly between her lips.

'Don't look so worried.' Rose said when Sylvia stammered out the news.

'The baby will be hours away yet.' She paused for a moment, turning sharply as the toddler hanging onto the back of her skirt slipped over onto the stone kitchen floor and let out a piecing scream.

Rose hauled the youngster to his feet in one hand and rubbed his knees which were now oozing a little blood, with a cloth that looked as though it had been used for wiping up the dishes.

'Be more careful.' She scolded the little fellow. 'I don't want to have to take you down the hospital.' The cigarette smoke the little fellow breathed in as his mother leant over him made him cough, Rose took no notice and still kept it firmly clamped between her teeth.

'Are you sure Janet be alright on her own?' Sylvia said quietly.

'Oh yes if she's anything like me she'll cope!' Rose said in a careless tone adding.

'Best thing you can do is get to work! There is nothing you can do up at the lodge.' She took another long pull on the cigarette.

'I'll make my way up as soon as I can.' Rose looked thoughtful for a moment, then said

'Perhaps you could just drop by and tell the district nurse the situation on your way to the bus stop.' This was Rose's passing shot as she turned her attention back to the breakfast table behind her where an argument going on between two of her boys, and she seemed more interested in their squabbling over cereals than her daughter, shouting at her brood before turning again to Sylvia and in what seemed to be an afterthought said.

'Tell the nurse will be down as soon as I have got this lot off to school!'

With that Sylvia was dismissed, Rose quickly closing the door as soon as she'd turned round on the doorstep to leave.

Going down the road towards Nurse Hudson's house, Sylvia felt rather relieved that the baby had decided not to arrive in the middle of the night when she would have had to run the gauntlet of the dark lane that led to the lodge with its overhanging trees to fetch help, she wondered what Rose's reaction would have been if she had arrived on her doorstep then!

Nurse Hudson answered her rap at the door of her house.

'The midwife thought that baby might arrive a little early.' The Nurse declared when Sylvia told her the situation.

'She said its head seemed well down when she examined her a few days ago.' She took in Sylvia's concerned look.

'Don't worry, Janet is a healthy girl, and first babies take a long time!' The nurse assured her.

'I will inform the midwife and will be up there to see that all is well quite soon, so it is alright for you to go to work.'

Sylvia suddenly remembered Rose's last words to her.

'Her mother said she'd be up after she gets the children off to school.'

'That's alright then.' The nurse said the expression on her face not changing at all, she waited at the door whilst Sylvia closed the garden gate behind her and made her way to the bus stop.

Sylvia managing to get her usual bus into town, but was on tender hooks all day.

When she arrived home it was to the news that Janet had been transported by ambulance to the local hospital for a possible caesarean section as the baby was likely in a breech position.

It was three days later that a healthy little girl was born naturally weighing in at six and a half pounds.

'Janet will have to stay in hospital for about ten days,' Rose announced when she came with the news just as Sylvia was about to leave for work.

'I suppose you will be alright here on your own.' She added as an afterthought.

Sylvia gave her small smile; she'd been alright on her own for the last three nights with no problems so why Rose was concerned now were her thoughts.

Peggy had at first insisted that her daughter return home.

'With your dad sleeping downstairs, you could sleep in our bedroom whilst Janet is in hospital.' She said resolutely.

'I am alright. It would mean moving a lot of my things back and it's for such a brief time it's really not worth it.' Sylvia was adamant that she was alright.

She did however take up her mother's invitation to dinner every evening after work for the duration of Janet's hospital stay, enjoying being part of the family again; she really hadn't realized how much she'd missed this!

Her mother insisted Mickey accompany Karl when he took her back to the lodge to sleep after spending the evening with them all, she didn't want to give Winnie Baker any chance to gossip about her daughter.

The week before Christmas the weather turned suddenly cold and Peggy was glad to get to the warmth of her kitchen when she went through the back door after finishing the chores at the Finches house. Glancing through to the sitting room, she saw Harry had nodded off in his armchair by the fire, so she went back through to the kitchen to begin preparing the vegetables for dinner.

She had just removed her hat and coat and reached for her overall, when she heard the sound of a motor car crunching on the stony lane outside the cottage.

Looking out of the Kitchen window Peggy's heart sank to her boots as she saw Miss Perkins draw up in her little dark green Austin Seven; 'what did she want' was the first thought that went through her mind as she watched the lady take her black handbag from the back of the car and smartly make her way to their door, her heels clicking on the path.

'Do come in.' Peggy invited as she answered her loud knock.

'Can I offer you tea?' She asked as she indicated a chair for her visitor to sit on.

'No it's a brief visit.' A slight smile hovered around Miss Perkins usual sharp features.

'I have good news about Michael.'

Peggy's heart lifted a little then sank, would Miss Perkins 'good news' mean that Mickey's mother had changed her mind and she wanted the lad back?

She steeled herself for Miss Perkins next words as the lady continued in her rather formal way.

'It has been agreed by the board that Michael can stay with you for the foreseeable future. I told them he is well settled and well cared for and no good would be obtained by moving him, especially as he has just obtained the scholarship to the Grammar school.'

For a moment Peggy wasn't sure she had heard the lady right; with all the difficulties of the past few weeks, could this be good news for a change?

'You mean Mickey—I mean Michael can stay here for good?' The words stumbled out.

'Yes.' Said Miss Perkins simply adding.

'For the foreseeable future at least is exactly what I am saying.'

Peggy's face beamed, no better Christmas present could she possibly receive!

'Thank you so much.' The words came out in a rush.

'Also.' Miss Perkins continued in her superior way.

'It has been agreed that as Michael's family has no interest in his wellbeing, the board will consider you and your husband as adoptive parents for the boy.' Miss Perkins whole face lit up as she delivered this last piece of news, She didn't add that the board were anxious to place displaced people like Michael in good homes under adoption, it was less expensive than paying for their keep!

Not that this news would have worried Peggy even with all the recent problems, she would have gladly managed if Mickey's happiness was at stake.

It was a beaming Peggy that saw her visitor over the doorstep about ten minutes later having signed papers for Mickey to be formerly fostered with a view to the adoption going forward.

She watched from the kitchen window as the lady climbed into her little car and then drive down the bumpy stony roadway to the main highway.

Wiping away her tears of sheer joy on her apron, she turned to see Harry standing in the doorway that led from the kitchen leaning heavily on a stick.

He took in the look on her face.

'You presumably heard what she said'

'The best Christmas present we could have!' Harry said holding out his arms.

She stood for a long moment before she moved towards him, reflecting how much Harry had changed in the last couple of months since the accident, although it had been hard, he'd learnt a bit of tolerance especially towards Karl who thankfully he had come to see in a different light.

Were they at last coming out of the dark tunnel that had been their lot in recent months?

CHAPTER TWENTY SIX

'I am taking it for granted you will you will come here for your dinner on Christmas day?' Peggy said as she and her daughter sat round the table drinking tea the Sunday before the event.

'Yes Janet is taking the baby to her mothers and staying overnight so I shall look forward to being here with you all.' Sylvia tried not to sound too excited, she didn't want her mother to realize how much she missed the family.

'How is Janet managing with the baby?' Was Peggy's next question.

'She has settled down very well, and sleeps well at night too'

'That's good, it wouldn't be much fun if you were kept up half the night when you have to go to work the next day.' Peggy observed, she gave a satisfied smile, she was looking forward to have her daughter back under her roof, even if it was for a brief time.

With all the males in now in the house she missed having some female company, especially her daughter company!

'Now that Dad's so much better, I suppose he might perhaps return to work sometime in the New Year?' Sylvia enquired.

'Yes that is the plan.' Her mother said before continuing in a heartfelt voice.

'I don't know how I would have coped without Ned and Karl; these two young men have been a godsend.'

Sylvia gave a quiet smile. 'I always told you that Karl was a real Gem.'

'Yes you did, and you have been proved right! I don't think your father can say anything about his race any more, and if he did everyone in this house and quite a few others would disagree with him!' Peggy reached across and squeezed her daughter's hand.

'You couldn't find a better man even if he was English.'

Sylvia's face glowed as she replied.

'I have always known that right from the first time I met him.'

'Ned and Karl are taking Dad's bed upstairs tomorrow; with a bit of effort he can manage the stairs now' Peggy said changing the subject.

'That's progress!' Sylvia observed.

'Well we will need the sitting room with all the family here for Christmas day, and there is the tree to bring in!' Peggy's eyes misted over.

'It wouldn't seem like Christmas without it.'

'No mum it wouldn't.' Her daughter agreed thinking back briefly to the many years it had been at the centre of their celebrations.

'Are you putting up any other decorations?'

'Not this year!' Peggy declared.

'Time has been against me and now Gisela's family have left, Mickey doesn't have anyone here to make paper chains with, and I will put a few bits of holly round the mirror and over the pictures though.'

'That will be nice!' Sylvia replied adding.

'Have you heard recently how Gisela and her family are?' She paused thoughtfully.

'We shall miss their company this Christmas wont we?'

'Yes without a doubt' Her Mother agreed, she gave a little sigh before continuing.

'The new people next door are very nice but there is nothing like the closeness I had with Gisela and the children. I think the war years had a lot to do with that; people had to rely on each other more.'

Peggy paused to drain her cup of its last dregs.

'And as to how Gisela and family are doing, well very nicely it seems according to her last letter, the girls are settled in their new school, but she is worried over Hugo and his relationship with his father!'

Sylvia gave her mother a sideways glance, then there was a serious tone in her voice.

'I have heard a lot of people have had difficult relationships with their off spring after they have been away for all those years at the war.' Adding.

'I have been so lucky having Dad at home even if he did work long hours. And it has been so good for Mickey and Ned too.'

'It makes you realize that the decorations don't really matter, families do!' Peggy said with real feeling in her voice.

Her daughter nodded in agreement.

'Hi there, nice to see you again.' Bridget said as she balanced a tray of sherry in one hand and tapped Sylvia on the shoulder with the other. The latter had just entered the Finch's house after church on Christmas morning

Sylvia turned round her face full of smiles, it was good to see Bridget and she gave her a quick hug almost knocking the tray out if her hands.

'Sorry!' She said as she quickly held out a hand to balance it.

'Never mind no harm done!'

'Can we talk?' Sylvia asked Bridget as she quickly glancing around at the throng that seemed to be coming through the Finch's front door in ever increasing numbers.

The two of them hadn't actually spoken since their last encounter on the bus quite a few months ago and Sylvia had every reason to be grateful for the information Bridget had gleaned and passed through a mutual friend about applying to the court for her and Karl to marry.

Sylvia felt she owed her thanks for what she had done.

Bridget put the tray quickly on a small occasional table in the hall and took two glasses of sherry from it, putting her arm round Sylva's shoulder she steered Sylvia into a small side room, just to the left.

'Come on spill the beans.' Bridget said in a teasing voice.

'I've been dying to know how you got on with the court business and all that!' Bridget paused for breath.

'No ring I see!' She said glancing at Sylvia's hand.

'So the court didn't give you permission?'

Sylvia blushed,

'Well actually it did give permission, but events have moved so swiftly since then that I'd almost forgotten about it.'

'Not with Karl now?' Bridget asked tentatively.

'Oh no nothing like that.' A smile spread across Sylvia's face and Bridget heaved a sigh of relief to know that she hadn't put her foot in it.

Sylvia pointed in the direction of the hall;

'Karl is out there with Ned now but circumstances changed our plans somewhat.' She went on to fill Bridget in about the events of the past two months, her father's accident and Karl's role in that, the early birth of Janet's little girl and how their living quarters had changed because of the situation.

'Well I must admit you have been busy!' Bridget said as Sylvia finished her explanations.

'That's the trouble with being away at school, I don't know what is going on locally, and I have only seem Mummy briefly since I got home, so there has been no time for a good talk; she has been so busy with the local Christmas arrangements and Dad. She paused before continuing.

'So I really didn't know how things were with you. How is you Dad now?' Bridget enquired.

'He is almost fully recovered, and Heinz says Janet will be able to join him shortly, when the baby has gained a little strength. So things are looking up!' Sylvia finished.

'So after that you and Karl can start to think of yourselves!' Bridget said firmly.

'Yes! To tell you the truth with all the problems, we haven't even told anyone about the court case.' Sylvia paused for a moment, suddenly remembering Bridget had her problems too.

'Do you know I haven't even asked how your Dad is, my mother said he'd come through the operation well.'

'He has been more comfortable since, but the surgeon said it would be a few months before he saw any real benefit.' Bridget turned towards the door.

'Come through and see him, he always welcomes visitors, although not too many at a time!' She turned the brass door handle behind her before ushering Sylvia across the hall to the small room opposite.

'I've brought Sylvia to see you.' She told her father as she opened the door and kissed him on the cheek.

Sylvia felt Claude's warm fingers against her own as she took his outstretched hand.

'I have heard of the sterling work your young man has been doing from your mother.' Claude told Sylvia.

'And Mr. Phillips and the vicar also speak well of him when they visit.' Sylvia blushed with pleasure.

'No one else about is there?' Claude said quietly.

'No just Sylvie and me.' Bridget told him.

'You got the courts permission I hear.' Sylvia turned her face towards him in amazement.

Claude gave his lopsided smile, and squeezed Sylvia's hand a little as he held it more firmly in his own.

'I can just imagine the look on your face now. Don't worry your secret is safe with me.'

'But how did you know?' Sylvia asked.

'I know someone well on the bench, and I guessed it was you when Bridget asked my advice about it some months ago.' Claude peered at her with his almost sightless eyes.

'It all fell into place, your mother talks to me sometimes about her problems, especially when she is worried about something.' Claude gave a little sigh.

'I suppose people confide in me because I have time to listen! But at least it makes me feel I am still useful in the community and with what people tell me I often put two and two together.'

'And you correctly make four!' Bridget said smiling at her father.

'I suggested to Sylvia about the court, and I didn't know the outcome but you knew all the time!' Bridget clasped her father's hand.

'Well I couldn't tell you could I you haven't been here?' Her father said simply.

'And as I can't see to write a letter that was out of the question.'

Claude turned his face towards their guest.

'And just in case you're worried Sylvia I never break a confidence, no one else will ever know what goes on in these four walls.'

'Thank you.' Sylvia said simply.

They heard Ned's dulcet tones calling Sylvia from beyond the closed door.

'Looks as though you are needed.' Claude said adding.

'Take care of your young man he is worth hanging on too.'

'Thank you I will.' Sylvia said her cheeks burning over the complements paid as she made swiftly for the door, waving her hand to Bridget in a last salute. Her friend bent low over her father, her fair hair blending against his grey, and she saw Bridget's love for him shining out of her eyes.

A lump rose in Sylvia's throat as she acknowledged to herself what a brave man he was and how lucky she was that her father's accident thanks to Karl had no such lasting results.

Pulling herself together she closed the door and joined Ned and Karl who were waiting for her by the open front door.

The three of them swiftly made their way back to the cottage for their lunch, Karl and Sylvia walking hand in hand; it was nice to hear he was well thought about in the community in the relatively short time he'd been here.

She gave him a few quiet sideways glances realizing for the first time how he had grown in statue and confidence in the past couple of months, it made her heart almost burst with pride.

'We missed you at church.' Were the first words Karl said to Harry as soon as they returned to the house.

'The new man doesn't have the same touch with the organ as you do!' Harry had a twinkle in his eye as he replied.

'Thanks for the compliment, you know I only took over the job when the regular man was called up for the war effort and somehow the job became mine when he didn't come back.' Harry smiled as he added.

'The new man is welcome to it, I am not sure I really want to do it again.'

'But you have such a good way with music.' Karl said.

'To tell the truth I prefer my squeeze box.' Harry admitted.

'It gives me a great deal of joy when people sing to the popular tunes I can conjure up! With all the extra work we had during the war years there was little time for socializing.'

'The war interfered with a lot of things.' Ned observed joining in the conversation.

'One thing is sure.' Harry declared with real feeling in his voice. 'This accident has taught me to make more time for more social occasions in the future. I hadn't realized how much I had let my work rule my life!'

Sylvia watched the ease of the two men together; although she wouldn't have wanted her father to go through these last few difficult months and the circumstances; she was pleased to know the outcome was the relationship that had become so much better between them.

A noise from outside leached into Sylvia's thoughts and she got to her feet rushing into the kitchen just as her mother was helping her Grandmother over the back doorstep with Uncle Bill following close behind.

Bill joined Harry and Karl in the sitting room for a smoke with Mickey and Ned joined them there, Peggy and her daughter retired to the kitchen to make the final touches to the Christmas lunch.

It was a jolly party that sat down to roast chicken, with vegetables and trimmings.

After they finished the washing up, every one retired to the small sitting room.

Harry now almost fully recovered was by the fireside in his armchair, Karl with his arm loosely about Sylvia's shoulder sat next to her on the Rexene settee with Mickey sitting alongside them.

Harry's mother occupied the other armchair, whilst Peggy sat on an old nursing chair that had seen better days and came down from the bedroom on occasions like this, Ned with Bill occupied two chairs brought in from the kitchen.

Peggy looking about her felt a satisfaction on how things had changed in the past year.

Then Ned wasn't sure whether he would be going back to London and Mickey now had the prospect of being adopted by them so would be the son Harry always longed for.

They had kept this information from him to release on this particular day.

Harry got up slowly from his chair.

'I will light the candles on the Christmas tree now.' He announced.

Mickey his face full of excitement looked up, this was the best time of the day when the parcels each one of them had put under the tree would be distributed amongst the assembled company.

Sylvia felt quite excited; the extra money Mr. Morishstein had given her for repairing the nylon stockings he had at her request put to one side for Christmas so she had been able to buy the family little extras this year, which gave her great pleasure.

Each gift carefully wrapped was passed to the recipient who opened it so that everyone could see the gift and admire it. Peggy was especially pleased with some new leather gloves her daughter gave, and Mickey with a new history book he'd wanted for some time.

Sylvia looked at the small collection of wrapped gifts now in her lap, one which looked like a small box intrigued her and she could feel the eyes of all of the assembled company on her as she opened it to reveal a pretty ring with three stones across it. Karl reached over took the ring from the box and slipped it on the third finger of her left hand.

Sylvia was overcome and couldn't speak, then she looked in the direction of her father and she could hardly believe that his face was wreathed in a smile.

'I gave Karl my permission a few days ago.' He said quietly.

'And I have to admit I was completely wrong about him, I am sad to say that it took this accident to make me realize it!' He paused and looked down for a moment at his feet before looking up into the eyes of Karl and Sylvia.

'I am sorry that I made life difficult for you both.' His eyes misted over before addressing his daughter.

'And you were right Sylvie there are good and bad in all nationalities.'

His next statement came as a bolt out of the blue.

'I promise I won't stand in your way again, what do you say to a spring wedding?'

For a long moment Sylvia and Karl looked at each other, not knowing how to answer.

'You mean with your consent.' Sylvia said.

'Yes and glad to, it isn't just that Karl saved my life, since the accident I have begun to see that people are more important than my principles.' He glanced across at Peggy.

'I was a very lucky man when I met your mother, at the time I didn't realize how much I put her through, which I have to admit now was sheer stubbornness on my behalf, thinking back I could have lost the most precious possession I have!'

He looked in the direction of his daughter and Karl, as Peggy red faced now squirmed with pleasure at these words.

'I don't intend to do the same to my daughter, who I can see has met a man who will love and look after her.' Harry paused to blow his nose heavily on a handkerchief he took from his pocket.

Getting to his feet he pulled a bottle of sherry from the sideboard cupboard and poured out a glass for each one of them.

Then he turned to Mickey.

'Before we raise our glasses, Mum and I have some good news for you.' He patted the lad affectionately on the head.

Miss Perkins called the other day, and we have been given permission to apply to legally adopt you!'

Mickey's face was a picture as he flung his arms round Peggy's neck.

It was the first Sunday after lent that Peggy slipped the satin gown she had worn at her own wedding over the head of her daughter and smoothed it down over her slender hips.

'You've altered it beautifully.' She said as she stood back to admire the slim shape and the wax orange blossom flowers her daughter had painstakingly sewn into the open sweetheart neckline of the dress.

'It gives me so much pleasure Mum to wear the same dress to marry Karl that you wore all those years ago, even if I have altered it a bit.' her daughter admitted.

Peggy picked up the pretty orange blossom headdress with its veil attached and put it onto her Sylvia's straight dark locks.

Looked at her reflection in the mirror Sylvia leant down to put on her white satin high heel shoes and gave a little twirl.

'Will I do?' She asked.

Peggy held out her arms in reply and Sylvia sank into them, a few minutes later her mother took her hand and holding up the dress from the back helped her daughter from her bedroom down the narrow stairs where Harry waited to escort his daughter to the church.

Leaving the two of them together Peggy got into Bill's car with Mickey for the short journey up the hill, after depositing them at the lynch gate Bill returned to their cottage to collect the bride and her father.

Ned who had agreed to be best man and had gone on ahead to walk to the church from the lodge with Karl.

The previous few weeks had been very eventful. Janet had left just two weeks ago to join Heinz in Germany, so it had been a rush for Karl and Sylvia to get the lodge ready for their occupation after the wedding, the whole family had pitched into help.

Jean Finch had completely surprised Peggy by insisting that she was going to be responsible for the entire reception at the 'Reading Room' after the wedding so that Peggy could enjoy her daughter's day uninterrupted.

Because of Peggy's past work for the village, it seemed everyone wanted to pitch in with help, with the rationing still severe food was a problem, where it came from wasn't questioned but a really nice spread was awaiting the guests which included most of the village people.

A small real fruit cake properly iced stood in pride of place waiting to be cut, Peggy had been amazed and delighted when Winnie insisted she had it made and iced out of her own rations.

On entering the church Sylvia's mother was really surprised to find a lot of the villagers sat on Karl's side of the church, close to tears she thought it a lovely gesture as they must have realized it was impossible for his family to be present. It was there way of showing their appreciation for the young man who had in the short time he'd been here made a good impression amongst them.

Everyone agreed the service conducted by the Reverent Hounsome was lovely; once the reception was under way and the food and toasts were finished Harry got his squeeze box out.

It was good to hear the old songs belted out under his fingers and the older element among the guests enjoyed a sing song whilst the younger ones got up to dance after Sylvia and Karl enjoyed their first dance as a married couple.

Later dressed in a pale green suit in the 'New look' length she'd chosen for her going away outfit, Sylvia and Karl said goodbye to their guests and with a special hug for her parents they made the short walk back to the lodge to begin their life together.

Later on they gazed out of the tiny bedroom window at the stars and watched the moon come up.

Sylvia beautiful in the moonlight wore a simple cotton white nightdress her dark hair curling at the ends falling softly on her shoulders gleaming as the light as the moon shone on it

Karl held her close, feeling the softness of her body, desire throbbing through him, he knew he would always love her; but that love would never be as great as this moment in time.